Dirk Bogarde

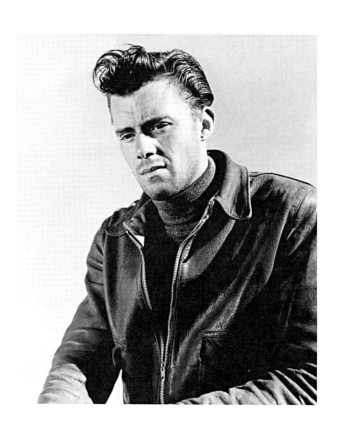

Dirk Bogarde

Matinee Idol, Art House Star

DAVID HUCKVALE

McFarland & Company, Inc., Publishers
Jefferson, North Carolina

ALSO BY DAVID HUCKVALE AND FROM MCFARLAND

Movie Magick: The Occult in Film (2018); *A Green and Pagan Land: Myth, Magic and Landscape in British Film and Television* (2018); *Music for the Superman: Nietzsche and the Great Composers* (2017); *A Dark and Stormy Oeuvre: Crime, Magic and Power in the Novels of Edward Bulwer-Lytton* (2016); *Poe Evermore: The Legacy in Film, Music and Television* (2014); *Hammer Films' Psychological Thrillers, 1950–1972* (2014); *The Occult Arts of Music: An Esoteric Survey from Pythagoras to Pop Culture* (2013); *James Bernard, Composer to Count Dracula: A Critical Biography* (2006; paperback 2012); *Visconti and the German Dream: Romanticism, Wagner and the Nazi Catastrophe in Film* (2012); *Ancient Egypt in the Popular Imagination: Building a Fantasy in Film, Literature, Music and Art* (2012); *Touchstones of Gothic Horror: A Film Genealogy of Eleven Motifs and Images* (2010); *Hammer Film Scores and the Musical Avant-Garde* (2008)

Frontispiece: Bogarde as Chris Lloyd in *Hunted* (dir. Charles Crichton, 1952)

LIBRARY OF CONGRESS CATALOGUING-IN-PUBLICATION DATA

Names: Huckvale, David, author.
Title: Dirk Bogarde : matinee idol, art house star / by David Huckvale.
Description: Jefferson : McFarland & Company, Inc., Publishers, 2019. |
    Includes bibliographical references and index.
Identifiers: LCCN 2019044376 | ISBN 9781476678030 (paperback : acid
    free paper) ⬡ |
    ISBN 9781476637099 (ebook)
Subjects: LCSH: Bogarde, Dirk, 1921–1999—Criticism and interpretation.
Classification: LCC PN2598.B647 H83 2019 | DDC 791.4302/8092—dc23
LC record available at https://lccn.loc.gov/2019044376

BRITISH LIBRARY CATALOGUING DATA ARE AVAILABLE

ISBN (print) 978-1-4766-7803-0
ISBN (ebook) 978-1-4766-3709-9

Front cover: Dirk Bogarde in the 1961 film *Victim* (Astor Pictures Corporation/Photofest)

Printed in the United States of America

McFarland & Company, Inc., Publishers
   Box 611, Jefferson, North Carolina 28640
   www.mcfarlandpub.com

Table of Contents

Introduction

Not long after the release of *Death in Venice* (dir. Luchino Visconti, 1971), a film society in the town where I lived with my family advertised a screening. My parents had been given a couple of tickets by a neighbor who had been unable to attend at the last minute; not knowing what to expect, they thought perhaps the film would be some kind of espionage drama. Both were very surprised and somewhat taken aback by what they experienced, especially as the sound system left much to desired. But despite this, the music of Mahler, which was still relatively unknown at that time, immensely impressed my mother in particular. Although I did not attend the screening, I was intrigued by their account of the evening, especially when, some years later, The Goodies, those comedy rivals to Monty Python, satirized the slow pace of Visconti's approach in a sketch on their BBC-TV show. That episode, "The Movies," was first broadcast in February 1975. Confronted with a long shot of a man shuffling along a sunlit beach in Visconti's latest movie *Death in Bognor*, Goodies Bill Oddie and Graeme Garden keep shouting, "Rubbish! Boo! Rotten! Boring!" Tim Brooke-Taylor, the third Goodie, appears and asks, "Have I missed much?"

"No," Garden replies, "just the first hour or two."

"What's happened?"

"Nothing."

"It's quite pretty," Tim concedes, but Bill is impatient.

"Come on, get a move on! Let's have the death then! Why are we waiting?! Come on you blighter, die! Come on, die!"

When the old man falls over, Tim asks, "Was that it?"

"No," Graeme groans, "another 90 minutes of it yet!"

"What happens?"

"Nothing. At least it's better than *Death in Venice*. Just die, for God's sake!"

I was only 11 years old in 1971 and knew nothing about *Death in Venice*, Thomas Mann, Visconti or Dirk Bogarde, but my interest in them all began

1

with this strange introduction to their work. A television viewing of *Death in Venice* many years later, after much more reading and comprehension, led to what I can only describe as a kind of intellectual epiphany, when I suddenly realized that, at long last, I understood what the story was all about, the disparate elements that had inspired Mann all marvelously crystalizing in my mind. These included Nietzsche's ideas about the Apollonian and the Dionysian, Mahler's musical expression of loneliness, nature worship and alienation, Wagnerian transfiguration and, not least, Platonic homoeroticism. I then realized that *Death in Venice* formed part of Visconti's immense trilogy about the rise and fall of German Romanticism, which ultimately led to the Romantic catastrophe of the Third Reich. As the world in which I found myself and with which I felt so uncomfortable had been largely created by that catastrophe, *Death in Venice* became the key with which to unlock modern history and explain all that I felt was wrong with the world. One of those three films, *The Damned,* also starred Bogarde, who was unfortunately absent in the opener *Ludwig,* about the Dream King of Bavaria, in which Trevor Howard created the cinema's most convincing and lifelike portrayal of Richard Wagner.

After the final credits of *Death in Venice* rolled, I walked out into the garden (it was a pleasant summer evening, I recall) and looked up at the silhouettes of the trees against the dying light, delighted by my intellectual breakthrough, which felt as wide and inspiring as the darkening sky. One or two stars had already begun to appear, along, appropriately enough, with Venus—Wagner's "Star of Eve." Though Visconti's film itself really only captures the surface of Mann's story, failing to address its philosophical kernel, I had, by that time, worked out by other means all that Visconti had omitted; but it was the extraordinary beauty of Visconti's vision that brought everything together, and central to its success was the enormous appeal of Dirk Bogarde's performance as Gustav von Aschenbach. I was compelled by the tiredness and sadness of Bogarde's expressive eyes, I was fascinated by the languid elegance of his movements and the mild warmth of his vocal tone. I was delighted by the cheeky smile he gives to himself when watching the boy, Tadzio (Björn Andrésen), on the Lido, and the careful way in which he contemplates the strawberry that will give Aschenbach cholera before popping it into his mouth and looking around him like a contented but still alert squirrel.

It was only with this film that I became truly aware of Bogarde as an actor, having missed his heyday as an Idol of the Odeons. I remained fascinated by his screen presence and, as I explored further, his off-screen personality as well. A major, if not the main reason for the appeal and necessity of Art is surely that it is about recognition, and in watching Bogarde I increasingly recognized much of myself. Of course, Bogarde was much better-looking—stunningly so, once out of his aging and grotesque make-up for *Death in Venice*—but I did feel psychologically in tune with him. I felt I understood him and why he had refused to come out of the closet. I also sympathized with his confession that he was not a dedicated actor with a passion for the stage (like his friend Sir John Gielgud) but rather a jobbing actor who almost by accident "became a film star" and worked professionally only to make a living. Unlike Mahler, the inspiration for *Death in Venice,* who "lived to compose," Bogarde acted to live, and much preferred a quiet day's gardening on his own to making films in a busy studio, rewarding though that process often was. He also seemed to be an intensely private, sensitive aesthete who, while fully aware of the sexual appeal of movies and "movie stars," was refreshingly Platonic in his idea of what love could and perhaps should be. "You can have a love affair without carnality," he often insisted, and such a view seemed an immensely refreshing and much-needed antidote to the always too prevalent belief that sex alone is the defining characteristic of what it means to be gay. Bogarde pointed out, without spelling it out, that sex was often rather a long way down the list of what really mattered to him and what really made the difference.[1]

He had an opportunity to state this in the last film he made, Bertrand Tavernier's *Daddy Nostalgie* (1990): He plays an ex-pat, curiously called Tony (the first name of Dirk's long-standing partner Anthony Forwood), who is recovering from a stroke and living in France. (So far, so autobiographical.) Tony offers this reply to a question from his daughter (played by Jane Birkin) about whether a sexual relationship can last forever: "Well, darling," he wisely explains, "frankly, it's the loving that counts."

I was born in 1961, the year in which Bogarde's "gay" blackmail thriller *Victim* (dir. Basil Dearden) was released. Bogarde, who starred as the homosexual barrister, Melville Farr, was 40 years old at the time and on the cusp of leaving behind his very British image as Rank's most bankable star to embark on a new international career of much more complex and challenging pictures. (Not that Bogarde ever looked down on his early films. He was immensely proud of them, even though he admitted that some of them were rubbish. "People like rubbish," he once said.[2]) *Victim* was a watershed moment for him: a serious role in a challenging drama that helped to raise awareness of the plight of homosexuals in Britain, without recourse to euphemism, grotesquerie, comic campness or subtextual innuendo, and the film consequently contributed to the abolition of an irrational, cruel and pernicious law. I too was 40 before I felt comfortable enough to reveal to my own very understanding and supportive parents that I was gay. In fact, I hadn't really worked it out for myself until about ten years before, and I was 55 before, in a development made possible by another commendable change in the law, I finally married my delightful husband.

I do not wish to concentrate exclusively on Bogarde's gayness in this study of his films, but it is nonetheless a central aspect of his screen persona and it is essential that it is addressed if we are to understand the complex nature of his appeal (ironically most of all to women), and the way in which he interacted with fans, the press, television interviewers and even members of his own family. Society has moved on since Bogarde's time, though there are now disturbing signs of a backlash against all the hard-won advances that have been made in liberal Western societies during the 1990s. Growing up in England in the 1970s, the only positive gay role models I could find on TV (my principal source of entertainment at the time) were comedians of high camp like Frankie Howerd (in *Up Pompeii*), John Inman (as Mr. Humphries in *Are You Being Served?*), Kenneth Williams and Charles Hawtrey in the *Carry On* films, Larry Grayson, high priest of the limp wrist,

who later took over from Bruce Forsyth as host of the popular BBC game show *The Generation Game,* and Kenny Everett on London's Capital Radio, whom I was later to be disturbed and disoriented to discover was a great fan of the British prime minister of the time, Baroness, then merely Mrs. Thatcher. Bogarde held similarly right-wing views until age and experience considerably softened him. It is heartening to realize that from a statement such as, in 1967, "With government handing out free medicine, social aid and all the other bits and pieces, no one need work at all,"[3] he was, by 1986, able to admit to TV interviewer Russell Harty

Kenneth Williams in *Carry on Cleo* (dir. Gerald Thomas, 1964).

that he liked listening to BBC World Service because "sometimes it's quite fun to see what Mrs. Thatcher has cocked up."[4] "My 'politics' have *radically* altered," he made clear, in the introduction to the collection of letters from which the former disdain for the welfare state is drawn.[5]

Only one of the individuals I have listed here ever "came out." Williams, Hawtrey and Grayson were so overtly camp they hardly needed to, and didn't, but Everett later did. He recalled on the BBC's long-running radio show *Desert Island Discs*[6] that as soon as he made headline news, he had to cope with builders wolf-whistling when he was walking to the London radio station where he worked; and it was then that he appreciated the advice of his straight black masseur, who told him that he now knew what it was like to be black. Everett's analysis of the problem was that people had a lot of spare hatred and needed targets (it didn't much matter which kind of target) at which to unleash that hatred. Even when that edition of *Desert Island Discs* was broadcast in 1993 (when Everett was HIV positive, and just before he developed the AIDS virus that killed him), there was a certain frisson in his quietly defiant admission: "I like gay people. I think they're fun." His attempt at marriage to "a lovely lady" (as he described his former wife, Lee Middleton) did not "cure" him as he hoped it might, and he realized that "you're born gay" and there is nothing you can do about it. He came to terms with who he was and became "absolutely happy," as he put it; but his earlier desire not to be gay was one very definitely felt by Dirk Bogarde, as we shall see. (Bogarde's biographer John Coldstream passes along an uncorroborated account of Bogarde, at the end of the 1950s, taking aversion therapy at London's University College Hospital, which is described as "a week on the ward, where he would be shown erotic pictures of men while being administered drugs to make him vomit,"[7] and suggests the appalling brainwashing techniques Anthony Burgess satirized in his dystopian novel *A Clockwork Orange*.)

It is some measure of how uninformed and unaware, not only of gayness in general but of my own reality in particular, that it never really occurred to me that all these people were gay (I hadn't yet discovered Dirk). They merely made me laugh and in ways that seemed quite natural. Only much later did I put two and two together. Gayness really wasn't something anyone talked about when I was growing up, other than in chillingly clinical terms. To add another example, it never occurred to me (how on Earth could it not?, I now wonder) that Bobby Crush, the popular pianist in the stride piano tradition of Mrs. Mills, was also gay. When, many years later after his 1970s heyday, he looked back on his TV appearances at that time, he tearfully confessed that he was "upset by it all."

> I looked very young and carefree, but that wasn't the entire truth because at that time I was also coping with realizing that I was gay, and at the same time I was being thrust into the spotlight. I never expected it to make me feel as emotional as I do tonight. I have to say that when I look back, my memories, really, are mainly of the inside of theaters and the inside of hotels, but I don't remember having an awful lot of fun. Most people in their late teens, early-twenties are using that time to go out and have relationships. That never really happened for me. At that time, we had no "out" gay pop stars, we had not "out" storylines in soap operas and what have you. It was all terribly closeted, you know. It was really frowned upon. I regret not coming out to my parents, because I was afraid of disappointing them.[8]

Albert Finney's performance as Alfie Byrne in Barry Devlin's *A Man of No Importance* (dir. Suri Krishnamma, 1994) perfectly encapsulated the dilemma of gay men in an unsympathetic society (Dublin in the 1960s), which never discussed let alone countenanced such a thing. Finney's middle-aged gay bus conductor has never come out, but secretly longs to dress and behave like Oscar Wilde; and, when not conducting buses, he directs amateur dramatic productions of Wilde's plays, full of longing for Rufus Sewell's handsome young bus driver. His despairing line "It's too late!" struck a desperately resonant chord in my own subconscious when I first heard it, prompting me to get on with being who I was before the same could be said of myself.

Defining gayness is rather like peeling an onion. When all the layers are taken apart and analyzed, we soon discover that many of them are not incompatible with so-called "straight" orientation. When trying to tease out a "confession" from Bogarde in his 1986 interview with him, Russell Harty drew attention to Bogarde's interior furnishings as a way of trying to establish the exact nature of Bogarde's relationship with Forwood, whom he described as "your manager and closest personal friend." Harty continued:

> But it's more than an agent and client relationship isn't it? … You share this house with him. … It is a house of exquisite taste and it seems to have a kind of unity on it. I wondered if you created it together.[9]

Bogarde, of course, refused to be drawn, but it is obvious that Harty was suggesting that a taste for interior furnishings is an obvious indication of a gay personality. It is not, of course. I have personally encountered many gay men who are interested in neither vacuum cleaners nor home improvements—who, indeed, have no interest in the arts and dislike classical music. Quentin Crisp was famous for living in squalor: "There is no need to do any housework at all," he famously insisted. "After the first four years, the dirt doesn't get any worse." Traditionally, of course, housework has been a feminine occupation, as the Victorian critic John Ruskin put it in 1865:

> Now, the man's work for his own home is, as has been said, to secure its maintenance, progress and defense; the woman's to secure its order, comfort and loveliness.[10]

However, a desire for tidiness and "sweet ordering," as Ruskin termed it, was a gay stereotype that did indeed fit Dirk, as he made clear in the title of his third volume of autobiography, *An Orderly Man*. Rather like his habitual use of Anthony Forwood's surname to suggest a kind of military relationship, the phrase "Orderly Man" also suggests a military "orderly"—an enlisted soldier assigned to perform various chores for a commanding officer, or even a hospital attendant. Bogarde thus manages to turn his desire for the neat and tidy into something less—or perhaps more—"gay." He even disguises his need for orderliness by suggesting from the outset that he would actually rather be much more scruffily "masculine":

> I am an orderly man. I say this with nonsense of false modesty, or of conceit. It is a simple statement of fact. That's all. Being orderly, as a matter of fact, can be excessively tiresome and it often irritates me greatly, but I cannot pull away. I sometimes think that I would far prefer to live slumped in some attic amidst a litter of junk, dirty underclothing, greasy pots and pans, paints and canvases strewn about everywhere, an on-the-point-of-being-discarded mistress weeping dejectedly on the stairs, fungus on the walls, and an enormous overdraft at the bank or, better still, absolutely no money at all. Unvarnished, muscles, Puccini, but it just won't work for me. I have to live in an orderly manner; I'd tidy up the attic in a flash, scrub the pots and pans, stack the canvases, exterminate the fungus, label the paints and send the mistress back to her mother or husband. And keep what money I had as frugally as a miser, in a sock beneath my mattress. Orderly is what I am....
>
> What instinct makes me behave in this extraordinary fashion? Is it something which I have inherited from my father: a man who was always correct, contained, persistent and fully planned all his life? Or is it some hideous subconscious sign of some monstrous flaw in my otherwise apparently serene make-up. God knows.[11]

Well, since he asks, this is my cue to apply a little psychoanalysis to the situation. It is, after all, an extraordinary way to open a volume of memoirs. As if it mattered. Is being tidy so very significant to merit an entire page about it? In the same year that Bogarde filmed his interview with Russell Harty, Antony Easthope brought out a collection of essays under the title of *What a Man's Gotta Do*. His argument, rooted in Freudian theory, is that masculinity, like all matters of gender, is a social and psychological construct. But it is particularly vulnerable to anything that it perceives to be undermining it.

> Anal eroticism affects men and women in three ways especially. Pleasure can attach to the idea both of the active explosion of feces or urine and to that of being passively penetrated. Secondly, since producing a turd is one of the first ways we learn to control ourselves and our bodies, different meanings can be symbolized by giving up or keeping feces. Surrendered, they can mean a gift ("Do it for mummy") and so an expression of sexual desire; retained, they embody narcissistic pleasure, something we want to keep for ourselves....
>
> A third aspect of anal eroticism concerns tidiness and order. Dirt is matter in the wrong place. And so getting rid of dirt by putting it in the right place yields an anal

pleasure, or rather, it sublimates anal eroticism by turning it to another end. Piling up money through the effort of putting things in order is doubly a form of anal eroticism and, as has often been remarked, has a close association with capitalist accumulation and enterprise....

But it is the view of psychoanalysis that while men seek to separate the genital from the anal and maintain an opposition between them, women are much less concerned to draw a firm line. If this is the case, there may be several reasons for a male wish to reject and exclude the anal [which] focuses male homosexual desire. To a would-be perfect masculinity, anal eroticism must be rejected along with the femininity of which it might become a bearer.[12]

Bogarde might thus be said to have had his question answered by Easthope here, the most significant part of his argument being that perfect masculinity must reject banality and femininity. It must "struggle to keep itself together, to close all gaps, watch every move, meet aggression with aggression. The purpose of the masculine ego, like that of the castle, is to *master* every threat.... To maintain its identity, it must not only repel external attack but also suppress treason within." And Easthope also points out that the "enemy within" is the masculine ego's own femininity.[13] For Easthope, masculinity "aims to be one substance all the way through. In order to do this, it must control what threatens it both from within and without. Within, femininity and male homosexual desire must be denied; without, women and the feminine must be subordinated and held in place." Masculinity "wants to present itself as an essence—fixed, self-consistent, pure. In fact it has no essence and no central core."[14]

It seems to me that this analysis, together with homosexuality's rejection of what one might call the primitive prime directive of childbirth, accounts for much of the world's homophobia. Bogarde insisted that, far from hiding his own nature, everything was in fact available for inspection:

There is a complete totality of a picture, as far as I'm concerned. It's all there, if you want to read it, but if you're not very bright, you won't get it. You have to read between the lines of everything I ever write anyway.[15]

This, coming as it does from the horse's mouth, gives me some license to do just that (though not exclusively) with regard to his performances in over 60 films, which variously cast him in a diversity of parts. Robert Tanitch has listed some of these characters as

bookie, speedway champion, Borstal boy, drug addict, penniless street-musician, army deserter, Dutch refugee, cheese salesman, medical student newlywed, ship's doctor, gardener [...] Mexican bandit, defrocked priest, barrister, research psychologist, Harley Street surgeon, manservant, intelligence officer, Oxford don, master code-breaker, British consul, schizophrenic chocolate manufacturer, and camp villain on a cartoon strip.[16]

Bogarde claimed that he had never played himself in any film.[17] In his correspondence with the mysterious Mrs. X, later published in *A Particular Friendship,* he insisted:

> To be fair, when, if you see *Accident* you will not really see "me" ... you will see me being someone else: I hope. But don't get carried away that the character I play is anything remotely like the man who owns the house you once owned. T'aint so. And I don't smoke a pipe, or drink sherry, or watch cricket matches or wear a gown and tweeds ... and as far as I know, I haven't had the change in life. Yet.[18]

To quote Hamlet, it seems to me that here Bogarde "doth protest too much." And he adds, "I hope," which suggests that even he thought there might not be much of a difference between him and "Stephen" in that film. And, anyway, the superficial differences he lists are nowhere near as significant as his physical presence. Most if not all of Bogarde's films in fact reveal different aspects of his own personality, a personality that becomes all the more fascinating precisely because of the enigma made out of it. The fact of the matter is that Bogarde was really always Dirk, in different settings, different costumes, different stories, but always filtering himself through the camera and his various roles. This was why his name was so often above the title of the films in which he starred. It was Dirk Bogarde, not the characters he played, who carried those movies, and it was Dirk Bogarde whom audiences came to see. Such is the nature of being "a movie star," despite being an excellent performer as well; the movie was never entirely the main point in a film with Bogarde's name above the title, even in those masterpieces of the cinema directed by Joseph Losey. If Bogarde was starring, the film was simultaneously always about him.

In 1992, I wrote Bogarde what was a fan letter disguised as a request for an interview. I didn't really expect a reply, but to my complete surprise, one morning a envelope of thick blue laid paper, inscribed with a florid script in black ink, landed on my doormat. The card inside read:

> 30.1.92
>
> Thank you for your very kind letter. I much regret that there is not the remotest chance of an interview! All that is far behind me—& I have written it, been asked & questioned until I could weep.
> Sorry! But my writing really demands my time—
>
> Sincerely
> Sir Dirk Bogarde

I wondered if meeting him in person would have made any real difference to me, as by then I felt I knew him rather well, having applied my own interpretation to his often unreliable autobiographies and his rather more revealing performances. The interpretations of others also played their part, in particular the magnificent "authorized" biography by John Coldstream. But I felt Bogarde's sustained contribution to gay liberation through those performances, about which, ironically, he often deluded himself, deserved more attention. At a time when gay rights are once more under threat, I hope this book, along with its more general overview of his films, confirms just how much how society in general has to thank Sir Dirk Bogarde for.

Chapter One

"It's too horrible to watch!"

There had been many coded references to homosexuality in American cinema before *Victim* came along, but none of those films had a direct impact on legislation. They did, however, help the cause by a slow form of cultural osmosis, at least when stereotypes were not reversing it. Edward D. Wood professed to have adopted a serious approach to transvestism in his 1953 *Glen or Glenda,* but that film was too far outside the mainstream (the protagonist explains that he fought in World War II while wearing woman's underwear) to make much legislative impact at the time. Vincente Minnelli's *Tea and Sympathy* (1956), about a classical music–loving, theatergoing 17-year-old boy at a macho prep school, was compromised by the Motion Picture Production Code's prohibition of any overt mention of homosexuality in the screenplay. The supposedly gay hero anyway ends up happily married to a woman, his sexual ambiguities resolved. Richard Brooks' 1958 film adaptation of Tennessee Williams' *Cat on a Hot Tin Roof* removed all overt references to homosexuality, as had Elia Kazan's 1951 film version of *A Streetcar Named Desire,* much to Williams' annoyance. (In the stage version of the latter, Blanche DuBois' husband committed suicide after a homosexual affair.)

The relationship between Stephen Boyd's Messala and Charlton Heston's Ben-Hur in William Wyler's *Ben-Hur* (1959) could be interpreted as homosexual (the gay screenwriter Gore Vidal certainly thought so), but again, the film's historical setting weakened its impact. *Suddenly Last Summer* (dir. Joseph K. Mankiewicz, 1959), which Vidal adapted from another play by Tennessee Williams, deals with the propositioning of young men for sex. More explicit than the two earlier Williams films about this subject, its approach was nonetheless compromised by its negativity. "Since the film illustrates the horrors of such a lifestyle," claimed the Production Code Administration (successor to the Motion Picture Production Code), "it can be considered moral in theme even though it deals with sexual perversion."[1]

Ironically, the much more famous case of Oscar Wilde, the subject of two films in 1960, the year before *Victim,* did not have quite the same impact.

The story was, of course, well known—indeed, infamous—but both films were costume dramas, distancing the immediacy of the issue. Robert Morley, the Wilde of the first film (*Oscar Wilde,* dir. Gregory Ratoff), gave a serious and compelling performance in a role that had marked his Broadway debut in 1938, but the larger-than-life nature of both Wilde and Morley combined made the subject seem exceptional rather than applicable to everyday life. In fact, the story is much the same as in *Victim,* concerning blackmail, the love of an older man for a younger, the involvement of barristers, social scandal, and Wilde's own impassioned defense of "the love that dare not speak its name," which anticipates the rather more concise confession of Bogarde's Melville Farr with the boy he falls in love with ("I wanted him!") in *Victim.* Wilde's own words from the trial on April 26, 1895, are performed with great sensitivity and seriousness by Morley:

> What is the "Love that dare not speak its name"?—"The Love that dare not speak its name" in this century is such a great affection of an elder for a younger man as there was between David and Jonathan, such as Plato made the very basis of his philosophy, and such as you find in the sonnets of Michelangelo and Shakespeare. It is that deep,

Robert Morley (left) as Oscar Wilde, with John Neville as Bosie in *Oscar Wilde* (dir. Gregory Ratoff, 1960).

spiritual affection that is as pure as it is perfect. It dictates and pervades great works of art like those of Shakespeare and Michelangelo, and those two letters of mine, such as they are. It is in this century misunderstood, so much misunderstood that it may be described as "The Love that dare not speak its name," and on account of it I am placed where I am now. It is beautiful, it is fine, it is the noblest form of affection. There is nothing unnatural about it. It is intellectual, and it repeatedly exists between an elder and a younger man, when the elder man has intellect and the younger man has all the joy, hope and glamour of life before him. That it should be so the world does not understand. The world mocks at it and sometimes puts one in the pillory for it.[2]

Morley's Wilde drama was filmed in black and white, as was Bogarde's *Victim.* In an attempt to add greater realism to the story, Ken Hughes' *The Trials of Oscar Wilde* starred Peter Finch as the doomed poet, this time filmed in sumptuous color, with Finch, in stark contrast, presenting Wilde in a much less florid manner, verging on making him "straight-acting" with all the camp extravagance converted into more understated urbane wit. Emphasis is laid on Wilde the happily married family man, further to "normalize" the story and engage audiences in supporting the cause. (Like Morley, Finch was not gay himself.) The film was not popular, despite critical acclaim, and neither of these Wilde dramas had the impact of *Victim.* While the comedy cross-dressing of Billy Wilder's *Some Like It Hot* (1959) may have helped loosen the censorious control of Hollywood's Motion Picture Production Code, its two obviously straight characters (Tony Curtis and Jack Lemmon) play with homosexual stereotypes in a way that cordoned off the subject within the traditionally "safe" quarantine of comedy.

One intriguing fact is that many of the films that deal with this subject belong to the horror film genre (or Gothic romance), which was, for so many years, treated with as much contempt by critics as homosexuals were by society at large. The horror film had always, until relatively recently, been situated on the fringes of film culture, and was consequently well placed to explore a variety of "fringe" subjects, or, conversely, those subjects that are central to human experience but regarded as too dangerous to enter the mainstream: our obsession with power, the trauma of birth, the inescapable agonies of death, the irrational and polymorphous manifestations of the sex drive, and the fluid nature of identity, gender and even "reality" itself. It is significant that the horror film has now, by 2019, become a mainstream genre, as so many of the social taboos it has traditionally discussed are now no longer taboos. Consequently, the "horror" genre has largely lost its *raison d'être.*

Dirk Bogarde never made a horror film as such, but his output is curiously related to it in its exploration of similar taboos, particularly in the films he made during the second half of his career. As an outsider, to a great extent, he would have been well suited to the genre's many themes of exclusion, for the horror film is indeed the genre for outsiders *par excellence*. Horror films almost invariably concern duality, either heroes who are self-divided or villains who challenge the established order of things from outside society. Colin Wilson has called Hermann Hesse's novel *Steppenwolf* "A Treatise on the Outsider." The hero of that novel, Harry Haller, is a "being self-divided, [and] his chief desire is to be unified."[3] The loosely employed "werewolf" imagery of the novel symbolizes this:

> To explain his wretchedness, Haller has divided himself into two persons: a civilized man and a wolf-man. The civilized man loves … order and cleanliness, poetry and music (especially Mozart); he takes lodgings always in houses with polished fire-irons and well-scrubbed tiles. His other half is a savage who loves the second world, the world of darkness; he prefers open spaces and lawlessness; if he wants a woman, he feels that the proper way is to kill and rape her. For him, bourgeois civilization and all its inanities are a great joke.[4]

Hesse explains that Harry wished "to be loved as a whole and therefore it was just with those whose love he most valued that he could least of all conceal and belie the wolf."

> There were those, however, who loved precisely the wolf in him, the free, the savage, the untamable, the dangerous and strong, and these found it peculiarly disappointing and deplorable when suddenly the wild and wicked wolf was also a man, and had hankerings after goodness and refinement, and wanted to hear Mozart, to read poetry and to cherish human ideals. Usually these were the most disappointed and angry of all; and so it was that the Steppenwolf brought his own dual and divided nature into the destinies of others whenever he came into contact with them.[5]

It is not hard to find a popular parallel to all this in Lon Chaney Jr.'s Larry Talbot, the doomed title character in *The Wolf Man* (dir. George Waggner, 1941), one of the most melancholy and tragic of all horror films. Bogarde, the urbane and civilized orderly man, often explored his own Steppenwolf in film roles as diverse as juvenile delinquent Tom Riley in *The Blue Lamp* (dir. Basil Dearden, 1950), wife murderer Edward Bare in *Cast a Dark Shadow* (dir. Lewis Gilbert, 1955), the sadistic Barrett in *The Servant* (dir. Joseph Losey, 1963) and the sado-masochist Nazi, Max, in *The Night Porter* (dir. Liliana Cavani, 1974).

The pathos of horror films lies always in the division between social norms and transgressive outsiders. "Can you imagine anything worse than living forever?" Christopher Lee once said of his most famous character, Count Dracula, adding, "I thought of Dracula as rather human, with a terrible solitude of Evil."[6] Peter Cushing's Baron Frankenstein, on surveying the damage done by marauding villagers on his laboratory in *The Evil of Frankenstein* (dir. Terence Fisher, 1964), laments, "Why can't they leave me alone? Why can't they ever leave me alone?" Carlos Clarens, one of the earliest historians of the horror film itself, asked, "Didn't Mr. Hyde become more recognizably human as we learned to accept what our forefathers endeavored to conceal and repress?"[7] He continued,

> There are unforgettable horror moments in non-horror films: the autopsy in Bergman's *Ansiktet*; the episode of Gelsomina and the monstrous child in *La Strada*; or recurring in the work of Luis Buñuel. Yes these films are not to be regarded as horror films; these shudders are means to an end, not an end in themselves. This same manipulation of the audience—or rather, its absence in modern cinema—accounts in part for the present artistic lethargy of the genre. The key word nowadays is distantiation, as opposed to the involvement of classic cinema, and the shock punctuation of horror has been replaced by steady, pervasive anxiety of our times, as in the work of Jean-Luc Godard, the most contemporary of our filmmakers. Still, a chilly draught from Nosferatu's castle can be felt in the corridors of Marienbad.[8]

Similarly, there are many elements in Bogarde's films that are related to the horror genre but not, strictly speaking, part of it; it is the aspect of the outsider that brings them together. Bogarde also worked with a great many people who *did* make horror films—indeed who specialized in them. Intriguingly, Dirk's future partner and business manager Anthony Forwood had appeared in five early murder mysteries for Hammer Films in the company's pre–Gothic days, which nonetheless foreshadowed that company's later series of psychological thrillers. In the first, *The Man in Black* (dir. Francis Searle, 1949), Forwood, as selfish cad Victor Harrington, accidentally murders the gardener who works for a Yoga expert. (Both roles are played by a pre–*Carry On* Sid James in the antithesis of his later saucy persona.) The Yoga expert disguises himself as the gardener to unmask a plot, masterminded by his second wife and stepdaughter, to kill him for his money; and everything is played out in Hammer's favorite location of Oakley Court, the pseudo–Gothic architectural style of which later graced such horror classics as *The Brides of Dracula* (dir. Terence Fisher, 1960) and *The Plague of the Zombies* (dir. John Gilling, 1966). Indeed, we first glimpse Forwood's Harrington as he parks his automobile in the *porte cochère* of the mansion, giving us an opportunity to observe the griffons (soon to become much loved icons of Hammer horror) on either side of the main entrance.

In Forwood's second Hammer, *The Black Widow* (dir. Vernon Sewell, 1951), he plays the lover of a married woman (Christine Norden), and he plots to murder her husband and acquire both the woman and the husband's property. Having already murdered a gardener in the previous film, Forwood's best (though perhaps unexpected) line here is, "I must say, I don't particularly like the idea of murdering my best friend," to which Norden replies, "But you don't mind having an affair with his wife?" In the end, the husband (Robert Ayres) finds out about their plot, shoots Forwood in self-defense. Just as the police arrive, Norden turns the pistol on herself.

In Forwood's third Hammer film, *The Gambler and the Lady* (dir. Patrick Jenkins, 1953), he played a suave aristocrat, Lord Peter Willens. His wife (Naomi Chance) is having an affair with Dane Clark's eponymous American gambler, who is caught up in gangland violence. A small role in *Mantrap* (1953) followed, in which Paul Henreid played Hugo Bishop, a man falsely accused of murder who, on his escape from prison, tracks down the real culprit. It was directed by Terence Fisher, who would go on to create the world-famous brand of Hammer horror; but in 1950, Fisher had also directed Bogarde in the Gainsborough production *So Long at the Fair,* an abduction melodrama that has a great deal in common with Hammer's *The Kiss of the Vampire* (dir. Don Sharp, 1963). In both films, one of the characters is bewildered by a conspiracy, which makes them think they are losing their sanity. In *So Long at the Fair,* Jean Simmons plays Vicky Barton, who is on holiday in Paris with her brother Johnny (David Tomlinson). Overnight, Johnny vanishes, and the entire hotel staff insist that she arrived there alone. Only Bogarde's George Hathaway is willing to help her learn what happened: Johnny had been taken ill with what a doctor diagnosed as plague, and the city authorities, anxious to avoid panic and the loss of business revenue during this time of the International Exhibition, arranged the deception. In *The Kiss of the Vampire,* Edward de Souza's Gerald Harcourt attends a costume ball organized by Noel Willman's Dr. Ravna, a vampire. Gerald is drugged while his wife Marianne (Jennifer Daniel) is initiated into the vampire cult. The following morning, Dr. Ravna and his family insist that Gerald arrived alone and throw him out. Only Clifford Evans' Prof. Zimmer is willing to listen to Gerald's story and help him rescue Marianne before it is too late.

Forwood's fifth Hammer film was, appropriately, *Five Days* (dir. Montgomery Tully, 1953), in which Dane Clark starred as a bankrupt businessman who persuades his best friend to kill him so that his wife can collect the life insurance money. Clark changes his mind when his fortunes unexpectedly improve; unfortunately, another partner in the business is *also* trying to kill him.

Several of the actors who appeared in these early Hammers went on to grace their more glamorous Gothic shockers: Warren Mitchell, Kathleen Byron, Mona Washbourne and George Pastell all made their mark in the House of Horror, and if Forwood had not met Bogarde, it might well have been the case that he would have followed them. His connection with the fringes of horror continued when he appeared with Boris Karloff in an episode of *Colonel March of Scotland Yard*, a British TV series. The *Colonel March* stories were based on the book *The Department of Queer Complaints,* which used the term in its conventional sense: Colonel March has a penchant for investigating locked-room mysteries and "supernatural" crimes.

None of these films had homosexual resonance, beyond what we now know to have been Forwood's own sexuality, but this aspect of the horror film can be found in many others. Alfred Hitchcock's adaptation of Daphne du Maurier's *Rebecca* (1940) emphasized the lesbian nature of Judith Anderson's crazed housekeeper, Mrs. Danvers, having her lovingly finger the dead Rebecca's underwear to the luscious sound of composer Franz Waxman's celesta chords. She explains that these garments had been made specially for Rebecca by the nuns in the convent of St. Clare, and later, in a departure from the novel, she sets fire to the house to prevent the new Mrs. de Winter from replacing her former mistress, whom she so obsessively loved. But *Rebecca* is a "Romance," where, as we all know, anything can happen, and very little of what does happen has much relation to reality. Val Lewton's famous horror film *The Seventh Victim* (dir. Mark Robson, 1943) juxtaposed possible lesbian attraction with Satanism, though not in the standard manner of "gay villains." In Manhattan's liberal, "artistic" and consequently "gay-friendly" Greenwich Village, Jacqueline Gibson (Jean Brooks) is attracted to a fellow cult member, Francis Fallon (Isabel Jewell). The ambiguities of this film in general, together with its then peripheral position as a horror film, again did nothing to change the perceptions of public opinion.

Horror films have an appeal to both gay and straight people, but one of the reasons they appeal to homosexuals is because they are so often about outsiders—monsters who are rejected by the joiners-in. The situation of the Frankenstein Monster has no doubt struck a chord with many an alienated and persecuted gay adolescent. The similarly isolated Dracula at least had power on his side, and that was something else which, if we can't exactly identify with, we can at least fantasize about along the lines of "if you can't join 'em, beat 'em." Such monsters, along with mad scientists distrusted by conventional society, and reanimated mummies seeking love or wanting revenge, can just as easily serve a gay perspective as a heterosexual one. A persecuted werewolf is not only relevant to the hormone-fueled fixation of heterosexual horror fans on the breasts of such films' nubile starlets. In 1931, *Dracula* (dir. Tod Browning) showed Bela Lugosi as the vampire count looming over a *male* character, Dwight Fry's Renfield, which film historian, Gary D. Rhodes, reminds us was rather a brave transgression not only of Universal's insistence that Dracula should "go only for women and not men" but also of the *Code of Ethics for the Production of Motion Pictures,* which insisted: "Sex perversion or any inference of it is forbidden."[9] The 1936 sequel *Dracula's Daughter* (dir. Lambert Hillyer) brought lesbianism to horror films, with implications that were so *outré* at the time that many people failed to realize what was actually going on. The scene between Countess Zaleska (Gloria

Holden) and Janet (Marguerite Churchill) contains what became known as "the longest kiss never filmed,"[10] while the countess' seduction of Lili (Nan Grey), who is attacked by this female vampire, served only to emphasize the perceived "wrongness" of this kind of attraction at the time.

An even "gayer" horror film is *Bride of Frankenstein* (1935). It was directed by the homosexual James Whale and also co-starred the ultra-camp Ernest Thesiger, embroiderer *extraordinaire* in private life and, cast as the waspish Dr. Pretorius in the film, given some memorably effete lines, which he delivers with the quintessence of queenliness. Having been booted out of university for knowing too much, he explains: "'Booted,' my dear Baron, is the word … for knowing too much. Do you like gin? It is my only weakness…." "The creation of life is enthralling," he adds. "Science, like love, has her little surprises." Whale's inversion of the traditional Romantic iconography of Hollywood romance—a love affair between two monsters (and the two scientists who create them) extended even to the way the film was marketed, the posters showing Elsa Lanchester's Nefertiti grotesquerie as the "Bride," complete with scars, gazing up at Boris Karloff's famous Monster with an adoration she does not feel when encountering him in the film itself, whereupon she screams and croaks with horror. This subversion, along with the iconoclastic religious imagery (the Monster crucified like Christ and overturning funerary monuments), all point towards Whale's subtextual gay agenda.

Hammer's *The Brides of Dracula* was released the year before Bogarde's *Victim*, and the assembly of available young women in this adventure seem to be wasted on David Peel's apparently gay vampire, Baron Meinster. He attacks his own mother, Martita Hunt, in an Oedipal outrage after we have heard that in the past there had been "gay times" at the chateau. The relationship between the baroness and her sinister female servant (Freda Jackson) also echoes that of Danvers and Rebecca. The baroness has chained up her wayward son to keep him from infecting others with his decadent taste for blood (which in this context might be a metaphor for semen). Peel indeed does rather resemble Bogarde with his, expressive brown eyes, *retrousée* nose and elegant delivery of lines. He was also suspected to have been gay, bringing his pet poodles onto the sound stage during filming, and dubbed "a confirmed bachelor" by Hammer's publicity department.

It was not until after *Victim* and the liberalization of society's approach to homosexuality that gay vampires were "outed" in Roman Polanski's *The Fearless Vampire Killers* (1967), a film largely modeled on Don Sharp's *The Kiss of the Vampire*. In the latter, Barry Warren's piano-playing Carl, the charming vampire son of chief vampire Dr. Ravna, could also be regarded as gay. He plays the piano, after all, but the evidence is not conclusive. There is no doubt, however, about the orientation of Iain Quarrier's vampire, Herbert von Krolock, the undead son of Ferdy Mayne's Count von Krolock in *Fearless Vampire Killers,* who is first discovered drawing himself a bath in his nightshirt. Taking a fancy to Polanski's Alfred, one of the vampire killers, he sits next to him and discusses the art of love. He remarks admiringly on Alfred's long eyelashes ("They look like golden threads") and then reads from Alfred's love manual:

> Place the left arm around the shoulders of the loved one. Put the left hand on the left shoulder like a little birdie alighting the branch. Good. Excellent. Then let an angel pass. Shall we allow an angel to pass? Once the angel has passed, bend the face towards the locks of the loved one and brush them with the lips.

Unfortunately for Herbert, his fangs get stuck in the covers of the manual rather than Alfred's neck.

As British society became more permissive, Hammer became more sexually explicit. Female nudity was introduced in *The Vampire Lovers* (dir. Roy Ward Baker, 1970), in which Ingrid Pitt's lesbian vampire bites various exposed bosoms ("Laura, I feel that we'll be such good friends," she sighs to her first victim). But again, homosexuality is presented as an aberration. This lesbian vampire is a social outcast. She must be staked through the heart and decapitated to enable heterosexual normality to prevail once more. Indeed, this lesbian spin on vampirism caters primarily for the heterosexual male gaze.

Baker returned to helm Hammer's sex-twist production *Dr. Jekyll and Sister Hyde* the following year, in which the good doctor (Ralph Bates) turns into an evil female alter ego (Martine Beswick). But this transgender story did not point towards the current promulgation and support of the transgender community as, once again, such fluidity of gender is presented as morally wrong and unnatural. There is also an intriguing gay moment, when Jekyll, still himself but under the influence of Sister Hyde within him, encounters his very heterosexual neighbor, Howard Spencer (Lewis Fiander). Mrs. Hyde has already enjoyed a sexual encounter with Howard, and recalling this from the other side of his personality, Jekyll touches Howard's cheek, amorously gazing at him whilst softly whispering his name. Fiander's bewildered expression tells us all we need to know about the film's underlying attitude to homosexuality.

As we shall see, some of Dirk's films approach the horror genre, even if only in tenuous ways (*Our Mother's House* perhaps being the closest he ever got to it). *A Tale of Two Cities* (dir. Ralph Thomas, 1958), in which Bogarde played the self-sacrificing hero Sydney Carton, has many intriguing, if only coincidental, parallels with the famous brand of Hammer horror. Most obviously, the film's year of release coincided with that of Hammer's *Dracula* (dir. Terence Fisher), in which Christopher Lee plays the title role. In *A Tale of Two Cities,* Lee plays a comparable villain, the Marquis de Saint-Evremond, who peers out of the window of his chateau like the count in the much later *Scars of Dracula* (dir. Roy Ward Baker, 1970). In fact, Lee's performance is remarkably similar to his interpretation of his most famous role, not least Dracula's aristocratic hauteur and penchant for violence and rape. Saint-Evremond's death scene is very Draculine. He is dispatched with a knife, rather than a wooden

Christopher Lee as the Marquis de Saint Evremond in *A Tale of Two Cities* (dir. Ralph Thomas, 1958).

stake, through the heart, on which is speared a note: "Drive Him Fast to His Tomb." Composer Richard Addinsell even anticipates James Bernard's famous "Dra-Cu-La" theme of a falling octave in a scene in which Donald Pleasence's Barsac visits Rosalie Crutchley's inn. "It's too horrible to watch!" Cecil Parker's Jarvis Lorry laments during a riot scene—a line that could easily have been borrowed from a horror film poster. *Two Cities* also features a host of British character actors who would grace later horror films: George Woodbridge (the innkeeper in Fisher's *Dracula*); Douglas Lamont (here playing M. Defarge, but later to appear in Cyril Frankel's *The Witches*); Freda Jackson, whose interpretation of "The Vengeance" is hardly distinguishable from her crazed Greta in *Brides of Dracula*; Donald Pleasence is as grotesque as he would be in *From Beyond the Grave* (dir. Kevin Connor, 1974), in which Ian Bannen also appears, as he does in *Two Cities* (as the Marquis' manservant). Alfie Bass, the future Jewish vampire of Polanski's *The Fearless Vampire Killers*, plays a coach driver in *Two Cities*, and Rosalie Crutchley, future Egyptologist in Seth Holt's *Blood from the Mummy's Tomb* (1971), plays the sinister Madame Defarge. Even Leo McKern, later the archaeologist Bugenhagen in *The Omen* (dir. Richard Donner, 1976), plays the counsel for the prosecution, while Hubert Noel, who plays a border guard with a very English accent, would later play Count Sinistre, a vampire with an almost comically overdone French accent, in *Devil's of Darkness* (dir. Lance Comfort,

1965). *Two Cities* opens much like Hammer's Gothic entertainments, with a coach driving through misty woodland. Later, there's even a thunderstorm: "A storm indeed," says Jarvis Lorry, "enough to bring the dead out of their graves."

Gayness is perhaps less obvious in *Two Cities* but, with Bogarde in the lead, it is inevitably there. Ralph Thomas thought him perfectly cast, due to his "vulnerability" and his consequent ability to command immense sympathy—especially from women. Bogarde could also be convincingly *languid*, a quality that epitomized the lethargic and world-weary Carton, who "has the misfortune to be born without energy." Bogarde remains on the straight side of camp, but his performance is not so very far away from his super-villain Gabriel in Joseph Losey's *Modesty Blaise* (1966). There are all the characteristically weary smiles and the somewhat louche, tongue-in-cheek reactions, not to mention the famous raised eyebrow. Carton, of course, falls in love with the heroine (Dorothy Tutin), but feels himself to be unworthy of her returning his affections. "I am a disappointed drudge, sir," he says to his own reflection. "I care for no man on Earth, and no man on Earth cares for me," which lament does suggest to some extent that he craves a man rather than a woman. The embittered loneliness and studied Weltschmerz curiously foreshadow Bogarde's own feelings following Tony Forwood's death and his lonely life in London after all his happy years in Provence:

> I unpacked, suddenly felt dreadfully flat and weary. A fine rain spilled down the windows. On the terrace the pots and tubs were draggled and sere with the last of the summer. I'd deal with all that later.
> Emptiness sighs. Perfectly all right. No problem.
> Offenbach said, in one of his lyrics, "When you can't have what you love, you must love what you have."
> Fine, I'll go along with that.
> Why not?[11]

And Carton's love for Miss Manette could be said to have resembled Bogarde's own apparent infatuation with Capucine (Germaine Lefebvre), with whom he later starred in the Liszt biopic *Song Without End* (dir. George Cukor, 1960). In an astonishing flight of fancy even for a professional fantasist, Bogarde devoted an entire chapter in one of his memoirs to this "affair" with Capucine, whom he professed to have loved as much as Carton loves Miss Manette:

> "Cap, you do know, don't you, that I love you? I love you *very* much," and she kissed my cheek and said she loved me very much too![12]

But Carton's lethargy and cynicism concludes Bogarde's Capucine chapter, which, as Coldstream observes, does rather support the view of critic Keith

Baxter, who was of the opinion that the book as a whole expressed Bogarde's lack of "and kind of Faith in the goodness of life" and is "apparently bereft of Hope and devoid of the least hint of Charity."[13] Bogarde's description of Capucine's death is indeed singularly cruel and detached—and curiously suggestive of horror film imagery:

> Fastidious to the very end, and secretive, she had apparently fed her cats, locked the flat, climbed to the roof and typically of her, to avoid any distress to others, jumped out over the back of the block and landed sprawled among the dustbins. A slight figure, beautifully groomed and dressed for a lazy stroll round the lake in the afternoon sunshine. She wasn't discovered apparently until later, when the flies had started on her lips.[14]

Chapter Two

"I'm better on my own."

When Bogarde was born in 1921, homosexuality in England was a kind of secret society or, in more fortunate and sophisticated circles, an open secret. The novelist Hugh Walpole, the main literary rival of the predominantly gay (and unhappily married) W. Somerset Maugham, was also the unlikely friend of fellow traveler Virginia Woolf, who remarked in her diary on March 30, 1939 (when Dirk would have just turned 18):

> No, it was a good idea having [Hugh] Walpole alone. He gave me a full account of his sexual life, of which I retain these facts. He only loves men who don't love men. Tried to drown himself once over [Lauritz] Melchior. Jumped into a river; stuck in mud; seized a carving knife; saw himself in the glass; all became absurd. Reconciliation. Told me too of the Baths at the Elephant & Castle. How the men go there. Has had a married life with Harold [Cheevers] for fifteen years without intercourse. All this piles up a rich life of which I have no knowledge; and he can't use it in his novels. They are therefore about lives he hasn't lived which explains their badness. Hasn't the courage to write about his real life. Would shock people he likes. Told me how he had had a father and son simultaneously. Copulation removes barriers. Class barriers fade. Lives at Hampstead with Harold's family and friends completely naturally.[1]

Contrary to Woolf's claim, Walpole's "hidden" homosexuality did find its way into his novels. In *The Prelude to Adventure* (1912), Walpole's description of a rugby match (a game he personally much enjoyed as a spectator) is positively homoerotic. (Coincidentally, in his film with Judy Garland, *I Could Go On Singing* [dir. Ronald Neame, 1963], Bogarde's character also attends a rugby match, and somewhat unconvincingly cheers on his very muddy son: Dirk himself was certainly no football fan.) Walpole's description continues:

> He felt that the clouds were spreading behind him and a little wind seemed to be whispering in the grass—"Coming, Coming, Coming." His very existence now was strung to a pitch of expectation.
> As in a dream he saw that a Dublin man with the ball had got clear away from the clump of Cambridge forwards, and was coming towards him. Behind him only was Lawrence. He flung himself at the man's knees, caught them, falling himself desperately forward. They both came crashing to the ground....

He had a crowd of men upon him. Handing off, bending, doubling, almost down,
slipping and then up again—he was through them....
Surely never, in the annals of Rugby football, had any one run as Olva ran then.
Only now the Dublin back, and he, missing the apparent swerve to the right, clutched
desperately at Olva's back, caught the buckle of his "shorts" and stood with the thing
torn off in his hand.[2]

Even in unexpected places, Walpole is able to charge his descriptions
with homoerotic subtext. In *Rogue Herries* (1930), a young boy feels excited
by riding with his father:

But here he was pressed against his father's body, and he could feel the movement of
his thighs and above his head the throb of his heart, and in his face the wind was
beating like a whip.[3]

And in *Wintersmoon* (1927), Walpole almost ventures into lesbian incest in
his description of a woman's love for her sibling: "How many times she had
adored to busy her hands in Rosalind's lovely hair, to pull the head slowly
back to her breast and then bend over and kiss the smooth forehead and the
closed eyelids. When Rosalind was weary she liked that."[4]

I dwell on Walpole, not only because, as Bogarde said of his own writ-
ings, one has to read between the lines to get the message, but also because
Walpole's Platonic partnership with Harold Cheevers was similar to Bogarde's
later relationship with Forwood. However, Forwood was not the first man in
Bogarde's life. Dirk's sister Elizabeth recalled that there had been "Tony Jones,
John Nelson and there was another one—terribly nice chap, who died sadly.
He was in the army. It was during the war that he knew a lot of these. And I
used to go on the back of their motorbikes and have a lovely time. I didn't
care tuppence whether they were sleeping together or not. It didn't bother
me one bit. [...] Then he met Tony Forwood and that was it, absolutely 'it.'"[5]

One might also usefully compare the partnership of Bogarde and Forwood with that of British composer Benjamin Britten and singer Peter Pears.
(Intriguingly, both Britten and Visconti thought of adapting Mann's *Death
in Venice* around the same time, though Britten's opera is far more in touch
with what the novella is actually about.) Britten and Pears, like Bogarde and
Forwood, were always seen together, but euphemisms were required, the term
"friends" serving Britten and Pears, and "business manager" explaining away
Bogarde's reliance on Forwood. "Companion" also served both couples
equally well. Britten disliked identifying himself as part of a gay community.
In fact, he resented the use of the word "gay" to identify homosexuals, as he
found nothing "gay" (in the old sense of the word) in the social predicament
that it then was. "The word 'gay' was not in his vocabulary," Pears revealed
after Britten's death.[6]

But at least Britten and Pears were a couple out in the open, and their correspondence fully reveals the strength of affection between them. Bogarde, on the contrary, went to extraordinary lengths to avoid an admission of any emotional attachment, and famously burned all his letters and diaries in his later years to avoid anyone finding out about his private life. "I'm better on my own," he confessed on the BBC's *Desert Island Discs*. "I don't want anybody in my life. I never have."[7] Tony was virtually airbrushed out of the public picture and began to resemble "Everard," the imaginary "friend" of the comedian Larry Grayson, who always formed an off-stage presence during his routines. When TV interviewer Russell Harty asked Bogarde about Forwood, Dirk merely said, "Yeah, he's here," suggesting more a servant than a life partner; but as their housekeeper Agnes Zwickl remembered, Forwood was "awfully good-looking, very charming. All the women fell around him like crazy. He seemed to me to be a person to whom you could tell anything. He did everything for Mr. Bogarde. Whatever he touched came out right, whatever he arranged for Mr. Bogarde came out right too. I never heard an argument between them."[8] Of course, the reason for Bogarde's secrecy was primarily fear.

There were many precedents from closer to hand than merely Oscar Wilde to inspire such fear. John Gielgud, with whom Bogarde acted in two films, and who became a friend, very nearly had his career and reputation destroyed by a 1953 incident in a public lavatory. James Bernard, composer for many Hammer horror films, told me that one evening Gielgud rang the doorbell of the flat James shared with his partner, Paul Dehn, to discuss what he should do. Dehn was a great help, if only in a supportive sense, and Gielgud survived the ordeal, largely because of his immense reputation, which was not contaminated by the submerged resentment and outrage courted by Wilde before him. Even as late as the 1970s, homosexual scandals could destroy an actor's career. In 1975, Peter Wyngarde, internationally famous for the role of Jason King on TV's *Department S* (and apparently also known to some as Petunia Winegum), was fined for propositioning a crane driver in the public lavatory in Gloucester, after which he found himself in much less demand.

Similarly, Britten and Pears realized the importance of lying low. Unlike Forwood, Pears did not give up his own career to manage Britten's affairs. He kept on singing, and Britten kept on composing especially for his voice, the emotional partnership complementing the artistic one. But Britten also had constantly a need for the companionship of young boys—not, apparently, in any predatory way, but perhaps more in the manner of Aschenbach's need for Tadzio in "Death in Venice." ("He is a nice thing and I am very fond of him,—thank heaven not sexually, but I am getting to such a condition that I am lost without some children [of either sex] near me,"[9] he wrote of one such friendship.)

Similarly, Bogarde often claimed that he had yearned to be a father. His time working with children on *Our Mother's House* was, according to one of his remarks, a magical experience: "The children were fantastic, good actors, kind, funny, devoted and professional."[10] Bogarde's fantasies of fatherhood had earlier reached a level of unreality unmatched by his experience of that film. In *Hunted* and *The Spanish Gardener,* he had been paired with child actor Jon Whiteley, who had found Bogarde "a jolly and generous companion"[11] Later, Bogarde suggested that he had wanted to adopt Whiteley, to save him from an apparently unhappy family life. This, according to Whiteley, was "mind-boggling rubbish" as he had always enjoyed very happy relations with his parents. "I thought he must have been talking about somebody else, and the BBC had put the wrong picture up on the screen. There was no bearing on reality at all. Apart from anything else, we were a particularly close-knot family [...] I found the whole account very bizarre."[12]

Britten's fantasies, no less complicated, were reflected in his opera *Peter Grimes,* in which the eponymous fisherman, an outcast like Britten, is actually destroyed by his relationship with an apprentice, who ambiguously dies in Grimes' service. Britten had friendships with many boys: Robin Long, aka "the Nipper" (a fisher-boy friend, whom Britten also wanted "more of less to adopt," but who was killed in a road accident several years after the friendship ended), the child actors David Spencer (who created the role of Harry in Britten's opera *Billy Budd*) and David Hemmings (the original Miles in Britten's *The Turn of the Screw*), composer James Bernard, who was his amanuensis for a time, and Roger Duncan, son of Ronald Duncan, the librettist of Britten's opera *The Rape of Lucretia.* Once again, Britten wanted to adopt Roger, and even asked his father if he would agree: "Will you allow me to give him presents, visit him at school, and let him spend part of his school holidays with me—in other words, share him?"[13] Though the pedophilia paranoia of our own time might regard these liaisons with some suspicion, there is no evidence of any wrongdoing on Britten's part. But there remains the thorny question of his equal fascination of the corruption of innocence in his operas—a persistent theme throughout all of Britten's work.

Though Pears continued to work as a singer in his own right, Britten's tailoring of so many vocal works to his particular voice in some senses resembled Forwood's "promotion" of Bogarde in his managerial role. Both Forwood and Pears were intimately associated with their partners' creative careers. Pears was three years older than Britten. Forwood was six years older than Bogarde. Whereas Pears was always somewhat guarded and "mysterious"

("You never knew what Peter was thinking, never"[14]), Forwood was rather more lovable (to those who knew about him) than Dirk. "I think Tony liked himself much more than Dirk liked *himself*," recalled actress Helena Bonham Carter. "Dirk always had demons. But Tony was always happy within his skin."[15] Dirk, however, felt that nothing he could say or do "would ever convince him that people actually did like him *much* better than me!"[16]

Britten suffered more homophobic prejudice than Bogarde, presumably because Britten, though equally unable to "come out," did not disguise his relationship with Pears under any facade of Pears being merely his "manager." Consequently, he had to endure the innuendos of enemies, such as being part of a so-called a "buggers' alliance."[17] It is hardly surprising, given the climate of those pre–Wolfenden times, that Britten, like Bogarde, declined to discuss homosexuality in public. His works, however, frequently addressed the subject, even if only implicitly. His setting of Hölderlein's "Socrates und Alcibiades" is more explicit:

> Why, holy Socrates, do you court
> This youth all the time? Don't you know of anything greater?
> Why do your eyes gaze on him with love,
> As if you were looking at the gods?
> He who has pondered the most profound thoughts,
>   loves what is most alive;
> He who has seen the world understands lofty virtue.
> And in the end, the wise will often
> Bend toward that which is beautiful.

Britten's setting of the sixth of *Seven Michelangelo Sonnets* is an eloquent expression of any kind of love, but in the context of Michelangelo's own homosexuality, it obviously had an extra resonance for Britten. It also describes well the Platonic relationship of Bogarde and Forwood:

> If there is a chaste love, a heavenly pity,
> an equal fortune between two lovers,
> a bitter fate shared by both,
> and if a single spirit and one will governs two hearts;
> if one soul in two bodies is made eternal,
> raising both to heaven on the same wings;
> if love with one blow and one golden arrow
> can burn and pierce two hearts to the core;
> if each loves the other rather than himself,
> with a pleasure and delight so rewarding,
> that to the same end they both strive;
> if thousands upon thousands are not worth a hundredth
> part of such a loving bond of such a faith;
> then shall anger alone break and dissolve it?

Britten's setting of Herman Melville's *Billy Budd* has a particularly gay resonance, as have *Young Apollo,* the *Serenade for Tenor, Horn and Strings, Owen Wingrave, The Turn of the Screw, Les Illuminations* and many more. Pears' letter to Britten in 1974, when Britten was nearing his end, touchingly illuminates all this. Pears writes of *Grimes,* the *Serenade,* the *Michelangelo Sonnets* as having given him everything, describing himself as Britten's "mouthpiece," living in his music.

Bogarde and Forwood enjoyed a similarly symbiotic relationship. In managing Dirk's career, Forwood also lived Dirk's career. But before devoting himself to fostering it, Forwood, as we have seen, had cut a handsome figure as a supporting actor, standing 6'1", with none of the camp accessories of Bogarde's performance style; Forwood had been married to Glynis Johns, had had a son and was in every sense of the phrase more straight acting.

In *Traveller's Joy* (1949), Forwood was directed by Ralph Thomas, who would launch Bogarde's international career with the *Doctor* films. Forwood's uncredited appearance in Raoul Walsh's Napoleonic naval drama *Captain Horatio Hornblower R.N.* (1951) foreshadowed Bogarde's starring role in the very similar, though less lavishly photographed *H.M.S. Defiant* (dir. Lewis Gilbert, 1962). James Robertson Justice, Bogarde's nemesis in the *Doctor* films, and Stanley Baker, his sparring partner in Joseph Losey's *Accident* and *Campbell's Kingdom* (dir. Ralph Thomas, 1957), also appear in this, as does Christopher Lee as a Spanish captain, six years before his big break as the Creature in Hammer's *The Curse of Frankenstein* (dir. Terence Fisher, 1957). In Forwood's next film, Ken Annakin's 1952 *The Story of Robin Hood and His Merrie Men*, he played Will Scarlet (Robertson Justice was the obvious choice for Little John). Similar heroics were required of him in *Knights of the Round Table* (dir. Richard Thorpe 1953), in which he appeared as Gareth (coincidentally the name he and his wife Glynis Johns named their son, before Forwood left them to live with Bogarde).

Anthony Forwood as Will Scarlet in Walt Disney's *The Story of Robin Hood and His Merrie Men* (dir. Ken Annakin, 1952).

Forwood then gave up acting, tying himself to Bogarde's mast, though he did put in cameos in Bogarde's subsequent film *Permission to Kill* (dir. Cyril Frankel, 1975), having done the same in *Appointment in London* (dir. Philip Leacock, 1953) and *The Wind Cannot Read* (dir. Ralph Thomas, 1958). Otherwise, he became a shadowy figure to the public, always in the background but rarely mentioned, still less ever seen, though well known and respected within the film industry. It was obvious to insiders that Bogarde and Forwood's partnership was more than a mere business arrangement, but speculation was kept afloat in public until the end. And to that end, Bogarde destroyed any "compromising" information, though Forwood's later correspondence does contain fascinating insights behind the scenes of the film industry, particularly in this passage about Visconti's working method:

> He is unique in that his interest in detail is minute. Every part of every costume is scrutinized and all afternoon was spent sitting hunched in a chair on that set watching the set-dressing changed (including the carpet) towards something he would approve of. I suppose he is an anachronism, and his kind of film can only be made for large expenditure over as long as he needs to get it right.[18]

James Fox, who starred opposite Bogarde in Joseph Losey's *The Servant,* felt that Forwood had more class than Bogarde:

> On the one hand you felt that Tony was not in any way somebody who would be kicked about. He would send Dirk up. But Dirk would be quite bossy with him, and Tony did not seem to mind when he was being rude, abusive, domineering. He probably enjoyed being a little subservient. Obviously there must have been some sort of psycho-sexual thing going on, but who knows? Tony was the practical one, the one who drove the Rolls. I think Tony probably saw himself as the one who *should* be driving a Rolls. Later, Tony did the cooking, but I couldn't see him wanting to do the washing-up. Dirk did that. Nor can I imagine Tony making the sauce for the spaghetti, whereas I can see Dirk with his apron on, preparing his sauce—fussing, pottering, complaining, whistling.[19]

When the BBC suggested that Bogarde appear alongside Cliff Richard on Terry Wogan's chat show in the 1980s, Bogarde sensibly declined, and Tony remarked, "One sees what they would make out of it."[20] Indeed, the joint attempt to disguise this elephant in the room perhaps drew more attention to it than if they had faced the music and acknowledged it. As Coldstream reminds us, when Bogarde's novel *A Gentle Occupation* appeared, the *Daily Express'* "William Hickey" gossip column drew comparisons with novelist W. Somerset Maugham and his liaison with Gerald Haxton.[21] Haxton was a very different character from Forwood, but Maugham, like Forwood, had also married. As Maugham's biographer Frederic Raphael put it, when Maugham married Syrie Wellcome, he "split his bets and his personality. He married Syrie and divorced himself. Only his cynicism endured as a recon-

ciling factor."[22] Maugham needed to keep up a conventional front to please
his readers, as he was terrified of being identified as a homosexual. Like Forwood, Haxton was officially described merely as Maugham's "companion and
secretary." (Maugham's greatest contemporary competitor, Hugh Walpole,
similarly placed Harold Cheevers at the top of his list of "First Fifteen friends,
but went no further."[23])

Like Bogarde, Maugham dedicated one of his books (*A Writer's Note-
book*) to his "friend." Haxton arranged things for Maugham, as Forwood did
for Bogarde. Raphael describes Haxton as gregarious and charming, but
unlike Bogarde and Forwood, Haxton and Maugham often spent long periods
apart. When Maugham was in London, Haxton remained on the Continent.[24]
The terror of suffering the same fate as Wilde lay behind Maugham's refusal
to do anything about reforming the law. He never stood up for homosexuality
as Bogarde would do in *Victim,* and never spoke of his psycho-sexual reality
in public, even though, as Raphael reminds us, he attended a dinner in Wilde's
honor during the days of the author's disgrace, championing Wilde's wit and
brilliance, but drawing a veil over what had caused that disgrace. Forwood,
by contrast, relished having a statue of Wilde in the garden he shared with
Bogarde at Adam's Farm in Sussex, with "a Yucca up his arse."[25] Forwood suffered from Parkinson's disease, whereas Haxton drank himself to death, and
Maugham's grief over Gerald's passing was as great as Bogarde's over Forwood:

> You'll never know how great a grief this has been to me. The best years of my life—
> those we spent wandering about the world—are inextricably connected with him. And
> in one way or another—however indirectly—all I've written during the last twenty
> years has something to do with him—if only that he typed my manuscripts for me.[26]

This was the closest Maugham ever got to a public admission of his love for
Haxton, and it does indeed resemble Bogarde's guarded approach. He opened
up more than ever before in his sixth autobiography, *A Short Walk from Harrods* (1993), which describes Forwood's illness and death from Parkinson's
disease, Bogarde's own stroke and subsequent life on his own, but Sheridan
Morley observed, "The sound here is once again of closet doors being cau-
tiously half-opened and then slammed in our faces just as we were about to
poke about inside."[27] Of course, "keep them guessing" is a well-known way
of maintaining readers' attention, though Forwood's death is described in
both *A Short Walk from Harrods* and Bogarde's collection of reviews, *For the
Time Being,* in ways which make it hard to sustain any doubt about the truth.
Dirk was not better on his own:

> I experienced the despair when my manager and companion of fifty years lay dying
> in London, totally paralyzed with Parkinson's disease and terminal cancer and virtually

speechless. He was not shrieking, but was in deep, dire distress. When we lived in France I had promised that I would help him, but he had not put his request in writing, and we did not know about signing a "living will."

I would have done something—though I could not have stood in a court and proved that was what he wanted—but eventually he slipped into a coma. Almost his last words as his night nurse and I turned him were: "If you did this to a dog, they'd arrest you."[28]

I sat at his bedside looking silently at the dreadful demolition job being wrought on a good, kind, gentle man. It was quite enough to make anyone question any possible belief in God. […] I realized fully just how bloody useless I was on my own. There was absolutely no need for anything that I might do now. No morale to boost, no tray to set up, no sandwiches or takeaways for nurses. No Bloody Marys to soak in the cotton wool. No work. No future. Bewilderment all round. My carousel had ground to a halt. I had no idea how to restart it.[29]

Chapter Three

"You'll wake up in Broadmoor."

Bogarde shot to fame playing juvenile delinquents, and for a while he became typecast. The reasons for this are revealing, and they are intimately connected with misunderstood qualities of his own personality. What made him a convincing psychopath were the very qualities that disqualified him from being an action hero. (Military roles were an exception, for reasons discussed in the next chapter.) A less likely action hero than Bogarde it would be hard to imagine. By his own account, Dirk was hardly beefcake:

> Now, the fact that I was a scrawny as a plucked hen—and a skinny hen at that—didn't seem to matter. I mean, the Rank Organization did supply me with dumb-bells and great sets of wheels that I was supposed to do that with. All I did was to put on two sweaters and then put my shirt on and then put my jacket on, so everything was tailored that way. But it didn't matter.[1]

In Christine Geraghty's study of genre and gender in British cinema of the 1950s, she points out that Bogarde's "handsome good looks and tentative, tender, gentle manner was hugely appealing to women in a cinema otherwise dominated by rugged, silent types."[2] She also draws our attention to Andy Medhurst's observation that Bogarde "was at odds with the 'existing norms of masculinity' as expressed by stars like Kenneth More and Richard Todd."[3] And this helps explain the problem of all Bogarde's toe-dipping into the stormy waters of the action hero.

By contrast, his psychopaths and criminals were characterized by weakness, which is not at all the same thing as gentleness and sensitivity. But all Bogarde had to do was channel these qualities into a mirror image, so to speak, and combine them with his "feminine" (and, by implication, "hysterical") features to excel in a series of what he called "dirty mackintosh" roles. Those early roles led to much bigger things, principally because Visconti admired one of Bogarde's latter forays into the territory of criminal weakness in Jack Clayton's *Our Mother's House*. Bogarde recorded the conversation he had with Visconti about this in *Snakes and Ladders.* They were discussing Bogarde's possible casting in *The Damned,* which Visconti equated with the story of *Macbeth.* "Macbeth is weak, a weak man," he insisted.

"I have to play so many weak men," Bogarde complained.

"Maybe you play them well?" Visconti observed, listing the roles of Stephen in *Accident,* Barratt in *The Servant* and the "Pappa" in *Our Mother's House* as examples of weak characters. "I must have a *strong* actor to play a weak man, not a weak actor," Visconti insisted.[4] This was a highly perceptive understanding of Bogarde's particular quality, which both launched his career and helped redefine it after he had left dirty mackintoshes far behind him.

However, Bogarde began his film career as a Victorian footman with a talent for gambling on the horses in the 1948 adaptation of George Moore's *Esther Waters* (dir. Ian Dalrymple and Peter Proud). Bogarde thought his performance as William Latch and the film in general were disasters,[5] but neither were as bad as that. In fact, Bogarde was rather well cast as the charming but selfish servant, who gets poor Esther pregnant and then abandons her in favor of the aristocratic daughter of his employer. There is also one unwittingly apposite line, uttered by Mrs. Latch (William's mother, the cook, played by Mary Clare): "A man needs a woman to keep him straight." Homosexuality is not intended here, but it nonetheless has a certain resonance. *Esther Waters* is a kind of Victorian *Cathy Come Home* (Ken Loach's famous TV play about single mothers, first broadcast on the BBC in 1966). Esther's descent into squalor after her abandonment makes her resistant to William's later blandishments when they meet again, he being by then reasonably well-off and wearing a mustache as a signifier of supposedly greater maturity. But William falls ill and Bogarde has the first of his many subsequent death scenes.

William Latch is not a villain in the strictly criminal sense, but he is certainly irresponsible and selfish, and Bogarde's ability to convey Latch's charm and weakness, vulnerability and determination secured his second film role. In *Quartet* (dir. Harold French, 1948), he played an aspiring pianist who commits suicide on being informed that he will never be good enough to succeed in a concert career. Such a highly strung character (an outsider, in many ways, from the pleasant but dull aristocratic family from which he comes) initiated Bogarde's later succession of criminals, spies, outsiders and social misfits. There is, indeed, a connection between the "artistic" and the criminal types in his career, which Thomas Mann, an author with whom Bogarde was subsequently to have much to do, felt was almost inevitable. In "Tonio Kröger," Mann writes:

> I know a banker, a grey-haired business man, who has a gift for writing stories. He employs this gift in his idle hours, and some of his stories are of the first rank. But

despite—I say despite—this excellent gift, his withers are by no means unwrung: on the contrary, he has had to serve a prison sentence, on anything but trifling grounds. Yes, it was actually first *in prison* that he became conscious of his gifts, and his experiences as a convict are the main theme in all his works. One might be rash enough to conclude that a man has to be at home in some kind of jail in order to become a poet. But can you escape the suspicion that the source and essence of his being as artist had less to do with his life in prison than they had with the reasons that *brought him there?* A banker who writes—that is a rarity, isn't it? But a banker who isn't a criminal, who is irreproachably respectable, and yet writes—he doesn't exist.[6]

The Borstal drama *Boys in Brown* (dir. Montgomery Tully, 1949), which appeared one year after *Esther Waters*, cast Bogarde as the splendidly slippery and soft-spoken Welsh lad, Alfie Rawlings. Bogarde's villains in this early part of his career are far more convincing than his later ones, lacking, as they do, all traces of camp. Alfie is a scheming, double-crossing charmer with what Bogarde himself called "the reckless daring which springs from cowardice,"[7] and it was the inherent vulnerability in Bogarde's persona, that febrile sensitivity, which could so easily be made malicious and misanthropic, which directors correctly identified as being so appropriate for such roles. Director Tully described Alfie as having "blue eyes, an angel face and an ingratiating manner. There is a sinister quality of Sadism about him."[8] If Bogarde's later performance in *Accident* was, as he claimed it to be, his Hamlet, Bogarde's Alfie is his Iago. He greets Richard Attenborough's nervous, shame-faced Jackie Knowles (a hapless getaway driver for a couple of jewel thieves, whose car won't start after the robbery has taken place), with all the lilting charm of a Welsh wizard; but when he offers to be Jackie's pal, Jackie, desperate to get through the experience of Borstal with a good record and rightly suspicious of Alfie's manner, decides he would be better off looking after himself. Michael Medwin's cocksure "Sparrow" Thompson, says, "That Alfie don't 'arf give me the creeps," and, indeed, this is one of Bogarde's most unnerving performances, mainly because it is so understated. His lean, sharply chiseled features, dark eyebrows, liquid eyes and casual grace all help to suggest this fallen angel, who sets about trying to destroy Jackie's chances of going straight—to "grind him down." In fact, the performance is very much a demonstration of the "motiveless malignancy" that Coleridge identified in Shakespeare's Iago:

> The last speech, [Iago's soliloquy,] the motive-hunting of motiveless malignity—how awful! In itself fiendish; while yet he was allowed to bear the divine image, too fiendish for his own steady view. A being next to the devil, only *not* quite devil—and this Shakespeare has attempted—executed—without disgust, without scandal![9]

Playing on Jackie's weakness (both Bogarde and Attenborough both specialized in this quality, though in rather different ways), Alfie manages to inveigle him into an escape plan with several other ne'er-do-wells. But Jackie changes his mind at the last minute, sensibly thinking it best to obey the rules and play the system. If he is to persuade Jackie to change his mind back again, Alfie must somehow make him hate the system as much as he does. His principal means of achieving this is sneakily to show Jackie the photo of Jackie's girlfriend Kitty (played by Barbara Murray), which he has found in the drawer of fellow conspirator Bill Foster (Jimmy Hanley). Bill had been released at the start of the story, met Kitty, reoffended and returned. Kitty remained faithful to Jackie, but Jackie is persuaded to think that Bill has stolen her from him. (Bill was merely meant to pass the photo on to Jackie, as a keepsake from Kitty, but he doesn't do so until it is too late.) The scene in which Alfie sets up all this is just as powerful as the way in which Iago works on Othello's jealousy by manipulating the business with Desdemona's handkerchief:

IAGO

Nay, but be wise: yet we see nothing done;
She may be honest yet. Tell me but this,
Have you not sometimes seen a handkerchief
Spotted with strawberries in your wife's hand?

OTHELLO

I gave her such a one; 'twas my first gift.

IAGO

I know not that; but such a handkerchief—
I am sure it was your wife's—did I today
See Cassio wipe his beard with.

OTHELLO

If it be that—

IAGO

If it be that, or any that was hers,
It speaks against her with the other proofs.

OTHELLO

O, that the slave had forty thousand lives!
One is too poor, too weak for my revenge.
Now do I see 'tis true. Look here, Iago;
All my fond love thus do I blow to heaven.
'Tis gone.
Arise, black vengeance, from thy hollow cell!
Yield up, O love, thy crown and hearted throne
To tyrannous hate! Swell, bosom, with thy fraught,
For 'tis of aspics' tongues!

The sly smile Dirk gives to Alfie, his *sotto voce* delivery and languid move-ments create the finest villainy he ever conveyed, far outshining his much less believable and far less virile Nazi, Bruckmann, in Visconti's *The Damned*. The plan works: Jackie's sense of betrayal makes him think there is no point in obeying the rules, and he rejoins the gang.

But the plan goes wrong when one of the "screws" discovers Jackie up to no good, and Jackie hits him on the head. There is some doubt as to whether the man will survive. When the boys are rounded up, they all refuse to talk; but at the last moment, Alfie claims that he did the deed, knowing full well that this will make Jackie confess. That way, Alfie gets Jackie to incriminate himself and face being hanged if the charge is converted to mur-der. It is a particularly nasty thing to do, and all for no other real reason than the desire to destroy someone whom Alfie rightly thinks can be easily manip-ulated. Bogarde said at the time that he enjoyed playing Alfie, claiming that he played the part "with the deepest love than an actor can give a character."[10] It shows, especially at the end when the other boys round on him for being a double-crosser. On his knees before the governor, he reveals the terrified and abused boy beneath the sly veneer:

> They went on hitting me, like my dad did the first time he caught me stealing. He thrashed me, sir. I swore I wouldn't do it again. I promised. I promised. I begged him to stop, but he wouldn't stop, sir. I can't bear being hurt. I can't stand it, sir, but I can't be blamed for being scared, sir. You see, they all hate me. They all hate me here. They know I'm a coward, see, they know it, and they'll bash me up—they'll bash me every time they get a chance, they'll bash me, sir.

Bogarde's most celebrated villainous role is surely Tom Riley in *The Blue Lamp* (dir. Basil Dearden, 1950), in which he famously shoots Jack Warner's policeman at a time when such a thing was almost unheard of in Britain. In many ways, Dearden's later *Victim* is a companion piece to *The Blue Lamp,* each film discussing, as they do, a pressing social issue of the day. In *The Blue Lamp,* it's what to do about juvenile delinquency. Seen from today's perspective, Bogarde's performance is the most interesting thing about the film, the heartiness of the policemen now seeming almost absurdly out of date, especially when we observe them lustily rehearsing their male voice choir. Bogarde's splendidly shifty Tom Riley, however, is just as relevant today as he was in 1950. Constantly on the lookout for the police, with roving eyes, furtive movements and bluff bravado which turns to blind panic when he is caught, Bogarde epitomized the feelings British audiences had about youth in this postwar period, when traditional social structures seem to have been broken down by a war that propaganda had suggested would bring everyone together.

Bogarde as Tom Reilly holds up Doris Yorke in *The Blue Lamp* (dir. Basil Dearden, 1950).

The Blue Lamp is about social outsiders, and, as a homosexual in 1950, Bogarde knew all about how it felt to be an outsider. Simply by being homosexual at the time, Bogarde was indeed a criminal, even if an un-prosecuted one, and *The Blue Lamp* is not so very different from *Victim* in the way it conveys the anxiety (and thrill) of living against the law. Although it is not about homosexuality, it is definitely about sex. Bogarde and Dearden knew full well the phallic power of a gun. "When you've got one of these in your hands, people listen to you," says Riley, fondling his weapon in a sexually charged manner. "I reckon a scare is good for your insides." For him, the thrill of crime is orgasmic: "Makes you think quicker. You're all keyed up and then, afterwards, you feel terrific, like...." At which point he kisses his girl (Peggy Evans), words thereafter being redundant. (A screaming train whistle obliges instead, to underscore the implication.) Later, he tries to strangle the girl in a desperate attempt to silence her, and there is a distinctly Sadean feeling to this as well.

Tom is described in the documentary-style voiceover at the beginning of the film as one of many "restless and ill-adjusted youngsters." They "lack the code, experience and self-discipline of a professional thief," who, presumably, would never shoot a policeman, and would always concede to a "fair cop" if they were caught. To signify his character's dubious nature, Bogarde wears absurdly wide lapels, as he did when he played the less villainous outsider role in *Once a Jolly Swagman* (dir. Jack Lee, 1948).

That film, also known as *Maniacs on Wheels,* contains no actual criminality (if we discount the Nazis who inhabit the fringes of the story). But Bogarde's performance as a working-class speedway hero (surely the most unlikely of roles for a man who had no affinity with cars and mechanics) could easily have moved in that direction. His tough portrayal of Bill Fox again avoided all traces of camp but did reveal his vulnerability. Like an artist (and, according to Thomas Mann, a criminal as well), Bill has no interest in working a steady job. Instead, he takes up speedway racing as a means of getting rich quick. His working-class parents disapprove of this, his mother (Thora Hird) at first refusing the money he offers her from his ill-gotten gains (she eventually relents), while his father (James Hayter) reprimands him: "A job's a job, son. You'll learn that one day." His morally upstanding brother Dick (Patric Doonan) goes off to Spain to fight the fascists, while Bill falls in love with a Nazi-loving society girl known as Dotty Liz (Moira Lister). She displays a photograph of herself having a jolly night out with SS men at a Nuremberg Rally, which she describes as having been "a thrilling experience." Bill, whose success allows him to dress in jackets with those impossibly wide reveres, could so easily have melted into the criminal underworld, but for this film, speedway racing is disreputable enough to illustrate the alternative to conventional society's work ethic. When war comes, Bill's army comrade (Cyril Cusack) points out the dangers of being unhappy with your lot. "There are some people who are never satisfied," he says, meaning Hitler and the Nazis, but Bill takes this to heart, realizing that he would have been happier if he'd not left his grindingly boring job in a factory making glass bottles and stayed at home with his family, instead of making lots of money and being mobbed by hysterical female fans. In this respect, the film also anticipates Bogarde's own career and his professed hatred of "stardom," with its equally intrusive admirers. "Go on and sign the autographs," Bill's manager (Sid James) insists. "You're going to be a star!" And this film is indeed a critique of stardom in general. "Who do you think you're working for? Yourselves?" Bill's brother asks him later. "Yes, you make money. A lot of it too; but where do you think the really big money goes?"

BILL: We do all right. It's just a sport, that's all.
DICK: In Spain, they call bullfighting a sport.

BILL: It's a blood sport.

DICK: And speedway's not? You believe that? Oh, I know. For you, it's just a job, for all you riders. A way to make a living. But the crowd—you don't think they want to see you smash yourself up? Don't kid yourself. They want to see you swept up into little pieces.

This dialogue curiously foreshadows Bogarde's line in *Song Without End,* in which he plays the role of the similarly mobbed piano virtuoso Franz Liszt. For Bogarde's Liszt, the audience is like a dragon that comes "every night for your blood and every night you have to kill it. And the next night it's back again, breathing fire, and you have to kill it all over again."

Bogarde's first film with Joseph Losey, *The Sleeping Tiger* (1954), also exploits the psychopathic type. Like Bogarde himself, his character in this film, Frank Clements, doesn't like sport and can't ride a horse. Instead, unlike Bogarde, he holds up passersby, one of whom turns out to be a psychiatrist, Dr. Clive Esmond (Alexander Knox), who decides to invite him back for treatment as a resident patient in his own home. Though this is not a horror film, we do have here a very similar situation to the one we find in Hammer's *Hands of the Ripper* (dir. Peter Sasdy, 1971), in which Victorian psychiatrist Eric Porter takes into his personal care a pretty homicidal murderess (Angharad Rees), whom he discovers actually to be possessed by the spirit of her father, Jack the Ripper. The psychiatrist defends his patient even though he knows she is guilty of murder, and ultimately pays the price. Similarly, in *The Sleeping Tiger*, Esmond risks perjuring himself: When the police accuse Clements of robbery, Esmond provides him with a false alibi.

Bogarde is just as pretty as Angharad Rees and even more incorrigible than Jack the Ripper's daughter, committing his crimes purely on his own account without any prompting from the spirit world. Always elegant in his delinquency, Bogarde excels at insolent stares, cynical smiles and violence (early on, he deliberately trips up a female servant). Analysis reveals that Clements hated his bullying father and, after his mother was forced out of the family home, he hated his stepmother just as much as he hated his father. He wanted his father to die and when his father eventually did just that, he could never get over his sense of guilt. "Hate, guilt and fear" is Esmond's diagnosis. All this boils down to a simplified outline of Freud's contentious Oedipus complex, with its concomitant homosexual implications. Clements wanted his father to die, which according to Freud is quite normal (according to the theory, all boys want to take their father's place next to mother in bed), but the Oedipal theory suggests that "normal" boys overcome this desire, identify with the father and therefore become heterosexual. The gay ones don't. In identifying with the aggressor, the boy diminishes his castration anxiety and defends himself against the father's wrath as the two contend for the mother. Fear of "castration," to which Freud refers symbolically as the father's ability to render the son powerless, eventually resolves the conflict. The boy absorbs the masculinity of his father. Fear of "castration" (the father's ability to render him powerless) eventually prompts abandonment of this death wish and the boy instead identifies with him. The resolution of the conflict between the drives of the id and the ego is the defense mechanism of identification through which the boy internalizes the personality characteristics and the masculinity of the father. In identifying with the aggressor, the boy diminishes his castration anxiety and defends himself from the father's wrath as the two contend for the mother.

> It is the fate of all of us, perhaps, to direct our first sexual impulse towards our mother and our first hatred and our first murderous wish against our father. Our dreams convince us that this is so. King Oedipus, who slew his father Laïus and married his mother Jocasta, merely shows us the fulfillment of our own childhood wishes. But, more fortunate than he, we have meanwhile succeeded, in so far as we have not become psychoneurotics, in detaching our sexual impulses from our mothers and in forgetting our jealousy of our father. Here is one in whom these primeval wishes of our childhood have been fulfilled, and we shrink back from him with the whole force of the repression by which those wishes have since that time been held down within us.[11]

According to this theory, a boy's failure to identify with his father results in the boy identifying with his mother, and focusing his libido onto the shared object of attraction, leading to a homosexual outcome. In fact, it is now increasingly accepted that our sexual destinies are determined in the womb. Though *The Sleeping Tiger* seems to be informed by Freudian analysis, Clements seems to be suspicious of it. He explains to Mrs. Esmond that he has spent his afternoon reading one of her husband's books: "In it, he said that childhood is the thing that counts—you know, parents and children, but he's wrong." Then, in a close-up that not only emphasizes the point but also draws our attention to Bogarde's own personality, he adds, "People are born the way they are." Clements then argues with Esmond, who suggests that some of his problems are due to "the kind of home your stepmother gave you."

"Why do you always bring her into it?" Clements snaps as he folds his newspaper. "It's almost as if you were implying there was something between us." Esmond, of course, thinks that Clements looks on him as the father he hated.

Clements is a particular kind of psychopath, and though not overtly presented as a homosexual, there are plenty of clues that he might be—one being that Bogarde has been chosen to play him. Mrs. Esmond says of Clements, "Beneath all that bravado, there's something rather appealing"— a rather telling choice of words, which reflects exactly what it was that made Bogarde such a success with his female fans. Mrs. Esmond's increasing infatuation with Clements does rather resemble Bogarde's adoring followers, who were all barking up the wrong tree. Appealing Clements may be, wandering around in riding boots (as one famous photo of Dirk at home echoes), but he is also a misogynist. When Esmond's wife Glenda (Alexis Smith) becomes infatuated with Clements, she persuades him to take her to a sleazy Soho club. Clements agrees, but only if she will "go upstairs and put on something a little cheaper." Dancing with him at the club, a curious exchange takes place. She asks him if he feels as though he were dancing with one of his girlfriends. "But you're not one of my girlfriends," he replies, nibbling her ear. "No, you wouldn't like a girl like me," she stammers. He grabs the back of her neck and squeezes. "You're hurting me," she complains, at which he snaps, "Don't fool around, Glenda."

The housemaid doesn't like Clements either, and prepares to leave. Just as Clements deliberately spills ink over the clothes she has packed in a suitcase, Mrs. Esmond rushes in, sees what's happened and says, with frustrated anger, "I wish I were a man." She is about to strike him, but Clements grabs her and kisses her. This is complicated, but can be disentangled: If Mrs. Esmond were a man, her affair with Clements would have been much easier and perhaps more meaningful. Clements, like Don Giovanni before him, seduces and corrupts the women he despises, but only because he can't have the men he secretly desires.

The plot now begins to resemble yet another horror film of a later period in British cinema: Michael Reeves' *The Sorcerers* (1967), which features a comparable juvenile delinquent called Mike (Ian Ogilvy). After being telepathically connected, through a novel process of mind control, to the consciousnesses of an elderly couple (Boris Karloff and Catherine Lacey), Mike's actions are dictated by and his experiences channeled back to "the sorcerers," who vicariously enjoy his sensations of car chases, robbery, murder and sex. In the case of *The Sleeping Tiger*, it is Mrs. Esmond who begins to enjoy Clements' lifestyle, though not vicariously. Trapped between her prim self and her infatuation with Clements, she loses control. "Don't look at me as if I was a juvenile delinquent," he snarls—but that is exactly what he is, because in the very next scene, he indulges in armed robbery.

Esmond finally breaks through to Clements and "cures" him, but this means that Clements has no further need for Mrs. Esmond. He claims that he is abandoning her out of "decency"—he can't keep on abusing the doctor's trust—but he really means that he was never really interested in her to begin with and, as she describes it herself, now flips her away like a used cigarette.

As Dr. Esmond puts it, explaining the title of the film in the process, a sleeping tiger prowls in the dark forest of every human personality, and Esmond has his own tiger: At the end of the film, after his wife appears bleeding from one of Clements' blows, he pretends to shoot his protegé. Mrs. Esmond is distraught, but then understandably goes off her head when he confesses that Clements isn't dead after all. Apparently he has merely disappeared. Consequently, Mrs. Esmond drives off, picks Clements up in her car and then drives to her (and his) death through the poster of an Esso Oil tiger mascot, for the benefit of those who haven't yet understood the title.

The film would lose all its interest if Bogarde had not brought out the gay subtext to all this rather overblown nonsense. Indeed, it wouldn't have been made in the first place if Bogarde had not been involved. Losey, blacklisted by Hollywood due to his Communist sympathies during the McCarthy witch hunt, was out of work and desperate when Bogarde agreed to watch one of his earlier films in a freezing Pinewood Studios projection room. Bogarde later felt embarrassed that Losey "preferred to walk about outside in the slush like an expectant father, and quite unaware of the importance for him, then, of my acceptance or not of his work…. [The] one person I wanted to work with most was kicking his heels in the car-park in a long blue overcoat waiting for my verdict."[12] Losey thought *The Sleeping Tiger* had a "lousy cheap story,"[13] but reading between the lines was fruitful. The gay subtext is somewhat incognito, like Losey, who directed it under the then necessary pseudonym of Victor Hanbury.

Bogarde explored another kind of homosexual psychopath the following year in *Cast a Dark Shadow,* in which the cuddly connotations of his character's name, Edward Bare, were at odds with his murderous personality. It is perhaps rather a gay thing to do to date a woman old enough to be your own mother, but certainly only a psychopath would do this merely to be in a more convenient position to kill her for her money. This is exactly what Edward Bare does in this story. In fact, he attempts to commit this crime twice, the first time with sweet old Mona Washbourne as Monica Bare, who wants to change her will. Edward doesn't realize there is an earlier will leaving all her money to a sister he's never met, and it is this will that his elderly wife wants to change, so that everything will go to Edward. Misunderstanding her motives, he decides it's time to kill her before she endangers his inheritance. He does this by turning on the gas and making her murder look like an accident (the same tactic that Peter Van Eyck uses in Hammer's *The Snorkel,* directed three years later by Guy Green). The languid sound of a nightingale ironically accompanies this murderous scene, which may well have inspired Jack Clayton's use of birdsong to accompany the troubling conclusion of *The Innocents* (1961). Only after Monica's death does Edward realize that he should have let events take their course: If she had revised her will, the money *would* have come to him. As it is, he gets nothing but the house.

With no ready cash, Edward now uses his charm to seduce someone else, whom he meets in a rundown seaside cafe, where the entertainment is amusingly provided by an trio of elderly women called "The Rocketeers." Margaret Lockwood, playing against type as Freda Jeffries, provides Edward with a suitable candidate: a vulgar ex-barmaid made good, with plenty of money for the taking. Bogarde was by this time well practiced at gazing affectionately at his female victims, while simultaneously expressing murderous thoughts via arch smiles. Perhaps Freda suspects what Edward is after when she explains that her former lovers were after the moneybags "and not the old bag herself." And when she persuades Edward's fussy old housemaid to open the former marital bedchamber, she hits the nail on the head in response to Edward's fury at such an intrusion: "Anyone would think it was Bluebeard's chamber"—which it is, of course.

Bogarde as Edward Bare, finishing off Mona Washbourne's Monica Bare in *Cast a Dark Shadow* (dir. Lewis Gilbert, 1955).

Cast a Dark Shadow, as its title suggests, could easily have been marketed as a horror film, or at least as the kind of psychological thriller Jimmy Sangster often wrote for Hammer, but the presence of Bogarde diverted it into something less troubling. After all, in *The Snorkel*, the villain is a nasty German. In *Cast a Dark Shadow*, the villain is played by a British heartthrob, whose fans had no idea that he or the character he was playing was gay. Once again, though, there are clues. Monica's lawyer Philip Mortimer (Robert Flemyng) suspects what Edward has been up to, and contemptuously remarks, "You make me sick," which is perhaps not just because Edward is a murderer.

A third woman enters the story in the form of Charlotte Young (Kay Walsh), whom we eventually learn is Monica's sister. She knows "what an unbalanced mess" Edward really is and wants to "drag out the rottenness" within him, which again suggests something rather more than mere murderousness. Edward doesn't know who she really is, and decides that she would make a very good third victim: He therefore plans to leave Freda and marry Charlotte. When he learns the truth, he decides to kill her instead, which will mean that Monica's money will flood back to him. He tampers with Charlotte's car and believes she has been killed in an accident, but in fact he has been framed: Charlotte returns. "I think I'm dreaming," Edward stammers. "You'll wake up in Broadmoor," says the lawyer, who has been a party to Charlotte's plan all along. Edward throws a drink in Mortimer's face and drives off, forgetting that he's chosen the tampered-with car, which Charlotte had carefully avoided. Laughing, he thinks he has escaped them, but then he realizes his mistake and plunges over a cliff to the death he had planned all along for Charlotte. As Tanitch observes, Bogarde was very good at conveying "the essential weakling underneath the ruthless, cold-bloodied exterior," and this all depended on those "gay" characteristics so often misconstrued as "weakness" but are in fact sensitivity, charm and gentleness.

All these qualities were brought to the fore in *Our Mother's House*. At first, Bogarde was wary of involving himself in this project, which required him to play father to a house full of children. "That's the last thing I should do," he said, "to be father to a lot of kids."[14] Despite the juvenile cast, this is perhaps the closest Bogarde ever got to a horror film in the manner of the Tigon and Amicus psychodramas of the 1970s such as *The Beast in the Cellar* (dir. James Kelley, 1970) and *What Became of Jack and Jill?* (dir. Bill Bain, 1972). (In the latter, Mona Washbourne, continuing the kind of thing that happened to her in *Cast a Dark Shadow*, finds herself playing an elderly granny, whom her grandson murders for her money.)

The house in which *Our Mother's House* is mostly set is suitably Victorian Gothic in style on the outside and distinctly dreary on the inside, though in the hands of a director like Freddie Francis it might have looked more sinister. The suburban, autumnal streets outside, however, summon exactly the kind of mood Francis would have created to convey the sense of isolation, alienation and unnerving melancholy of a story in which a group of bereaved children bury their deeply religious mother in the back garden to prevent them all from being sent to an orphanage. Séances take place in a makeshift tabernacle the children erect over the grave. The eldest child, Diana, played by Pamela Franklin (another stalwart of British horror films), communicates with "Mother," rocking back and forth in a sinister, creaking rocking chair and working herself into a trance. "Mother is here. Mother is listening. Does anyone want to speak to Mother?" she asks. The movie develops into a kind of suburban *Lord of the Flies*, with trials taking place, and "Mother" punishing anyone who misbehaves. One child has her hair cut off, merely for having asked a passing biker for a ride.

Into this deranged state of affairs comes Bogarde's Charlie Hook, a Cockney ne'er-do-well who reveals that he was married to the children's mother. At first he seems to be a loving father, but as the children become inconvenient to him, preventing him from enjoying the attentions of various women friends who visit with increasing frequency, he turns on his charges and brutally reveals to them that they are all illegitimate, that their mother was nothing more than a common prostitute and that Charlie merely gave them his name, not his DNA. None of the children are his. In despair, Diana, who loved Charlie more than any of the others, kills him with a swift blow on the head with a fire poker.

Charlie's essential misogyny, related via his weakness of character to the gay characteristics identified above, is revealed when he tells one of the boys, "They're very dangerous, you know—women. They're not like us. We have our little vices: a bit violent sometimes, a bit rough, but we do have a code […], but not women."

As mentioned earlier, Visconti's recognition of Charlie's essential weakness led to Bogarde being cast as an altogether more ruthless, though in the end considerably less convincing villain in *The Damned*. That operatic and sometimes incoherent parable of the Third Reich drew on a variety of sources: William Shirer's *The Rise and Fall of the Third Reich* ("a genuine Bible," according to Visconti[15]) Thomas Mann's novel *Buddenbrooks* and Shakespeare's *Macbeth*. Bogarde's role as Friedrich Bruckmann was not a gay character, but Visconti's own personal gay agenda very much colored the film as a whole. Originally, Bruckmann was to have been the principal character: a Nazi Macbeth, led on by a Lady Macbeth in the shape of Ingrid Thulin's Baroness Sophie von Essenbeck. But Visconti's infatuation with Helmut Berger, his boyfriend at the time, led to a major rewrite in which Berger, who plays Sophie's perverted son Martin, became the focal point, leaving Bogarde's performance severely cut and really rather irrelevant. This was a pity, as Martin's degenerate sexual obsessions are much less interesting than the corrupting influence of power experienced by Bruckmann.

Martin's pedophilia is dwelt on with unnecessary attention to detail, and could, after all, have belonged to any kind of prurient sex story. When Martin later descends into Oedipal rape, which destroys his mother's mind, the film really loses its focus. Sophie's collapse does, however, lead to the spectacular final wedding scene, in which she appears white-faced and mute alongside Bogarde's Bruckmann. After the marriage, they adjourn to a sitting room and commit suicide, echoing the last hours of Hitler and Eva Braun. The power of this set piece, alongside the film's earlier tableaux (the funeral cortège of Baron von Essenbeck through his steel works, the homoerotic orgy during an S.A. meeting, its subsequent bloody dénouement) demonstrate how much better the whole affair would have been if Martin's sexual peccadilloes and Visconti's obsession with them had been kept at bay.

The Essenbecks were in fact based on the real-life steel family of Krupp, whose business empire lay in Essen. Martin was Visconti's anachronistic real-

Bogarde's Macbeth in the guise of Friedrich Bruckmann in *The Damned* (dir. Luchino Visconti, 1970), with Ingrid Thulin as Baroness Sophie.

ization of Arndt Krupp, the mother-fixated playboy heir of the family business. He wore mascara, plucked his eyebrows, was adored by a harem of gay men and died of AIDS in 1986. Visconti regarded these industrialists, who capitulated to the Mephistophelian blandishments of Hitler, as the corrupted gods of capitalism. Indeed, his preferred title for the film was *Götterdämmerung*, after the final part of Wagner's epic *Ring* Cycle, and he aimed to demonstrate the capitulation of capitalism to the infernal gods of fascism in mythic terms. For him, these industrial magnates "still excite and disturb humanity today as the pagan deities, Wagner's gods, used to do. Money is the instrument of their power and factories bristling with smokestacks are the temples of their cult."[16]

But Visconti wanted to create more than just a historical film. *The Damned* was to be about the Nazis, yes, but also about "something more" reflecting his own Marxist ideology:

> I think that of all the interpretations of Fascism, the truest is the one that views it as the final phase of world capitalism, the final consequence of the class struggle taken to its final extreme, that of a monstrosity like Nazism and Fascism and that, naturally, can only precede a change to Socialism.[17]

As his biographer Laurence Schifano observes, Visconti was both fascinated and revolted by the excesses of Aschenbach, Sophie, Martin and Bruckmann, whose combined acts of rape, incest, parricide, pedophilia, murder and suicide are examined with unnerving attention to detail; and the distinctly lurid re-enactments of specifically homoerotic scenes suggest that the political agenda was on a lower level still than Visconti's own feelings of homosexual guilt. All the gay characters in *The Damned* are punished because, for Visconti, "love was always guilty." He regarded his own homosexuality as a "transgression" to be paid for with pain.[18] *The Damned* is hardly a glowing endorsement of homosexuality, with its main practitioners being good-looking SA storm troopers who are machine-gunned in their beds by the SS in a grotesquely queer *Liebestod*, after having indulged in a variety of male-bonding exercises. These include skinny-dipping, target practice with Luger pistols, folk dancing in lederhosen, a great deal of beer-swilling, performing a half-naked can-can wearing stockings and suspenders, and an out-of-tune sing-along to Wagner's *Tristan und Isolde*. The slaughter, when it finally comes, fully exposes the pornography of violence (a subject I will address in more detail later on) for what it is. It is all very decorous, however; one still photograph shows Visconti, ever the aesthete, carefully applying blood to the walls of the set. People die as in an opera rather than anything resembling reality. (Visconti's much-vaunted "neo-realism" is not quite as realistic as his admirers claim.) The blood is plentiful but it is splattered with loving care over handsome, well-toned male bodies either preparing for or in the midst of sexual congress. Bullets, blood and naked bottoms blend together in a manner in which perhaps only a gay director would indulge.

This is the film's homosexual core, but, as I said, Bruckmann is not presented as gay himself—quite the opposite. He depends upon Sophie's support for his murderous career to the top of the steel works, and without her, he is like a little boy frightened of the dark:

> I am not afraid, but Joachim–Konstantine—and tomorrow? God! The complicity grows and I know I'll be trapped with Aschenbach all my life. Oh my God. I've accepted a ruthless logic and I can never get away from it.

Like Hitler himself, Bruckmann is curiously asexual, which may well reflect the supposition that, if Hitler was indeed gay himself, his homosexuality was repressed to the point of complete denial (a state of psychological affairs that might help to explain the subsequent prohibition of homosexuality by a movement whose bodyguard was run by the notoriously homosexual Ernst Röhm). The distinctly camp Martin, to whom we are first introduced wearing drag as a Marlene Dietrich lookalike, is actually more interested in little girls and incest with his own mother than in anything male. (The historical reference here is to Hermann Goering, who similarly liked wearing nail varnish and makeup.) But both Martin and Bruckmann are presented as variants of the cancer that destroyed Germany in the 1930s. Everyone is tarred with the same brush, and they might just have well as been gay like the SA boys and Konstantine himself. The implication is that everyone has been perverted. Homosexuals in Visconti's film are just as damned as everyone else, as the title of the film suggests. It is indeed an uncomfortable film for a gay man to have directed and gay actors to have appeared in, but it is equally uncomfortable for any human being to watch, as it demonstrates how we are all driven by the Will to Power and are all equally vulnerable to the corruption of power.

Bogarde made a rather more convincing Nazi in *The Night Porter* (dir. Liliana Cavani, 1974), in which he plays Max, an ex–SS officer who, in postwar Vienna, takes a job as a hotel night porter. Politically unrepentant, he awaits the time when National Socialism will once more regain control, but his plans are complicated by the arrival of Lucia (Charlotte Rampling), with whom he once had a distinctly kinky, perversely loving sado-masochistic relationship in the death camp over which he presided.

There is seemingly nothing very gay about all this, but there is something rather Gothic, and the Gothic, as we know from the history of those literary and artistic movements, has often attracted gays (Horace Walpole, William

Charlotte Rampling as Lucia and Bogarde as Max in *The Night Porter* (dir. Liliana Cavani, 1974).

Beckford, William Kent, possibly Bram Stoker, certainly James Whale, etc.). As Richard Davenport-Hines, quoting Mark Edmundson, has eloquently explained, "S&M and gothic literature was not coincidental: 'you cannot have Gothic without a true hero-villain; without a cringing victim; and without a terrible place, some locale, hidden from public view, in which the drama can unfold.... S&M is where Gothic, in a certain sense, wants to go.'"[19] *The Night Porter* has all this, though without the traditional Gothic trappings of pointed arches and brooding forests. Instead, we have the terrifying interior of a condemned tuberculosis sanatorium in the outskirts of Rome, which stands in for a Nazi concentration camp. And Bogarde was chosen by Cavani to play this role because Max's sexuality is by no means straightforwardly heterosexual.

To begin with, Bogarde's very civilized persona is highly appropriate here because that was exactly how many Nazis appeared to be: highly cultured and charming individuals like the leader of the Hitler Youth Organization, Baldur von Schirach. Nazis were indeed brutal and barbaric but they did not all appear to be so, and in many cases were not *entirely* so. It is, as they demonstrated so appallingly, quite possible to appreciate Beethoven string quartets in a death camp. That Bogarde at first seems an unlikely Nazi is exactly the point. Also, he was particularly good at playing servants who become masters, as we shall see when discussing *The Servant*; but whatever personal demons Bogarde might have been exorcising in this role, there is no doubt that the film opened itself up to misinterpretation as a kind of perverted porno film. Though it was ostensibly an anti–Nazi movie, Bogarde confessed to an identification with the SS officer he was playing:

Walking, or perhaps I should say strutting, through the empty huts and wards, the long dim corridors and the decaying scraps of abandoned garden surrounding the place, in my fine black-and-silver uniform and high-peaked cap with its Death's Head insignia, cracking my boots with a thin silver-topped whip, I had no illusions at all that I was *not* the man I was supposed to be playing. I felt exactly right. I felt frightening; powerful; commanding. The uniform did that; at least externally. […]

   The uniform itself had a curious effect on the inmates of the camp. Perfectly ordinary paid-up members of their actors' union, they had been carefully chosen for their thinness, drabness, age and general feeling of decay. They scurried away as I walked past them or hid, crouching, in corners, huddled nervously; and the more that they huddled and scurried, the taller I stood, the wider I strode. It was an interesting experience. The SS uniform had been extremely well designed for the purpose it was to serve: fear.[20]

Heinrich Himmler had no doubt that the uniform of the SS was effective for this purpose: "I know there are many people who fall ill when they see this black uniform," he confessed; "we understand that and don't expect that we will be loved by many people."[21] Manufactured by the fashion house of Hugo Boss, the SS uniform was originally designed by the decorative artist, porcelain manufacturer and SS officer, Karl Diebitsch (1899–1985), in collaboration with the SS graphic designer, Walter Heck. Its power-drenched symbolism subsequently made it an attractive fetish object for individuals with sado-masochistic inclinations. Susan Sontag, in her 1974 article "Fascinating Fascism," was one of the first people to explore this aspect of Nazi imagery:

In pornographic literature […], the SS has become a referent of sexual adventurism. Much of the imagery of far-out sex has been placed under the sign of Nazism. Boots, leather, chains, Iron Crosses on gleaming torsos, swastikas, along with meat hooks and heavy motorcycles, have become the secret and most lucrative paraphernalia of eroticism. […] Why has Nazi Germany, which was a sexually repressive society, become erotic? How could a regime which persecuted homosexuals become a gay turn-on?[22]

Sontag's answer to this question is Hitler's own metaphor of rape when discussing how best to lead the people. Hitler was quite clear about this:

In the morning and even during the day people's will power seems to struggle with the greatest energy against an attempt to force upon them a strange will, a strange opinion. At night, however, they succumb more easily to the dominating force of a stronger will. For, in truth, every such meeting represents a wrestling bout between two opposing forces.[23]

The sexual connotations of such imagery are hard to ignore. Sontag points out that "Nazism is 'sexier' than communism (which is not to the Nazis' credit, but rather shows something of the nature and limits of the sexual imagination)."[24] She adds, crucially, "Sadomasochism is to sex what war is to civil life: the magnificent experience. As the social contract seems tame in comparison with war, so fucking and sucking come to seem merely nice, and therefore unexciting…. The color is black, the material is leather, the seduction is beauty, the justification is honesty, the aim is ecstasy, the fantasy is death."[25]

The sexual excitement of the uniform is central to the power, indeed *meaning* of *The Night Porter*. Another of Bogarde's memories of filming in Vienna supports this. After appearing in SS regalia in the streets one night on location, a crowd gathered to watch and afterwards shouted "Sieg Heil!" to an enormous roar of laughter and applause. Bogarde was appalled. Charlotte Rampling accused him of taking things too seriously: "They loved it. Just loved it!" she laughed.

"Not the 'acting' alas: the uniform."[26]

Thomas Carlyle, incidentally one of Hitler's favorite authors, identified the importance of clothes to human behavior in his 1836 book *Sartor Resartus*: "Society, which the more I think of it astonishes me the more, is founded upon Cloth."

> Lives the man that can figure a naked Duke of Windlestraw addressing a naked House of Lords? Imagination, choked as in mephitic air, recoils on itself, and will not forward with the picture. The woolsack, and the Ministerial, the Opposition Benches—*infandum! infandum!* And yet why is the thing impossible? Was not every soul, or rather every body, of these Guardians of our Liberties, naked, or nearly so, last night; "a forked Radish with a head fantastically carved"?[27]

A naked SS officer is almost a contradiction in terms. Indeed, in the *Damned* scenes in which we see SA troops being shot by SS, it is the SA men who are naked—hence powerless. We are all powerless without our clothes, and the SS made a conscious point of dressing to kill. Sontag observes that sadomasochistic fantasies can be both homosexual and heterosexual, "although it is among male homosexuals that the eroticizing of Nazism is most visible."[28] Bogarde thus brings a sub-textual homoeroticism to his *Night Porter* role, despite the fact that Max's "affair" is with a woman.

And there is more. Max films the naked inmates of the concentration camp—both male and female victims, not only suggesting the character's own narcissism, but also reflecting the audience's complicity in the allure of Nazism, for we too are "filming" the experience by watching what has already been filmed by Cavani. There are also more overtly homosexual references. At the beginning of the film, before we know anything about his Nazi past, when Max is working at the hotel, he wakes up a younger member of the hotel staff called Kurt (Geoffrey Copleston) to attend (we presume sexually) to a particularly demanding countess, a long-established resident of the establishment. "You asked for a month's wages in advance," Max reminds him, holding up the fellow's underpants and stretching them suggestively. "All of it. I like people who honor their contracts." He then hurls the underpants at Kurt and accuses him of smelling of fried food. "I'm dripping with Helena Rubinstein's Eau de Cologne for men," Kurt insists. "For men of distinction"— all of which suggests an intimacy between the two men that is more than merely professional. Indeed, despite the female pin-ups in the room, they seem to be lovers having an argument, an impression that is strengthened when Max zips up Kurt's fly in the elevator. "Thanks," Kurt smirks, as Max raises an eyebrow. Later, Max shines a spotlight on male ballet dancer Bert (Amedeo Amodio), another hotel resident. We later learn he had been one of Max's fellow concentration camp SS officers. In a flashback, Bert is shown dancing naked (but for a jockstrap) before his fully dressed Nazi comrades. Max sits, jack-booted with legs crossed (all the seated SS officers cross their legs, incidentally), which, in the popular semiotics of homosexuality, suggests why he might have wanted to shine the spotlight on Bert in his hotel room and gaze at him with such intensity. ("Men who cross their legs are obviously gay […]. Sitting with your legs wide open is the sign of a real man, it shows you're not afraid to get kicked straight in the crotch."[29]) Max's wrists hang limply as he rests his arms over the case of the gramophone during this performance, while a portrait of Himmler gazes down on them all, like Parsifal before his gay Grail Knights.

Returning to the hotel, Max prepares an injection for Bert, who needs drugs to help him sleep. "If I were rich, I'd hire you to do everything for me," Bert confesses, exposing his buttocks. "Be careful," he warns Max, before the needle goes in. As the camera pulls away, we see a brief expression of pain/pleasure on the dancer's face as he says, "You're very good at it. You never hurt." Cavani's camera then swings around to show Bert's hand holding Max's wrist. Thus is the gay context of this heterosexually sadomasochistic "love" story set up.

Max's obsession with Rampling's Lucia is a deeply misogynistic one. His idea of love is possession and degradation, in which Lucia is, of course, complicit; but the dynamic of their affair has much in common with the tensions experienced by gay men in those less enlightened times. Max and Lucia's affair not only began in a hostile environment but it is also impossible for them to admit to its continuation, which takes place in secret, behind closed doors—to the extent that they are unable to go out to buy food, and consequently begin to suffer from the effects of malnutrition. Also, in the concentration camp scenes in which Lucia dances for Max, she is "rewarded" with the severed head of a fellow prisoner, making a direct connection with Oscar Wilde's transgressive play *Salomé*, in which Salomé dances before Herod and receives the similarly severed head of John the Baptist in return. This macabre moment is played out amid a scene in which the now topless Lucia sings the Marlene Dietrich classic "Wenn ich mir was wünschen dürfte," ("If I Could Wish for Something") wearing an SS peaked cap and watched by SS officers who are festooned with feather boas as they drink champagne in this

'THE NIGHT PORTER'

DIRK'S MOST CONTROVERSIAL MOVIE

● MAKE way for another daring and 'hot' movie — The Night Porter which has at last found an English distributor. The film has already met with protest and a strong reaction. It's playing in Paris and it was re-opened in Rome after the Italian courts declared that the film was not obscene but rather a work of art, and all the prints that were confiscated on the film's original opening were returned to the distributor.

It's being launched here by Joe Levine, and stars Dirk Bogarde and Charlotte Rampling. It concerns the relationship between a former SS guard at a Nazi concentration camp and a young Jewish girl who re-discovers him working as a night porter in a Viennese hotel. Instead of denouncing him as her seducer and torturer years previously when she was 14 years old, she is strangely drawn to him again.

He then seduces her away from her husband, lures her to his room and chains her to the washstand. The couple then indulge in a series of masochistic passions.

Miss Rampling in a recent out-burst could not understand why the film took so long to reach British screens. She accepts the fact that it may upset some people but adds, "the upset could not be from the sex scenes. The power of the sex scenes are minimal, compared to the overall strength of the film itself. It has an undercurrent of menace running right through. It isn't an intellectual film. But it's a pretty powerful film that's certain to move anyone — particul-arly women — who see it." We sus-pect it could also move a lot of people right out of their cinema seats! Dirk Bogarde also defends this explicit movie, a movie which he des-cribes as being "a strange experience for me". Dirk says, "To me the film is a love story not a film about ex-Nazis. Some of the scenes are explicit. They have to be." ☐ END

Charlotte Rampling plays a Jewish girl and Dirk Bogarde is the SS guard at a Nazi concentration camp in The Night Porter. It is a strange story of seduction and an undeniable passion

The Night Porter reviewed in *Photoplay*, November 1974.

makeshift cabaret, which is surely a recapitulation of Visconti's equally decadent, though more specifically homoerotic scene set at Bad Weissee, in *The Damned*. Nazi decadence is thus contextualized within the broader *fin-de-siècle* decadent movement, of which the homosexual Wilde was so outspoken a champion.

Far from being pornographic, *The Night Porter* is a clinical analysis of depravity. Bogarde was appalled by the way the film was promoted as pornography, recalling that its American preview "was held in a theater lined with black leather, and the critics sat in black leather seats with chains across them, and there were match-hooks with whips on them."[30] The British critical response was quite balanced. Alexander Walker of the *London Evening Standard* "slammed us with a scathing attack spread across two pages,"[31] but Felix Barker, Margaret Hinxman and Virginia Dignam were full of praise. It may well be that the moral (as opposed to artistic) disapproval of *The Night Porter* is really the rage of Caliban staring at his own reflection. One may be bored by it, but moral censure is compromising. Bogarde's stance has much in common with Wilde's dictum, "There is no such thing as a moral or an immoral book. Books are well written, or badly written. That is all." Wilde continued:

> All art is at once surface and symbol. Those who go beneath the surface do so at their own peril. Those who read the symbol do so at their own peril. It is the spectator, and not life, that art really mirrors. Diversity of opinion about a work of art shows that the work is new, complex and vital.[32]

De Sade accurately analyzed the sado-masochistic impulse as perfectly natural. That it is not necessarily desirable is another matter. For de Sade, cruelty "is the primal sentiment Nature injects in us all."

> The infant smashes his toy, bites his nurse's nipples, strangles his pets long before the advent of reason; cruelty is stamped in animals, in whom … Nature's laws are more clearly to be discerned than in ourselves; cruelty thrives amongst savages, so much nearer to Nature than are civilized men: how absurd then, to maintain that cruelty is born of depravity. I insist, this doctrine is false. Cruelty is natural. All of us are born imbedded with a seed of cruelty, later cultivated by education; yet education does not belong Nature, and is as deforming to her sacred ways as arboriculture to trees. […] You see, cruelty is simply the energy within a man not quite totally corrupted by society; therefore 'tis a virtue, not a vice.[33]

This foreshadows Nietzsche's later observation that there is no morality in Nature, only necessity. ("[T]here is no one who commands, no one who obeys, no one who transgresses."[34]) Such an observation is undeniable, along with the fact of death. The exposure of truth, which has nothing to do with morality or indeed desirability, is de Sade's aim here, as is it Bogarde's, whose performance is disturbing precisely because he allows Max to be himself without censure. (Reminiscing about the Salomé head episode, Max, now inoffensively wearing his uniform as a servant of the hotel, lounges nonchalantly in a chair and casually admits that the severed head had belonged to a prisoner "who used to torment" Lucia. "She just asked me to have him transferred." He laughs: "I—I don't know why ... but suddenly, the—the story of Salomé came into my head and I couldn't resist it." He then giggles like a naughty schoolboy.) It is not an actor's job to criticize the character he plays; quite the opposite. He must identify entirely with him, and Bogarde's strength in roles to which he felt committed, such as this, is his perhaps shocking honesty. Having previously championed gay people in *Victim,* as we shall see later, he is not afraid here to reveal that gay, bisexual and "transgressive" personalities are not necessarily virtuous. This is perhaps a more contentious position now, at a time when minorities are more cherished than they were in the 1970s; and the complex nature of Nazi homosexuality is often ignored for fear of it contaminating acceptance of homosexual freedoms today. It should do no such thing, but neither should it obscure the truth that homosexuality was an important element in the formation of Nazism, of which its later prohibition was a perverse recognition and denial. The evidence that Hitler may have been gay is almost entirely circumstantial, despite Lothar Machtan's spirited attempt to convert it into a thesis to demonstrate that it defined the Führer's entire personality and career. There is great resistance among many homosexuals to accept a mass murderer into the clan, but there have been many heterosexual criminals, and this does not taint heterosexuality in general. If Hitler was indeed gay, the possibility that he repressed to such an extent would certainly explain why it became a personal and later political taboo. As Machtan points out at the end of his book:

> Hitler's sexual orientation does not supply *the* key to his career, but a knowledge of it gives scope for new interpretations—interpretations that in no way mitigate Hitler's crimes and Hitler's guilt or present his policies in a better light, but which can explain aspects of them more precisely. For the personal can be highly political; of that there can be surely no better proof than the story of Hitler's life.[35]

The problem here is that what is probable is not proof; but there is no doubt of Ernst Röhm's homosexuality, nor that of Rudolf Hess, who was known in gay Nazi circles as "Fräuline Anna" and was notorious for attending balls in women's clothing.[36] This observation, from Peter Conradi, the biographer of another presumed gay Nazi, Ernst Hanfstaengl, might usefully be compared with Goering's penchant for makeup and effeminate clothing. Conradi also mentions the remark of Roosevelt's emissary, John Franklin Carter: "One of the things I couldn't stand about Hitler was all the fairies he had around him. I don't like fairies."[37]

All this matters, because it exposes the hypocrisy of the official intolerance of homosexuals in the Third Reich, and might help to explain it. That Hitler crushed Röhm and the SA to disguise his own latent tendencies, can only remain a hypothesis, but the muscle-bound, hyper-masculine imagery of much Nazi art and propaganda does seem to be protesting too much to be taken on face value as conventionally "masculine" from within a purely heterosexual context. The juxtaposition of state-sanctioned homophobia with equally state-sanctioned, though unrealistic and idealized male pin-ups in two and three dimensions, is certainly worth noting. Antony Easthope believes that "paranoia actually *derives* from homosexual desire." He lists four distinct stages in this process:

> The first is homosexual desire, (1) "I love him." But the attempt to ward this off turns into its opposite, (2) "I do *not* love him—I hate him." The mechanism of projection changes it into another statement, (3) "He hates me, which justifies me in hating him." Generalized, this becomes, (4) "I do not love him—I hate him, because he persecutes me." These transformations try to explain what is noted as the main feature in paranoia, for it is the most loved person of their own sex that the paranoiac fancies as their chief persecutor.[38]

It was up to Cavani to frame the unpalatable truths of Bogarde's *Night Porter* performance within a moral context, but in Bogarde's view, what film executives "entirely failed to understand was all Lilly's [i.e., Cavani's] bitter anti–Fascist 'polemic' and argument, and so they had just concentrated on the Love Story, and found it appalling, and the idea that a woman could fall in love with her goaler completely unacceptable."[39] What may have been even more unacceptable was the simultaneous presentation of Max's—and his fellow SS officers'—homosexual desires. In Italy, Bogarde and Cavani were charged with obscenity, but were saved by a High Court judge who pronounced it "a work of art,"[40] which indeed it is.

Chapter Four

"All the nice boys like a soldier."

Bogarde played more military men than action heroes. Soldiers and airmen had the advantage of having the ready-made masculine connotations of military uniforms and a historical context in which combat and action is forced on individuals of all types rather than such activities being necessarily a personal decision. Bogarde was also a ex–military man himself, having served during the Second World War as an army intelligence officer. When asked by Russell Harty if he had ever killed anyone, he replied with an horrifically Sadean anecdote which, if true, no doubt informed his performance of the Salomé scene in *The Night Porter* (but there is always the possibility that it was his performance in that film that inspired the recollection).

> Personally, no. Indirectly, yes, I killed a lot of people, because I picked targets for the RAF—all over France, all over Germany, all over Holland; and sometimes we would warn them and drop leaflets and sometimes the wind took the leaflets out and blew them away, so quite a number of French villages went, especially in Normandy, and the Americans were great at doing that, except they didn't drop leaflets. They just bombed everything that moved. But to answer your question succinctly, yes, I was responsible at the age of 23 for a lot of deaths. I went to see quite a lot of them afterwards. I mean, I went back to the villages and saw what I'd done. I used to go painting, as you know, when I had any time off and I went to one village in Normandy and painted it because I had picked it particularly and it was a waste of time because everybody had got through, and I found what I thought, in the rubble, were a whole row of footballs, and they weren't footballs. I was sitting right beside them painting, and they weren't footballs, they were children's heads, and what it was, I discovered later, was a whole school of kids—a convent—had been pulled out of school and lined up in this little narrow alleyway between the buildings to save them from the bombing and the whole thing had come in on top of them. [...] That gave me a bit of a turn, yes. I didn't enjoy that.[1]

Gays were not, until recently, officially welcome in the British armed forces, but governments have always been quite happy to use anyone as cannon fodder in desperate situations, and Bogarde was conscripted regardless.

Of course, being gay in the military was—and is—nothing unusual. From Alexander the Great in ancient Greece to Ernst Röhm in the Third Reich, the military has always been a congenial place for certain types of gay men— and women. As in the theatrical world or the aristocracy (where gayness has always been much less problematic), it was not so much *what* you were that was the problem as being found out. Even for heterosexual soldiers, a military environment does indeed have many traditionally "feminine" aspects. As right-wing journalist A.A. Gill put it in an article entitled "Look Who's Stalking," soldiers "cook and sew, wipe surfaces, take out the rubbish, and kill."[2] Recruits, for whom ironing had previously always been strictly a task for their mothers, are often seen carrying ironing boards around with them as raw recruits.

The armed forces have long, if unintentionally demonstrated the fluidity of gender roles, just as they have also always sold themselves by means of sexual allure. Uniforms have that effect, but so too are many of the reported eroticisms of combat itself. A recent recruiting campaign in Britain was criticized by members of the military establishment for ignoring images of combat in favor of topics such as tolerance of Muslims, gays and emotional counseling, the argument being that young men are attracted to the military by images of combat, not by how well their post-combat trauma will be treated or whether they will be able to use a prayer mat on exercise. Of course, the reality of the situation is much more complex, but in terms of the way in which war is marketed as an aspect of popular culture, the erotic is a vital element.

Nineteenth-century novelist Anatole France, imitating a medieval style in his story "An Horrible Picture," was well aware of this symbiosis. France's narrator makes a distinction between "obscene" depictions of war and "heavenly" representations of the erotic, but the juxtaposition betrays their relationship:

> And like as it is (so he would say) obscene,—'t is the word Virgil writes of dogs wallowing in the mud and mire,—to depict murderers, whoreson men-at-arms, fighting-men, conquering heroes and plundering thieves, wreaking their foul and wicked will, yea! and poor devils licking the dust and swallowing the same in great mouthfuls, and one unhappy wretch that hath been felled to the earth and is striving to get to his feet againe, but is pinned down by an horse's hoof pressing on his chops, and another that looketh piteously about him for that his pennon hath been shorn from him and his hand with it,—so is it of right subtile and so to say heavenly art to exhibit pretty blandishments, caresses, frolickings, beauties and delights and the loves of the Nymphs and Fauns in the woods.[3]

The poet Rainer Maria Rilke, himself the scion of a military family, was the antithesis of everything military in his own life. Nonetheless he Romanticized military heroism in his poem "Der Knabe" ("The Boy"), in which he expresses the wish to be part of a cavalry troop "with torches like loose hair" ("mit Fackeln, die gleich aufgegangnen Haaren") with ten men wearing gold helmets, with one man beside him "blowing room for us with his trumpet, which flashes and screams,/blowing a black solitude for us." ("Und einer steht bei mir und blast uns Raum/mit der Trompete, welche blitzt und schreit,/und blast uns eine schwarze Einsamkeit."[4]) The imagery is so powerful because it is unmistakably erotic.

Novelist John Buchan also recognized gay militarism, though confined it to "decadent" Germans in his writings. In *Greenmantle,* published in 1916 during the First World War, he wrote of German officer Ulric von Stumm's taste in interior design. In fact, to have a sense of interior design at all seems highly suspect to Buchan, let alone this kind of decadent opulence:

> That room took my breath away, it was so unexpected. In place of the grim bareness of downstairs here was a place all luxury and colour and light. It was very large, but low in the ceiling, and the walls were full of little recesses with statues in them. A thick grey carpet of velvet pile covered the floor, and the chairs were low and soft and uphol-stered like a lady's boudoir. A pleasant fire burned on the hearth and there was a flavour of scent in the air, something like incense or burnt sandalwood. A French clock on the mantlepiece told me that it was ten minutes past eight. Everywhere on little tables and in cabinets was a profusion of nicknacks, and there was some beautiful embroidery framed on screens. At first you would have said it was a woman's drawing room.
>
> But it wasn't. I soon saw the difference. There had never been a woman's hand in that place. It was the room of a man who had a fashion for frippery, who had a perverted taste for soft delicate things. It was the compliment to his bluff brutality. I began to see the queer other side to my host, that evil side which gossip had spoken of as not unknown in the German army. The room seemed a horribly unwholesome place, and I was more than ever afraid of Stumm.[5]

One might be tempted to compare this passage with the more exotic Black Magic novels of Dennis Wheatley, but in fact, Wheatley has one of the characters on the side of good in *The Satanist,* express perhaps surprising sympathy for homosexuals: "I'm sorry for them, that's all. But if they are made that way I think they have as much right as other people to enjoy them-selves in their own fashion."[6]

In an astonishingly homoerotic passage from T. E. Lawrence's *The Seven Pillars of Wisdom,* Lawrence describes "one hundred Devon Territorials, young, clean, delightful fellows, full of the power of happiness and of making women and children glad,"[7] but then overrides this heterosexual context with an explicit admission of its opposite:

> The Arab was by nature continent; and the use of universal marriage had nearly abol-ished irregular courses in his tribes. The public women of the rare settlements we encountered in our months of wandering would have been nothing to our numbers,

even had their raddled meat been palatable to a man of healthy parts. In horror of such sordid commerce our youths began indifferently to slake one another's few needs in their own clean bodies—a cold convenience that, by comparison, seemed sexless and even pure. Later, some began to justify this sterile process, and swore that friends quivering together in the yielding sand with intimate hot limbs in supreme embrace, found there hidden in the darkness a sensual co-efficient of the mental passion which was welding our souls and spirits in one flaming effort. Several, thirsting to punish appetites they could not wholly prevent, took a savage pride in degrading the body, and offered themselves fiercely in any habit which promised physical pain or filth.[8]

In more up-to-date terms, Michael Herr's celebrated book of reportage of the Vietnam War, *Dispatches,* continues the juxtaposition, with soldiers confessing that the fear of death finally gave way in the excitement of male combat, which was like "undressing a girl for the first time."[9] Another famous passage concerns the sight of American Loach helicopters: "It was incredible, those little ships were the most beautiful things flying in Vietnam (you had to stop once in a while to admire the machinery). They just hung there outside those bunkers like wasps out of a nest. 'That's sex,' the captain said. 'That's pure sex.'"[10] Similarly, in Anthony Swofford's Gulf War memoir *Jarhead,* we learn:

> Vietnam war films are all pro-war, no matter what the supposed message, what Kubrick or Coppola or Stone intended.... Fight, rape, war, pillage, burn. Filmic images of death and carnage are pornography for the military man. With film you are stroking his cock, tickling his balls with the pink feather of history, getting him ready for his real First Fuck.[11]

People entered the Second World War with less military movie porn to sustain such enthusiasm, but it was part of the program nonetheless, as it had been during the First World War. Modris Eksteins reminds us that for the German sexologist Magnus Hirschfeld, "the uniforms, stripes and weapons were a sexual stimulant."[12] Even in *The Da Vinci Code* (dir. Ron Howard, 2006), Tom Hanks' Robert Langdon explains the significance of "the original icon for 'male'" by placing his fingertips together to form a symbol of "a rudimentary phallus. [...] Its known as 'the blade.' It represents aggression and manhood. It's a symbol still used today in modern military uniform." "Yes," Ian McKellen's Grail expert, Sir Leigh Teabing, adds, "the more penises you have, the higher your rank. Boys will be boys"—though this does not apply to British stripes, which are the other way round. From Quentin Crisp's overtly effeminate gay perspective, "any national dress or occupational outfit may be sexually stimulating and there are as many kinks as there kinds of costume. Uniforms appeal to devotees of the fearless man of action. They also pander to the Cophetua complex so prevalent among homosexuals. When any of my friends mentioned that he had met a 'divine' sailor he never meant an officer."[13]

While images of men dancing together may once have been (and might still be) deemed "disgusting," watching men *march* together would have been—and still is—a perfectly acceptable, indeed apparently desirable state of affairs. The sublimated male bond, which helps sell and maintain the military, has long been regarded as an essential, if disguised, part of its make-up, which is why it has taken so long for women to be allowed to fight alongside men on the front line. War films trade on all these tropes and are, in one way or another, inevitably part of the pornography of war. Audiences all want to be titillated by the excitement, the thrill of undressing their lover. Although the Second World War was greeted with much less enthusiasm at the time it broke out, the film industry has retrospectively milked it for all the eroticism and heroism it could force out of it. A large section of the public has an insatiable desire for war films as a substitute for the boredom of peace. Real war is regarded with some anxiety by many, but the *fiction* of war, which is how real war has always been sold anyway, never leaves the best-seller lists. Bogarde's war films are tamer than the likes of *Apocalypse Now* (dir. Francis Ford Coppola, 1979) and *Jarhead* (dir. Sam Mendes, 2005), but it was nonetheless his "prettiness" which helped to sell them, and they are no exception to the rule.

Bogarde always said he had grown "tremendously dependent on my fellow soldiers, which is why the only time I'm really happy in my life, is with a film crew or a camera crew like this, because we're a gang together."[14] But this contradicts what he said in an earlier 1981 interview for *Afternoon Plus*: "I simply like to be on my own. I like the silence. I couldn't live in the city."[15] This does rather beg the question how such a lover of solitude, who was so sensitive, remote and sophisticated, could have really enjoyed, still less come to depend upon that epitome of sociability that is service life. A May 8, 1941, diary entry, quoted by Coldstream, paints a rather more realistic picture, as Dirk (or Derek as he was then) set off to the war:

> Train crowded—Soldiers, old women, Conscripts like self. Journey awful—gaze out at receding Country—wonder if I'll die, and never see London again, hope not. Awful old bitch in Compartment says she'll vomit if I smoke—have to stand in Corridor—feel like going back to School.
>   Arrive Richmond Works at 6.45. Bundled into Army Lorry with 22 others. Arrive at Camp—bleak, barren and horrible—have awful supper—Sausages. Get shown to bunk-room—sleep on floor on Straw Buiscuits [sic]—4 blankets—lights out at 10:30. 25 of us here, all homesick dead tired—feel life has ceased forever—weep four bitter tears under my blankets.[16]

What are we to believe? With Bogarde, that is always hard to decide. He always claimed to have helped "liberate" Belsen, an experience that marked him for life, destroyed any possibility of the existence of God, and made everything else trivial by comparison. Coldstream, however, suggests that this might not have been quite as Bogarde so eloquently claimed in interviews and print. Coldstream refers to what he calls "confusion" with regard to Bogarde's accounts. "There is also an extraordinary, indeed perplexing contrast between these vivid accounts of being a witness to atrocity and the card he sent to Elizabeth [his sister] on 21 April, hoping she was having a 'gay time' with her current beau, asking for news, and reporting: 'We have been having the most beautiful weather here—I've been sunbathing, and got quite brown.'"[17]

Coldstream offers the possibility of this being an act of "total denial to others, if not to himself, of what he had seen, but given the exclusion zone around Bergen-Belsen in those early days after 2nd Army took it in hand; given the warnings about typhus; given the prohibition on access against all but essential personnel and a few accredited correspondents [...] what would Derek [i.e., Dirk] have been doing even at the gates, let alone inside them?" Coldstream's explanation of the anomaly is that the various descriptions he made of Belsen "are distilled in part from what Derek saw; in part from what he learned at second hand thanks to the unsparing newsreels and photographs of the time; and in part what was conjured in that ever-active imagination."[18]

In this respect, Bogarde's military performances are a continuation of his fantasies. His favorite film still is significant. It shows him as Patrick Leigh Fermor in *Ill Met by Moonlight* (dir. Michael Powell and Emeric Pressburger, 1957), wearing military uniform, a pistol nestling in the holster hanging from his waist, but with a certain brigand-like swagger about him created by the dirty white trousers, the unbuttoned tunic, the riding boots and his *contra posta* pose beside a fallen tree trunk. He turns his head into the distance, revealing his preferred left-hand profile, stubble decorating his perfect cheeks. It is all highly mannered—a fantasy of the military hero. Bogarde confessed as much in later interviews. He specialized in what he called "the little boy looking for God" or "staunch upper-lip brave captains."

> I took care to look pretty. [...] The cinema is a sexual thing. You go to the movies for sex. You may not go there to watch a porno movie, so I don't mean that kind of thing, but there's a sexual excitement. Nobody wants to go and see tea-cosies at work. [...] The reaction I was getting to my work and to being who I was was that people were turned on by me—when I was young, I'm talking about, not now; and there was an alchemy at work and so I used it. [...] It's all cheating. [...] The whole thing is fake. But then that's what sex is. It's an illusion. That's what the cinema is. It's illusion, but I was jolly sure that I was going to make every wing commander I played as physically possible [sic] and attractive as I could, as mischievous and flirty—whatever you like. I was totally aware of it.[19]

Martin Esslin, the critic who famously created the term "Theatre of the Absurd," was quite clear about the sexual appeal of actors:

Our interest in other people contains of necessity a strong erotic element. It is that which constitutes one of the basic characteristics and magnetic powers of drama: drama is basically *erotic*. Actors give the spectators who watch them a great deal of pleasure simply by being interesting, memorable, or beautiful physical specimens of humanity. Quite apart from their artistic and intellectual accomplishments, actors are people who, for money, exhibit their physical presence to the public. We all know that great stars derive their special magnetism from sex appeal. But what applies to the big stars contributes as well to the attractiveness and success of the lesser lights. In a sense all actors are exhibitionists: they enjoy being seen, being found appealing and worth looking at. Conversely audiences of drama are also, in a certain sense, voyeurs.[20]

Beauty and military heroism have always had a symbiotic relationship. Speaking of Bronze Age warriors, Adam Nicolson observes:

These killer chieftains were obsessed with male beauty. The great Greek heroes all have blond hair (unlike the Trojans, who are dark-haired), and they have lots of it, lustrous, thick hair being an essential quality of the hero.... Beyond their weaponry, carefully picked out on their memorial slabs, appears all the necessary grooming and beauty equipment.... Making the Bronze Age warrior beautiful is central to the idea he had of himself. Here is the handsome gang-leader, made more handsome by what he wears and how his body is prepared for its appearance among men.[21]

Bogarde's military men were, like their counterparts in reality, masculine *constructs* in the way that Antony Easthope has described. Bogarde's soldiers may have appealed to women, but that, ironically, was because they exude a gay sensibility; they are fully aware that they are constructs, in a way that heterosexual masculinity is not. Bogarde's military men fully understood, if only on an instinctive rather than analytical level, what Easthope has to say about male bonding in a military context:

The pain of war is the price paid for the way it expresses the male bond. War's suffering is a kind of punishment for the release of homosexual desire and male femininity that only war allows.[22]

Easthope cites *The Deer Hunter* (dir. Michael Cimino, 1979) to demonstrate this, arguing that the "sublimated homosexual desire" of Robert De Niro's character, Mike, "seems to be less than fully sublimated."[23] We also see this sublimated homosexual desire in many of Nazi sculptor Arno Breker's state-approved sculptures, which, as Peter Adam explains, were not ancient Greek idols but musclemen:

The sinewy bodies, trained in the gym, bursting with energy, represented the new ideal. All Breker's sculptures seemed to be destined for the sports field or the swimming pool. [...] Breker's statues were images of masculinity and power. Their aim was to seduce the young German into becoming a fighter and to identify with a carefully planned ideal of omnipotent manhood.[24]

Breker's statue *The Wounded* (1938) is a Nazi manipulation of Nietzsche's dictum "What does not kill me makes me stronger." A naked soldier sits (iron-ically based on a photograph of the French cyclist, André Leducq), one hand supporting his bandaged head, which is bowed to the ground. The compo-sition encourages us to admire the fortitude of strength overcoming adversity (though the statue in fact shows no actual wounds). The erotic energy of this Nazified version of Saint Sebastian is made greater not only by the fully exposed genitals that occupy a central position, but also the hardness of Breker's approach. While we admire many a Christian Saint Sebastian, we scent danger in Breker's work because of its associations. But the cult of the wounded man overcoming or ignoring his wounds is just as popular in con-temporary films such as the *Die Hard* series. Crucially, the self-conscious over-emphasis of *the masculine* suggests a lack of confidence: Either the het-erosexual perspective seeks thus to strengthen its self-image, or the homo-sexual plays with the component parts of the construct to create a more convincing illusion.

Bogarde's first foray into war movies took place in 1953, eight years after the end of the Second World War. The screenplay for *Appointment in London* was by John Wooldridge, a man who had flown 108 missions for the RAF. Bogarde's character, Wing Commander Tim Mason, was based on Wooldridge, but the number of missions he had flown had to be reduced to 90 in Bogarde's case, for reasons of credibility, truth so often being stranger than fiction. Bog-arde is indeed very pretty, so pretty, in fact, that he diverts attention from all the other men involved. He is also very much as one would expect: charming, authoritative, stiff upper-lip. In one scene he has to raise his voice in admon-ishment. He kisses his co-star, Dinah Sheridan, perfectly decorously, but Mason also has a softer side, being described as "highly strung" and having difficulty sleeping due to his nerves. His girlfriend wonders how he can carry on with bombing raids. His explanation: "By being scared that someone will see how afraid you are." This, however, does not stop him wanting to chalk up 90 raids, when, after his 89th, he is given every encouragement to retire from the field.

There are further chinks in his heterosexual armor. "Are you married," Sheridan asks him in the pub. Bogarde laughingly responds, "Me?" "No! No one's ever asked me."

Despite spending time with her, Bogarde's Wingco "doesn't like girl-friends around when the boys are flying. Doesn't matter who it is. He says it lowers morale." What keeps morale up is fun and games in the mess, which takes the form of the lads climbing onto piled-up chairs, dipping their feet in a bowl of mud and leaving filthy footprints on the ceiling. Once again, the "feminine" is perceived as a danger to the masculine myth of the military,

R.A.F. chaps having fun with mud in *Appointment in London* (dir. Philip Leacock, 1953).

despite the uniformed presence of the awfully proper Sheridan, who turns out to be part of Bomber Command. "Sometimes you can put a jinx on yourself getting mixed up with a girl," another airman tells the film's third male lead, Bryan Forbes, "and we don't want any jinxes in this outfit."

Apart from Bogarde, and possibly Sheridan, *Appointment in London's* other main attraction is the planes themselves. The obscenity of high-explosive bombs being loaded into place, with the usual grim humor of "Luv from the Skipper. 90 Today," and the inclusion of genuine footage of bombing raids over Germany, is, without putting too fine a point on it, the conversion of war into an entertainment. In their own way, the bombs, the excitement, Bogarde's good looks and the smart RAF uniforms are indeed a kind of pornography, for what else is there to enjoy in this kind of film?

They Who Dare (dir. Lewis Milestone, 1954) was Bogarde's second attempt in this genre, and once again, the SAS officer he plays is highly strung, but also incompetent. Bogarde's Lt. Graham gets a kick out of danger, learning, too late for the men under his command, "the ugly truth about myself." One of his men draws a caricature of him as a pirate. "If I'm a pirate," Graham insists, "so are you."

"With this difference," his comrade points out. "I was detailed to volunteer for brigandage; but you, you chose it and you love it."

To signal this brigand nature, Bogarde's lieutenant sports, first, a white silk cravat, later exchanged for a flamboyant polka dot variety. Obviously something of a poseur, Graham contrasts starkly with Denholm Elliott's more sensible, intellectual non-commissioned officer, Sgt. Corcoran, who ends up almost dead at the end. "I hate you," Corcoran shouts. "I hate you for never giving up. You don't think. You haven't the imagination to realize you're licked. Well, I know when I'm licked. Danger is your only kick." In fact, they aren't "licked," and Lt. Graham's determination *not* to be saves the day for them both in the end, but they are the only ones to make it back from their team's aborted mission to blow up an enemy airfield. Graham first of all endangers the entire troop by refusing to let them carry enough water (in order to save weight), and then insists on planting an extra, unnecessary bomb, when he should have been thinking about making his escape.

The story is dull. Only Robert Gill's score relieves the monotony (creating tension with sustained timpani rolls and, for two sequences, in which the men are in danger of being flushed out by the enemy, echoing the frantic string writing of Sibelius's *Tapiola*). Over an hour goes by before there is any action at all, and only one man is shot in the entire story, ironically demonstrating that the point that if a war film is to be entertaining, it must indulge in combat pornography. There are also one or two moments of sexual ambivalence alongside the silk cravats. The film opens in a restaurant where Lt. Poole (William Russell) is examining a menu. An eavesdropping floozie (presumably a dangerous pair of ears) inquires, "Been stood up?"

"Looks like it," Russell replies; but then Bogarde, looking as pretty as ever in his white cravat, enters instead of the girl we have been led to expect.

"I was about to give up on you," says Poole, immediately causing a potentially "queer" moment, which is, of course, immediately explained, allowing us to return to heterosexual normality. Careless of the eavesdropping floozie, Lt. Graham discusses their upcoming mission. This is his first act of selfish narcissism, which doesn't really lend itself to any kind male bonding, but the narcissism suited Bogarde's persona rather well.

Another war film followed the same year, this time directed by Lewis Gilbert. Bogarde starred alongside Michael Redgrave in *The Sea Shall Not Have Them,* a title that caused Noël Coward to observe, when passing the poster in Leicester Square: "I don't see why not. Everyone else has."[25] The film also caused a protest from British actresses, who felt unjustly excluded from the screen by the war genre. In fact, this kind of story had been handled somewhat better by Hitchcock in *Lifeboat* (1944), in which Tallulah Bankhead had proved herself perfectly seaworthy; but here it is four men who have been shot down into the sea and spend the entire film floating about in the freezing wind and rain. Nothing much else happens, and again it is Malcolm Arnold's music that keeps the pace going more than anything else. Bogarde, playing a sergeant who used to sell groceries in Luton before the war, is delightful—adorable, indeed. No wonder his female fans wanted to hug him, though this film was surely aimed more at the chaps. All he had to do was get very wet and act utterly exhausted, and he is indeed very good at conveying that his lips and fingers are numb with cold. The skipper of the plane they were all traveling in passes out and Bogarde's sergeant does his best to look after him, providing a tender moment of male affection, which only Bogarde could convey with the appropriate warmth (despite the implied freezing conditions): "We've been together two years, sir," he explains to Michael Redgrave's Air Commodore Waltby. "Others have come and gone, but we seem to have stuck. I don't know why." But perhaps the audience does. Bogarde's vulnerability and beauty are only enhanced by his worries about having stolen a can of petrol and being court-martialed for it. If nothing else, this film clearly demonstrates the qualities that made him a star. Christine Geraghty points out that his "good looks and tentative, tender, gentle manner was hugely appealing to women in a cinema otherwise dominated by rugged, silent types."[26]

There was more posing to come in *Ill Met by Moonlight*, a turgid "Boys Own" adventure, which even the towering talents of Powell and Pressburger failed to

Bogarde as Major Patrick Leigh Fermor in *Ill Met By Moonlight* (dir. Michael Powell and Emeric Pressburger, 1957).

rescue from mediocrity. But Bogarde livens things up by wearing a variety of costumes in his role as Patrick Leigh Fermor, one of which involves the mustache and outfit he hopes will turn him into "a latter-day Lord Byron."

He also wears civvies and, later, when clean-shaven ("I do feel naked without my mustache"), he exchanges his British uniform for German field dress (taken from a Nazi, played by Christopher Lee, whom Leigh Fermor shoots during a scuffle in a dentist's chair). Bogarde is dapper, charming and cheeky, dealing with Marius Goring's Nazi general, whom he and his chaps have abducted, in the most gentlemanly fashion. The Cretan freedom fighters with whom he works are all comedy types and the film hardly takes

Bogarde's Leigh Fermor in Byronic mode in *Ill Met By Moonlight*.

the nature of war very seriously. In that, it could be said to be a kind of soft porn: harmless enough, but not exactly exciting.

The Wind Cannot Read (dir. Ralph Thomas, 1958) was a romance in a military context. While in India learning Japanese, Bogarde's Flight Lt. Quinn falls in love with a Japanese girl (Yoko Tani) with a terminal illness. Throughout, Quinn and his fellow officers are victims of war rather than active combatants. Escaping from Burma in the prologue, Quinn is later captured by the Japanese.

After torture (hung by his arms from a tree), he escapes in time to see his girlfriend again before she dies. War is therefore presented as a backdrop to a romance which weakly echoes Puccini's opera *Madame Butterfly*. What makes the film particularly ironic, from a gay perspective, is that this conventionally "romantic" film is the only one of Bogarde's 63 other films in which he acts opposite Tony Forwood. The scene in question is short: Forwood plays an officer in charge of Japanese POWs, and there is, of course, no suggestion of the nature of their off-screen relationship. But there they are together, as in fact they always were.

The year after Bogarde had been truly brave by starring in *Victim*, he

Bogarde as Flight Lieutenant Michael Quinn (left) with Ronald Lewis as Squadron Leader Fenwick in *The Wind Cannot Read* (dir. Ralph Thomas, 1958).

starred as Sgt. Major Coward in *The Password Is Courage,* the irony of the character's name being somewhat lost on all concerned. Here, Bogarde is a kind of Cockney Simon Sparrow (the character he played in the famous "Doctor" films). Indeed, taking its cue from *Doctor in the House* (dir. Ralph Thomas, 1954), the film that might just as well have been called *Soldier in the Camp.* There was nothing camp about Bogarde's performance, though it wasn't exactly convincing, as the Cockney accent was not always as secure as it should have been. Supposedly based on fact, the story is really only one comedy situation after another: POW Coward escapes, is mistaken for a wounded German soldier, is taken to a German hospital, awarded an Iron Cross and then, when he is discovered to be British, is sent back to join his fellow POWs in an internment camp. On the way there, they set fire to a munitions train, which explodes spectacularly and gives the German soldiers an opportunity to gawp like the comedy stooges they are presented as throughout, with the exception of the noble, authentically Teutonic Ferdy Mayne. The POWs bribe the German "goons" (mostly played by British actors with cod German accents, which reduces whatever seriousness might have been originally intended to stiffen the film's backbone into a pilot for the long-running BBC sitcom 'Allo 'Allo).

The men attempt to escape by digging a tunnel, turning the proceedings into a kind of *Carry On Colditz*. It is misguided to take this film too seriously, but that is because it treats war as nothing more than a jolly joke, which of course it is not. When one of the Germans shouts, "Do you take us for idiots?" it is obvious that everyone, including the English actors playing them and their director, Andrew L. Stone, think exactly that.

Nigel Stock teamed with Bogarde in *The Password Is Courage* as a fellow soldier and smokes a manly pipe, as he would again in *The High Bright Sun* (dir. Ralph Thomas, 1965), which Tanitch rightly regarded as a retrograde step in Bogarde's career.[27] Here, Bogarde is much straighter, more cynical, more clipped in his delivery of lines and more aggressive, but femininity and homoeroticism is nonetheless suggested in two curious scenes. The first concerns his character's superior officer (Stock), who wears a Sam Brown belt with his uniform, smokes a pipe, but is also caught reading a copy of *Woman's Own* magazine. This embarrasses him. Stuffing it into a desk drawer, he burbles, "Extraordinary the, er … the, the, the letters these women write to these magazines. Terrifying questions." Questions of sex, one wonders? Why is this officer reading *Woman's Own*? Is it to reinforce, by contrast, Bogarde's overtly *masculine* role? Similarly, Denholm Elliott, who plays another intelligence officer, fondles his distinctly phallic automatic pistol with a certain loving swagger as he confesses, "I spend half my life groping very unattractive gentlemen to see if they carry arms." With regard to the man who has been following Bogarde's Major McGuire, Elliott smirks, "He's just mad about you. All the nice boys love a soldier."

Tanitch called *The High Bright Sun* a retrograde step in Bogarde's career because the previous year, 1964, Bogarde had made a much more important war film with Joseph Losey, *King & Country*. Of all Bogarde's war films, *King & Country* is by far the best, the most serious, the most compassionate and the most responsible. There is also a possible subtext of homoeroticism at work in the relationship between Bogarde's officer, Capt. Hargraves, and Tom Courtenay's Private Hemp, whom he defends from the charge of desertion at a court martial. Alas, he fails to save Hemp, who doesn't die when shot by the firing party, and so it is up to Hargraves to fire a *coup de grâce* at the end, in a grim parody of a *Liebestod*. Throughout the film, rain pours, mud squelches, rats squeal and the madness of military logic prevails. "It's a bit amateur to plead for justice," says the prosecuting counsel, played by the haughty James Villiers, pointing out that the law isn't necessarily on speaking terms with it.

Losey starts off with shots of Charles Jagger's heroic Royal Artillery Memorial at Hyde Park Corner in London, his prowling camera slowly questioning the sculpture's message of sacrifice and heroism against the noise of modern-day traffic. Suddenly, an explosion lurches us back to the mud of the trenches, accompanied by Larry Adler's specially commissioned and singularly melancholy harmonica score. Bogarde is entirely in control of his compassionate but realistic character, who eloquently argues, in close-up, for understanding and mercy in this case of a man who has been so overwhelmed by years of violence and shell-shock that he was unable to stand any more and simply started to walk away from the carnage.

> He has been out here for three years—longer, if I may say so, than some of us have been. He's seen it all. A man can only take so much. So much blood. So much filth. So much dying. In the shell hole he thought he was drowning in the mud. He thought his time had come and it had. After that, he was no longer responsible for his actions. He hadn't got the power to decide whether to stay or to go. He had one instinct only left: the instinct to walk—to walk home, to walk away from the guns. They've become a fact of our daily lives, so much so that we no longer ask each other why they are being fired. Is this war so old, and are we so old in it, that we've forgotten? Are we not fighting to preserve some notion of decency? Some notion of justice, to preserve for this court the right to choose? I beg to remind the court that if justice is not done to one man, then other men are dying for nothing.

This plea is rejected as merely "a matter of opinion" by the commanding officer, who, in the light of the pig-headed denial of shell shock from the battalion's doctor (Leo McKern), condemns Hemp to death. This film, very much a part of its time, was informed by the critical spirit that had created the 1961 *Beyond the Fringe* sketch "Aftermyth of War," in which Peter Cook and Jonathan Miller made fun of the heroic clichés that had been repeated *ad nauseam* by the British Film Industry since the outbreak of the Second World War:

> COOK: Perkins, I want you to lay down your life. We need a futile gesture at this stage. You'll raise the whole tone of the war. Go up in a crate, Perkins, pop over to Bremen, take a shuftie, don't come back. Goodbye, Perkins. God, I wish I was going too.
> MILLER: Goodbye, sir, or is it "au revoir"?
> COOK: No, Perkins.

This kind of thing, understandably, did not go down well with war veterans at the time, but it did represent the dawning of a new satirical age, the antiwar sentiments of which reached its ultimate expression in the BBC sitcom *Blackadder Goes Forth* (dir. Richard Boden, 1989), where the "futile gestures" of military heroism in the trenches brought that long-running series to a tragicomic ending, all the characters the audiences had grown to love being annihilated. Subsequently, in 2014, by which time the spirit of the 1960s had been gradually eroded by decades of right-wing ideology, the British Conservative politician Michael Gove criticized the Blackadder approach to war. The *Daily Telegraph* reported:

> Michael Gove has condemned left-wing myths about the First World War peddled by programmes such as the TV comedy *Blackadder* saying they belittle Britain and clear Germany of blame. The Education Secretary criticises historians and TV programmes that denigrate patriotism and courage by depicting the war as a "misbegotten shambles."
>
> As Britain prepares to commemorate the centenary of the outbreak of the war, Mr. Gove claims only undergraduate cynics would say the soldiers were foolish to fight. Mr. Gove wrote in the *Daily Mail* that he has little time for the view of the Department for Culture and the Foreign Office that the commemorations should not lay fault at Germany's door. The Education Secretary says the conflict was a "just war" to combat aggression by a German elite bent on domination.[28]

King & Country, perhaps even more strongly than *Blackadder,* remains as a sober antidote to Gove's revisionist view, blending compassion with criticism, and decency and courage in its deconstruction of militarism's heroic myth. Much of its powerful effect is due to Bogarde's elegant ability to combine authority with understanding, his highly expressive eyes and diction channeling his essentially compassionate nature. Perhaps only a gay actor could achieve this complex and finely shaded emotional balance.

That Bogarde much later agreed to appear in Richard Attenborough's *A Bridge Too Far* (1977), merely in order to raise funds to pay for a new fence around his Provence property, speaks volumes.[29] As it turned out, the fence cost him rather more than he bargained for, as his interpretation of Daphne du Maurier's husband, Gen. Sir Frederick "Boy" Browning, was deemed too effete and heartless for his annoyed widow, who described her husband as "an elegant and fastidious man but never effete."[30] Bogarde thought Browning "rather a prick,"[31] and despite his best efforts with a biased script, "effete" is really how his Browning turned out. Bogarde did get to say the actual title of the film in his dialogue, however, which refers to the attempt to capture and hold various German bridges, as this was how Browning himself regarded the one at Arnhem. The film suggested that Browning deliberately ignored evidence of German troops and tanks in the area around Arnhem, and continued with Gen. Montgomery's "Operation Market-Garden" merely out of bravado. Simplifying what had been in reality a rather more complex situation, Browning was depicted by Attenborough, his screenwriter, William Goldman, and consequently Bogarde, as the villain. When du Maurier learned that Bogarde was to be cast as her late husband, she voiced concerns that he might be portrayed as "effete and mincing [...]. I saw him in *The Servant,* and he was a homo in that. Whatever Moper [her name for Browning] was, he certainly wasn't a homo!"[32] The accusation of effeteness was not helped by the fact that Bogarde's Browning, in immaculate uniform, came to his decision after being shown evidence of a German presence courtesy of reconnaissance photographs, while sipping tea from a dainty cup and saucer.

Bogarde's own war experience had brought him into the area of Operation Market-Garden. He even claimed to have met Browning,[33] and was keen not offend anyone; but Bogarde's persona was such that any attempt to portray "fastidiousness" and "elegance" pushed many people's perception of the character he portrayed into that kingdom of camp, which he had undoubtedly commanded in *The Singer Not the Song* and *Ill Met by Moonlight*. Browning's son went so far as to say that Bogarde played his father as "a poofy waiter."[34] The disaster caused a major personal and professional rift between Attenborough and Bogarde, which never healed. However, there really is nothing particularly effete about Bogarde's "Boy" Browning. He has relatively little screen time anyway, and the amount of criticism he received seems to have been far more about him as an individual than his performance.

All this suggests a distinct homophobia. The language used to criticize Bogarde was hardly complementary—let alone what we would now call politically correct. The implication is that if Browning *had* been gay, it would have prevented him from being a good soldier; but far more troubling than a gay general, surely, no matter how inaccurate that may have been, is the kind of Boy's Own rhetoric given to Edward Fox's Lt. Gen. Brian Horrocks. Admittedly, if one is faced with the necessity for combat, morale has to be maintained. Shakespeare realized this, which is why Sir Laurence Olivier's *Henry V* (1944) was dedicated to the British Paratroop Regiment. But comparing war to a Western, which is what Fox's speech does, raises the problems about purportedly anti-war films, which Swafford identified. "Now, gentlemen," Fox begins, "I'm not saying that this is the easiest party that we've ever attended, but I still wouldn't miss it for the world."

> I like to think of this as one of those American Western films: our troops lacking substantial equipment, always short of food—these are the besieged homesteads. The Germans—well, naturally, they're the bad guys, and 30 Corps, we, my friends, are the cavalry on the way to the rescue.

Huge applause and cheering greets this modernization of Henry V's Agincourt speech; but the metaphor is revealing: war as a film. The metaphor would return during Vietnam, as writer and war correspondent Michael Herr records:

> "Life-as-movie, war-as-(war)movie, war-as-life."[35]

> "We all had our movie-fed war fantasies, the Marines too."[36]

"I'm just up there walkin' the ridgeline like a movie star and this zip jumps up smack into me, lays his AK-47 fucking right *into* me, only he's so *amazed* at my *cool*. I got my whole clip off 'fore he knew how to thank me for it."[37]

All the battle scenes, in which Bogarde does not appear, are far more distressing than quibbles about how gay his performance is. These realistic recreations of carnage and destruction are designed to demonstrate the futility of war, but those likely to be swayed by them hardly need so much information. Again, is it the case that what is intended to be an anti-war statement actually gets caught up in its own rhetoric and becomes a gruesome celebration of "heroism," vicarious bloodlust—an exercise in the sublime, indeed, experienced at a safe distance in one's cinema seat. A "safe distance" was exactly what Edmund Burke believed to be essential if one was to enjoy "the ideas of pain, and danger, that is to say, whatever is in any sort terrible."[38]

> When danger or pain press too nearly, they are incapable of giving any delight, and are simply terrible; but at certain distances, and with certain modifications, they may be, and they are delightful, as we every day experience.[39]

That reluctant horror star, Christopher Lee, who acted in a couple of films opposite Bogarde, was fully aware of the dangers of applying a sublime esthetic to matters of historical violence, as he explained in 1987, with regard to the horror films he made for Hammer:

> What we did was to create a morality play. It was a fairy story. It really was fantasy. It was magic. People knew it couldn't really happen. What they do today can happen, does happen, and will go on happening, and that is why I am against it, and that's why I haven't made a film like this for so many years.[40]

War films, no matter how well-intentioned, have the basic problem of having to revel in what they are supposedly criticizing. Any accusation of "femininity," as the furor around Bogarde's portrayal demonstrates, is inevitable; seen as a threat to the masculine myth of militarism.

Bogarde's action heroes are, of course, related to war heroes. Merging from his early typecasting as a juvenile delinquent, Bogarde became an IRA terrorist in *The Gentle Gunman* (dir. Basil Dearden, 1952). This character, Matt Sullivan, plants bombs in Underground stations in wartime London; but it is John Mills, as his pacifist ex-terrorist brother who gives the film its title. By the time of *Simba* (dir. Brian Desmond Hurst, 1955), Bogarde's image had been matured by the phenomenal success of *Doctor in the House* (dir. Ralph Thomas, 1954), and delinquency was replaced by heroism proper. *Simba* is the story of Bogarde's Alan Howard, a young man who comes to South Africa to discover that his brother has been murdered by Mau Mau terrorists. While there is obviously an attempt an demonstrate an enlightened approach to racism, the remarks of ex-pat British farmers, who convene in the town hall to discuss how to treat "native" violence, would fail to find their way into a script today, despite the fact that they were probably highly representative of views held at the time. In fact, there is so much about the film that is valuable as a reflection of the lost world of the 1950s, where ladies wore elegant frocks, nipped in at the waist, where vowels and consonants were all firmly in place, white men still ruled the waves, and "natives" were treated either as children or frightening savages. Indeed, the scenes featuring Mau Mau ritual would not have been out of place in Hammer's *She* (dir. Robert Day, 1965) or *The Plague of the Zombies* (dir. John Gilling, 1966). Christine Geraghty quite rightly points out that the contrast between black and white characters is used symbolically, with black men not only made up to look blacker but also filmed at night, while Virginia McKenna's "whiteness" is emphasized not only by her fair hair but also by her light-colored or pastel clothing. She doesn't even want a black doctor to touch her for fear of being contaminated.[41] Nevertheless, one key scene puts a liberal point of view firmly across in the words of the black doctor, who insists that he despises the Mau Mau, but also despises "any man who preaches violence and intolerance." This silences the distrustful Howard, who has only just been saved from being murdered himself.

Technically, the film is unconvincing by current standards, as all the actors were shot in England standing before back-projected footage previously shot in Africa. Stand-ins were also filmed in Africa for long shots, and it is often quite obvious they are not who they are supposed to be when we cut to the studio-bound close-ups of the British actors. Running alongside the political story of colonialism and rebellion, there is a romance between Bogarde's Alan and Virginia McKenna's African-born but still very English rose, Mary Crawford. Bogarde is also lit in the same flattering manner as McKenna, "emphasising his eyes and cheek bones."[42] Donald Sinden's armed and uniformed policeman, Inspector Drummond, is a much more commanding, masculine presence, having none of Bogarde's "feminine" appeal.

This particular quality of Bogarde's was presented at its romantic peak in *The Wind Cannot Read,* in which female audiences would have identified with Yoko Tai's vulnerable Japanese girl with whom Bogarde's character falls in love. His "gay" characteristics—gentleness, intuition, sensitivity—are the very things that such fans found appealing, while they simultaneously disqualified him from joining, convincingly, the ranks of the conventionally masculine military hero. *The Wind Cannot Read,* as we have seen, also grafts that military hero onto Bogarde's character, but it is hardly the point and merely legitimates the transgressive femininity he conveys in the romantic scenes. The action hero required none of these qualities, and Bogarde's equal lack of "beefcake" only compounded the problem. In attempting to turn him into a conventionally masculine sex symbol, Bogarde's producers and directors somewhat missed the point. What made him attractive to so many female fans was, ironically, not his masculinity, but his particular kind of homosexuality. These women would have been disappointed if they had ever managed to entice him into a bedroom, but he provided all those qualities women often failed to find in heterosexual men. Significantly, the far more flamboyantly gay Liberace's fan base was also female. So too is Cliff Richard's, even though no one officially seems quite sure what Sir Cliff's sexual orientation is. That Bogarde's portrayal of Franz Liszt in *Song Without End* looked so like Cliff Richard only helps to strengthen the comparison.

The romantic element in *Simba* was stripped down in Bogarde's next action hero. In *Campbell's Kingdom* (dir. Ralph Thomas, 1957), he played English invalid Bruce Campbell, who travels to Canada with the aim of drilling for oil on the mountaintop previously owned by his grandfather. All the evidence that there might be oil up there has been covered up by Stanley Baker's Owen Morgan, who wants, rather more ecologically, to build a dam and flood the land for hydro-electric power. The film is really an attempt at a colonial Western, just as *The Singer Not the Song* would be an attempt at a gay one. Everyone looks like a cowboy, apart from Bogarde (initially at least), in his English overcoat, suit and tie. Later, he wears a variety of very well-pressed lumberjack shirts, which do nothing to foster the tough image he was being told to create. In his attempt to outwit Morgan, Campbell blows up a bridge, explodes the side of a mountain, rides around on the running board of a truck, saves men from Morgan's crumbling dam, slides down rocky slopes and manages to drill for oil, all without getting his hands dirty. Compared with his nemesis, played by Baker, Bogarde really stood no chance. As the *New York Times'* reviewer put it: "Dirk Bogarde appears to be a man who would be more at ease in Mayfair than among the tough ruffians of the Rockies."[43]

Chapter Five

"Nature's played a dirty trick on me."

The fact that Bogarde never came out of the closet, makes the significance of *Victim,* which was so instrumental in helping to change the law on homosexuality in Britain, distinctly ironic. Bogarde always denied that he was homosexual. ("I do hope that seeing me slammed as a homo has not upset you," he wrote to his niece Alice. "It is actually quite untrue anyway ... and what about the ones who *are* and don't get onto the elegant list!" His participation in *Victim* was the furthest he ever got to a public declaration of his sexuality, and that was already quite a long way, particularly back in 1961.)

A few television programs on the subject had been aired in Britain in the late 1960s, ITV's *Man Alive* series, for example, in which "homosexual men" were exposed to the microscope in a documentary called "Consenting Adults: The Men." The apparently well-meaning and sympathetic journalist, Jeremy James, interviewed several individuals for this, but his use of "us" in his commentary seemed also to indicate his own position: "For many of us, this is revolting," he said, speaking over shots of a gay disco:

> Men dancing with men. Homosexuals today in this country break the law. It's estimated that one man in 20 is a homosexual. These men are a minority. They receive minority treatment. They face prejudice and intolerance. They stand accused of depravity and vice. In the heterosexual word, the homosexual disturbs conformist values, is shunned and perhaps misunderstood. Most homosexuals must lead a secret, dark existence.[1]

One interviewee, a senior gay doctor, observed: "I would say quite definitely in the olden days, it went against one if one was a churchgoer and if by any chance one came across the law, then all and sundry—judges included—thought not only were you a bloody homo but a bloody hypocrite as well. [...] The Earl of Dudley in the House of Lords last year gave us his opinion that prison was too good for all homosexuals." (One thinks of King George V's uncomprehending comment on homosexuality: "I thought men like that shot themselves.") James then suggested to this same doctor, "I think some people might be slightly appalled at the idea of having a homosexual doctor, particularly if they were going to take small sons to him, for instance. Did you find this?" No, the doctor did not find that to be the case; either his patients didn't know or were civilized enough not to worry.

Another fellow, a clerk, with his back to the camera, confessed that his mother, having found out that he had been with a soldier, threw him out of the family home. "Eventually, the police came to where I worked and told me I ought to go to the police station and give a statement about what happened. I didn't know the person's name [...] and I made a statement and we arranged to meet on the next week, and I think the police were in the doorways of the shops waiting for him to come but he never came. That was the beginning of it all." He was later arrested, his fingerprints taken, and he was locked in a cell from Saturday afternoon till Monday morning. He was taken in a Black Maria to court and sentenced to two years on probation.

These desperately sad stories are mere drops in the ocean of unjustified suffering into which so many gay men were plunged, and the stigma of merely being who one was amplified through family television screens across the land. Such prejudices had even formed part of Bogarde's 1965 film *Darling* (dir. John Schlesinger), during a scene in which he plays a TV interviewer. His question to Londoners on the street is, "What do you feel most ashamed of?" One man replies: "Talking as a Londoner in London itself—the amount of—um, how *rife* homosexuality has become in London itself." At which point the man looks up at Bogarde, who nods encouragingly, doubtless seething beneath his heterosexual shell. "I'm a tough nut to crack," Bogarde often used to say, most famously to Russell Harty in 1986: "I'm certainly in the shell and you haven't cracked it yet, honey."[2] His reluctance to come out of his shell is perfectly understandable, given the climate of his formative years.

One could also argue that one's private life is nobody else's business. Bogarde often did just that, despite having written seven volumes of autobiography. His sister Elizabeth explained that if anyone, even in his own family, ever attempted to ask if he was gay, he would swiftly prevent further discussion by snapping, "'Mind your own business.' Very sharply. And that was that. And I would never have wanted to fall out with him because he'd never have wanted to see me again."[3] People in the film business also knew, but Bogarde grew adept at avoiding the question. As Harty observed to his face in his 1986 interview, "You're also a highly polished answerer of oblique questions," to which Bogarde replied, "I know perfectly well that all my life, when I sit in front of an interviewer—and you're not excluded—that you dig—all of you— dig elephant traps—or tiger traps—and I know where they are. You can cover them with bamboo poles and bits of leaf, but I'll get round them. I have fallen into one or two in the past, and made up my mind that I would never do it again."[4]

In some ways, Bogarde's public denial of his own psychological reality resembled that of Liberace, who, like Oscar Wilde before him, foolishly dragged speculation about his sexuality into the courts. Unlike Wilde, Liberace got away with it, but not before making an absolute refutation of his true nature, which today is hard to believe could ever have been taken on face value. That such a state of affairs could exist in the 1950s is a measure of the relative naivety of British society at a time when it was still

Liberace, like Bogarde, managed to maintain the public persona of heterosexual heartthrob for a mainly female fan base.

possible to be outrageously camp on stage and maintain a heterosexual facade after the curtain dropped. It is also significant that Liberace's famous court case took place in England rather than America, where his persona did not clash so garishly as it did with the British establishment. This was a time when popular entertainment in the U.K. was epitomized by the cheery, uncomplicated humor of TV's *Billy Cotton Band Show*, which often featured that much more straightforward pianist, in the pub piano tradition, Russ Conway. He may have worn fancy waistcoats, but there was absolutely nothing camp about his persona. Tricky though his vamping style is to play, there was also nothing overtly "showy" about Conway's hits, such as "Side-Saddle" and "Snow Coach," in stark contrast to Liberace, despite his attempts at toning down his image at the time. British journalist William Conner—alias "Cassandra"—had started the row in 1956 with a piece in his *Daily Mirror* gossip column, where he described the pianist as "the summit of sex—Masculine, Feminine and Neuter. Everything that He, She and It can ever want."

I have spoken to sad but kindly men on this newspaper who have met every celebrity arriving from the United States for the past 30 years. They all say that this deadly, winking, sniggering, snuggling, chromium-plated, scent-impregnated, luminous, quivering, giggling, fruit-flavored, mincing, ice-covered heap of mother love has had the biggest reception and impact on London since Charlie Chaplin arrived at the same station, Waterloo, on September 12, 1921.

This appalling man—and I use the word appalling in no other than its true sense of terrifying—has hit this country in a way that is as violent as Churchill receiving the cheers on V-E Day. He reeks with emetic language that can only make grown men long for a quiet corner, an aspidistra, a handkerchief, and the old heave-ho. Without doubt, he is the biggest sentimental vomit of all time.

Slobbering over his mother, winking at his brother, and counting the cash at every second, this superb piece of calculating candy-floss has an answer for every situation. Nobody since Aimee Semple MacPherson has purveyed a bigger, richer and more varied slag-heap of lilac-covered hokum. Nobody anywhere ever made so much money out of high speed piano playing with the ghost of Chopin gibbering at every note.

There must be something wrong with us that our teenagers longing for sex and our middle-aged matrons fed up with sex alike should fall for such a sugary mountain of jingling claptrap wrapped up in such a preposterous clown.[5]

Liberace, adored by so many women, felt that this fairly accurate representation of his public persona was a threat to his predominantly female fan base, and he took action accordingly, the court case commencing in 1959. He was eventually awarded damages of £8000 pounds and, in his own now-famous words, "cried all the way to the bank." One can imagine Bogarde cringing with distaste at the whole affair, but also nervously identifying with the root cause of the problem, for he too was a pin-up at the time, also adored by yearning females, and, along with Liberace, what that self-styled "Stately Homo of England" Quentin Crisp described in his autobiography *The Naked Civil Servant* as a "hoax":

Publicity is annoying to some homosexuals because they enjoy living incognito. This allows them to practice a hoax upon society and particularly upon its women, with whom they carry on teasing flirtations. [...] Possibly this perpetual confidence trick satisfied the hatred these men felt for the outer world.[6]

Telling people to mind their own business is not quite so easy to sustain when you are a major international film star, who, in the case of Bogarde, increasingly challenged his "official" status as a heterosexual heartthrob by turning in performances that were either overtly gay, or otherwise often examples of camp high and low, sexually ambivalent, mannered or somewhat unconvincing attempts to convey conventional masculinity. That so many women fell for him only emphasizes this duality: As already mentioned, women have always found gay men attractive at a distance, only to be disappointed when it comes to matters of intimacy. It seemed to me that many of Bogarde's films were a

Quentin Crisp as Queen Elizabeth I in *Orlando* (dir. Sally Potter, 1993).

kind of confessional for him—not in any sense of wishing to be absolved from any sense of sin, but rather as an elliptical way of admitting what he could never spell out in any other way. Even when playing straight roles, Bogarde often informed them with gay sensibility. Sometimes, as we shall see, when Bogarde is being as manly as he could muster, other characters make curiously ambivalent comments, which cast some doubt…

The homophobic state of affairs in my own formative years may well have contributed to a denial of my own personality, as it seemed so much safer not to engage with myself, let alone anyone else, than expose myself to such catastrophes experienced by the interviewees on that *Man Alive* documentary. In that respect, I later learned, I was in some ways rather like Bogarde. Indeed, I have always agreed with what he said in his last major television interview, *Dirk Bogarde: By Myself*: "You can have a love affair without carnality. It is a lot to do with respect, and respect for somebody's mind and intellect, that is higher by far than one's own."[7] Sexually, Bogarde was very probably more of a narcissist than anything else. In a TV interview from 1981—the first occasion on which he had allowed a film crew into his Provence house—he confessed, "I am totally the most selfish man that exists. I made a plan for myself after the war, which was look after me. I don't want to share it with anyone. I don't want to share it with family, or children or kiddies. I don't want any of that crap. I don't want it. I can't be more truthful than that."[8] Well, not quite, as there was Forwood, conveniently hidden away behind the scenes in the Selfish Giant's castle. Bogarde's relationship with him had, by then, become entirely platonic. To remove the elephant from the room entirely, Coldstream offers this important piece of evidence with regard to the nature of the rela-

tionship. Talking to the British journalist John Fraser, Bogarde "smiled enig-
matically":

> "We've been together a long time," he said. "Now, we're like brothers." Fraser described
> how he pressed him further and was led up to the house's extensive attic, where on a
> point stood a gleaming Harley Davidson, facing a gigantic picture on the wall of Dirk
> in *The Singer Not the Song*. The account of how Dirk achieved a form of ecstasy during
> ten minutes of "bedlam" astride his mean machine sent the staff at a Sunday tabloid
> newspaper into almost as great a frenzy—much to the subsequent dismay of Dirk's
> family and friends. […] He wanted only to "come clean" about the love that Dirk and
> Tony had for each other and to illustrate the harmless, if somewhat noisy, way in which
> a celibate and "huge narcissist" sought gratification.[9]

This approach does seem to confirm what Quentin Crisp has to say
about onanism:

> Masturbation is not only an expression of self-regard: it is also the natural emotional
> outlet of those who, before anything has reared its ugly head, have already accepted
> as inevitable the wide gulf between their real futures and the expectations of their fan-
> tasies. The habit fitted snugly into my well-established world of make-believe.[10]

One of the problems with society's perception of gay mentality is that it is presented so often in purely sexual terms, which are in fact only part of (and perhaps the least interesting part of) the many things that make the difference. It has a lot to do with humor, with taste, with perception and, more radically, with social deconstruction and philosophical detachment. Gayness is indeed deconstructionist, a challenge to matters of gender and identity, to established social structures and the accepted rules of power politics. As I said, I was too young to have watched the *Man Alive* program in 1967, but the prejudices exposed in it, so

Bogarde and a photo of himself as Anacleto in *The Singer Not the Song* (dir. Roy Baker, 1961).

infrequently discussed but ever-present by implication as part of the dominant ideology of the time, profoundly affected my own self-confidence in an insidiously subliminal manner.

The continued horror of homosexuality that is still active in so many countries always perplexed me until I discovered, online, another question posed to Quentin Crisp, during his first television interview (which was never conventionally broadcast) in the wake of the publication of *The Naked Civil Servant* in 1968. Interviewer Bernard Braden summed up the underlying homophobia of so many cultures and civilizations by remarking, "Because [homosexuals] are not concerned with reproduction of the species, they therefore have a sense of detachment about other things in life, which would probably make them very good leaders—rulers." Crisp disagreed with the idea that gays would necessarily make good leaders, and didn't comment on the first part of the observation. But, to me, Braden had isolated a key point: Homosexuality is a challenge to "the prime directive." Spinsters used to be pitied because they were considered to have been unfortunate. Homosexuals were, and in some countries still are proscribed because they were considered to be unnatural. Gay people certainly go forth but they do not multiply, and because they have for so long stood outside the mainstream, they are a continual challenge to it—a deconstructionist subversion of received opinion, of moral platitudes, of the whole meaning of Christian civilization. Thus also spoke Friedrich Nietzsche, another closet homosexual, whose sexual orientation informed an entire philosophy. Long before Nietzsche, the Marquis de Sade had questioned the censure that homosexuality had suffered for so long:

What is the only crime which can exist here? Surely not placing oneself in such or such a position, unless you wish to hold that some parts of the body are different from others, that some are pure and others impure, but as it is impossible to advance such absurdities the only possible crime can be in the waste of semen. But I ask you is it probable that that semen is so precious in the eyes of Nature that it cannot be wasted without crime?[11]

Fortunately, by 1968, some societies were catching up with de Sade and Nietzsche, increasing tolerance and understanding; but Crisp's explanation for that change was not that it was the result of enlightenment but rather of boredom: Gays, like feminists, are gradually accepted because people are bored by the noise of protest:

You know, Mr. Bronowski invented "the arrow of time," which always points in the direction of diminishing difference. That seems to me to have been a wonderful thing to have said; and, of course, it's here. Once there was a difference between the classes, then there was a difference between the sexes. Now there's almost none. You can only speak of *actions* as being homosexual, and repeated actions lead to a homosexual life, but the idea of a homosexual person is passing. Even homosexuals themselves have ceased to think of themselves as apart—as a special group, a people apart. They are allowed to mix with the real world and so they tend to do so. [...] Basically, I'm a person.[12]

This view was considerably ahead of its time, as my own experience was to demonstrate, but time did indeed eventually catch up with it. Alas, for those of Bogarde's generation, it was all rather too late. They'd had to make quite a different bed on which to lie, and that environment formed not only Bogarde's persona but also the roles for which he was most celebrated. There is still a pressing need for vigilance against homophobia, and for films to address it both at home and abroad, but *Victim* was a landmark. It was not the first film about homosexuals, but it was the first film to feature a mainstream heartthrob star in the traditional male role of a married lawyer, who is also homosexual. It was by placing the subject in a conventional context that made the difference.

Victim was released on August 31, 1961, and soon followed by Tony Richardson's *A Taste of Honey* in which Murray Melvin also broke ground by sympathetically portraying a gay working-class character, though one that was much more overtly "camp" than Melville Farr. Before *Victim,* homosexuality in Bogarde's films had only ever been subtextual. Knowing, as we now do, Bogarde's personal orientation, it is perhaps possible to regard fugitive pieces like *Hunted* (dir. Charles Crichton, 1951) as allegories of the gay predicament. In *Hunted*, Bogarde played a murderer on the run, and though playing a straight character (he has killed his unfaithful wife's lover), his situation was not that different from the fugitive lifestyle of many gays at the time. At one stage, a policeman says, "Let there be no place where this man can hide or rest in safety: no cellar, no barn, no ditch, no field." Similarly, in *Desperate Moment* (dir. Compton Bennett, 1953), Bogarde's character is also on the run trying to clear himself of a murder to which he confessed out of loyalty to his comrades, but did not in fact commit. Constantly dodging pursuing policemen, as he does here, this could easily have become something similar to *Victim,* and one line unintentionally expresses the homophobic spirit of the times in which it was shot. Commenting on a dog that's playing in his office, an American soldier calls him a "cute guy," to which his British police colleague replies, "If guys can be cute, I suppose he is."

Someone like Quentin Crisp was an obvious target of police attention due to his flamboyant effeminacy. (Policeman: "You're dressed as a woman and you'd better catch a bus quick or there will be trouble. People don't like that sort of thing [pointing at my flyless trousers and my high-heeled shoes]."[13]) But Coldstream also quotes from the much more straight-acting gay actor Richard Chamberlain, who observed, "It's hard for those who weren't around in the '40s and '50s to appreciate how deeply terrifying it was to imagine being labeled a faggot, a pansy, a pervert. It seemed to me then that even traitors and murderers were generally held in higher esteem that I would be if anyone ever found out the truth about me."[14] Crisp writes of gay life in the 1930s: "The police thought of homosexuals as North American Indians thought of bison. They cast about for a way of exterminating them in herds."[15]

The relationship that develops between Bogarde's character Chris Lloyd in *Hunted* and the boy, Robbie, played by Jon Whiteley, is a kind of gay one without being in any way pedophiliac. After all, it would have been quite a different film if the abducted child had been a girl rather than a boy. The male bond is essential for the film to work in the way it does. It is, indeed, a love story, which also embraces issues of loyalty, trust and compassion; and these are also the typical values of the war movie. *Hunted* was, in many ways, the perfect vehicle for Bogarde's celibate homosexuality to express itself—all those qualities apart from "carnality" that defined his own personality. Chris' relationship with his wife Magda (Elizabeth Sellars) is based entirely on lust,

TRAPPED. After leaving the Scottish mainland in a stolen fishing boat, Robbie falls sick with a fever. Lloyd's conscience tells him he must return to port but, waiting there, are the police and the end of freedom.

DIRK BOGARDE
with KAY WALSH
ELIZABETH SELLARS
and introducing JON WHITELEY

HUNTED

Screenplay by JACK WHITTINGHAM
Produced by JULIAN WINTLE

Directed by CHARLES CRICHTON
AN INDEPENDENT ARTISTS PICTURE

Bogarde as Chris Lloyd (right) with Jon Whiteley as Robbie in *Hunted* (dir. Charles Crichton, 1952).

but that with Robbie is entirely based on love—to such an extent that when he thinks they are home and dry, steaming out to sea on a stolen boat, Chris sacrifices himself to save Robbie, who has become dangerously ill. Christine Geraghty sees these qualities as representing a break with the stereotype of the "masculine," traditionally authoritative father. She sees Bogarde's performance as emphasizing "the feminine aspects of Chris' role; he is seen feeding Robbie, putting him to bed and telling him bedtime stories."[16] Chris carries Robbie in his arms and embraces him to keep him warm. Ultimately, he sacrifices his own freedom to save the boy.

There were other personal resonances in the story. Robbie is adopted and lives with an abusive Scottish couple with whom he is miserable. This is why he runs away and ends up falling in with Chris. Bogarde would have been able to identify with Robbie's plight, having been sent to stay with his own Scottish relatives when his brother Gareth was born. The experience scarred him, and inspired several highly critical passages in his autobiographies, which hurt his well-meaning relatives, who never intended any harm. The abrupt contrast between southern and Scottish ways was a particular shock:

> The first time I offered to kiss my uncle on the cheek before I went to bed, he recoiled as if I had physically assaulted him and, with a crimson face, gruffly said, "We don't do that sort of thing here." And offered me his hand. My aunt received her kiss as if I had threatened her. She winced uncomfortably. The Lavatory became the "Bathroom." You never spoke of Birth, only ever of Death. If a woman was pregnant, she was "a wee bitty under the weather." And one was never seen in the corridor of the house in pajamas.[17]

The Spanish Gardener (dir. Philip Leacock, 1956) also had a gay subtext, which was much more pronounced in the original A.J. Cronin story on which it was based. Rank hushed this up for the film, but Bogarde certainly knew what it was all about. The story concerns the possessive love of diplomat Harrington Brande (Michael Hordern) for his son Nicholas (again played by Whiteley). Brande is separated from his wife for reasons that are not explained beyond Brande's insistence that his wife left him "of her own volition, without cause or motive." The motif may well have been his lack of interest in her, which he certainly doesn't lack with regard to Bogarde's peasant gardener, José. Bogarde sounds neither Spanish nor like a peasant, but he is very good-looking. Nicholas has been the only man in Brande's life up to this point. He fusses over him, looks on adoringly as the boy says his prayers, and keeps explaining, in his tight-lipped way, that "my son is delicate." Brande is indeed buttoned-up, always immaculately turned out in three-piece suits and ties, and obviously sexually repressed. Bogarde, ironically, plays an entirely heterosexual man (he has a girlfriend) but José nonetheless understands what Brande's problem is. This is not only jealousy of his own son, who enjoys the company of José rather more than helping his father unpack his collection of Dresden china figurines, but also Brande's own attraction to the gardener. "It is as a man that you have failed," Brande's superior (Bernard Lee) informs him. "For Heaven's sake, try and behave like a human being." But to do so would require him being honest with himself.

"I don't know what evil is in your mind," says José during his big confrontation with his confused employer, "but I pity your son." The camera bathes in a close-up of Bogarde's big brown eyes during this, which contrast superbly with Hordern's constrained features. Having falsely accused him of stealing Nicholas' watch, Brande is overcome with guilt. He knows that his corrupt servant (Cyril Cussak) is responsible, and when he sees José in handcuffs, he asks, "Are those things necessary?" José smiles up at him, knowing full well that Brande is attracted to him. On the train that takes José to his trial, the rhythm of the wheels suggests the words, "José is good, José is good," to Brande's tortured mind. In the end, all accusations withdrawn, he begs José for forgiveness, tending his wounds, and the final shots between them are full of Brande's averted gazes and downcast eyes. José assures him that Nicholas will forget the injustice he has suffered.

"He won't forget you," Brande replies, adding, with great significance, "Nor shall I." There is nothing overtly gay about any of this, but, as Bogarde said of his autobiographies, all you have to do is read between the lines and everything becomes clear. Reading between the lines, however, wasn't necessary when viewing *Victim,* where everything is out in the open. Its screenplay was written by the husband-and-wife team of John McCormick and Janet Green, who had been under contract with Rank until 1959 when they collaborated with Basil Dearden for the first time on *Sapphire. Sapphire* was also what the critic Victor Perkins called a "thriller-problem" film. These, he felt, worked "neither as thrillers nor as examinations of a problem, and particularly not as films."[18] This is an extreme view, which perhaps overlooks the context in which Dearden's problem-thrillers first appeared. *Sapphire,* like *Victim* two years later, examined taboo subjects, long-overlooked by British cinema as a whole before. In the case of *Sapphire,* Britain's "hidden" black community was put under the microscope, along with the prejudicial attitudes of white Britons at the time. A girl is found murdered on Hampstead Heath. The girl is what is referred to as a "lily-skin"—a black who looks white. But as the proprietor of a black nightclub (Dan Jackson) later explains to the investigating policemen (Nigel Patrick and Michael Craig), "Your chick was a lily-skin, wasn't she? It's in the evening papers. I think I would have remembered if she'd been in here. Oh, you can always tell, 'cause once they hear the beat of the bongo…" at which point, the camera pans down to catch the tapping, twisting feet of another "lily-skin" as she responds to the rhythm accordingly. "Yes," the nightclub owner continues, "no matter how fair the skin, they can't hide that swing." Ironically, as this is a film about the contrast of black and white, *Sapphire*, unlike *Victim*, was shot in color, though this does help to suggest the vibrancy of black culture in London nightclubs with its blue drainpipes, yellow walls and pink lampshades, not to mention a red taffeta skirt we will encounter later. When Sapphire's obviously black brother calls at the boarding house where she had been living, he initially has the door closed in his face by the landlady (Grace Arnold), who informs him that she only takes in white students. This cold shouldering was the lamentable fate of many of the so-called "Windrush Generation" who arrived in postwar England, encouraged by official offers of hospitality to colonials only to discover that this failed to mean much when they found themselves on the streets of London. The landlady is appalled that she has been housing a black girl who only *looks* white. She asks Patsy (Jocelyn Britton), one of her other (white) guests, "That girl that you brought here, did you know she was colored?"

"What girl?"
"Sapphire."
"Yes. Yes, I did."
"When did she tell you?"
"Well, *she* didn't. A friend told me."
"This house is my living. If it got round that I took colored students, certain white people wouldn't allow their children to stay here."
"Well, I think it's a damn silly prejudice!"
"I'm not saying it isn't, but I can't afford to have my rooms empty. To think that she could be so sly."
"It's people like you who made her sly. Well, you've jolly well got another room empty now."
"Patsy! You took Sapphire home to Guildford, didn't you?"
"Yes."
"Did you tell your father and mother she was colored?"
"No."
"Well, then, don't be so quick to call me prejudiced."

Sapphire's murderer is eventually discovered to be the very white middle-class sister of David Harris (played by Paul Massie), who has brought dishonor to the family by getting Sapphire pregnant. By first leading the audience to expect a black murderer, Dearden creates extra shock value when revealing a white culprit, further exposing the mood of racial intolerance that the film addresses. "Red taffeta under a tweed skirt," says Patrick's policeman, considering the evidence. "Yes, that's the black beneath the white all right," Craig's counterpart exclaims, in an exchange that was to be echoed in *Victim* in a similar scene between two other policemen, one sympathetic, one less so.

Sapphire anticipated Kenny Everett's *Desert Island Discs* recollection of the remark made by his masseur soon after Everett had officially "come out": "Now you know what it feels like to be black." Having shown racial prejudice to be alive and well in Britain, Dearden and Green now turned their attention to homophobia with an equally fixed gaze. The topic was timely, with the Wolfenden Report on "Homosexual Offenses and Prostitution" having been published in 1957. This had recommended that it was not the function of the law "to intervene in the private life of citizens, or to seek to enforce any particular pattern of behaviour," but by 1961 there were still six years to go before homosexuality was no longer a crime, and *Victim* played a significant role in bringing about that change.

It was not alone, however. Before being made into a film, the 1958 stage production of *A Taste of Honey* also made an impact on the Lord Chamberlain's Office, and stirred calls for reform. At this time it was illegal not only to be gay but also to portray gay characters on stage, which latter could only

Bogarde as Melville Farr in *Victim* (dir. Basil Dearden, 1961).

be achieved by means of innuendo. Thus, Geoffrey Ingham is only gay by implication, such as his explanation of why his landlady has thrown him out of her boarding house: "It isn't what I've done, it's what she thinks I do. She doesn't like the way I walk."

Responding to the spirit of the times, Green and McCormick were keen to write a screenplay on this subject, especially after having read the Wolfenden Report, but many actors were reluctant to accept the leading role of the barrister Melville Farr. James Mason, Stewart Granger and Jack Hawkins all turned it down, which was just as well, as their refusals left the field open for Bogarde—a man who, if not openly "out," knew all too well what the problem was from the inside. He made every attempt to cover his tracks, however, claiming that there were no gay people actually involved in making the film. "We had a lot of very straight heterosexuals camping themselves silly in it," he insisted,[19] choosing to ignore not only his own reality but also the very obvious exception of Dennis Price. "The set was closed to all visitors," Bogarde recalled, "the press firmly forbidden, and the whole project was treated, at the beginning, with all the false reverence, dignity and respect usually accorded to the Crucifixion or Queen Victoria."[20] It was decided to call "these people," as he referred to gays, "inverts," and, as is now well-known, explained that the tension on set was broken by a chippie, who shouted one morning, "Watch yer arse, Alfie!"[21] (Or "Charlie," as he has it in *Snakes and Ladders*.) Sylvia Syms, who played Farr's wife Laura, recalled the emotional power that lay behind Bogarde's performance in the key scene 112, when the secret comes out, for which Bogarde rewrote the dialogue:

> All right—all right, you want to know, I'll tell you. You won't be content until I tell you, will you—until you've *ripped* it out of me? I stopped seeing him because I *wanted* him. Can't you understand—because I *wanted him*. Now what good has that done you?

Syms has said, "You just need to see the pain, really," and it was Bogarde's astonishingly expressive eyes that conveyed it.[22] The personal connection to what he was playing here seems to have been of a similar intensity to that witnessed by Freddie Francis when directing Peter Cushing in *The Ghoul* in 1975. Cushing was still at that time still in deep mourning over the death of his wife Helen, and he had arranged to have enlarged photographs of her to stand in for those the dead wife of the doctor he plays in that film. ("On the screen they're this big," he explained, "so at last we made a film together."[23]) However, when he delivered the line, "My wife is dead..." his co-star, Veronica Carlson, remembered, "You knew that he wasn't acting at all and he was literally breaking down in front of everybody."[24] Similarly, Bogarde's camera operator, Bob Thomson, realized that during the filming of *Victim* that Bog-

Peter Cushing and Veronica Carlson in *The Ghoul* (dir. Freddie Francis, 1975).

arde was giving "such a sincere performance. It gave an atmosphere, and made us think we were making a film that was different from the normal run."[25]

The power of *Victim*, which on the surface is a fairly straightforward blackmail drama, rests not only on the controversial subject but also in the remarkable strength of Bogarde's performance and personality. Without him and his emotional commitment to the film, it almost certainly wouldn't have made the impact it did. "I had achieved what I had longed to do for so long," he admitted, "to be in a film which disturbed, educated, and illuminated as well as merely giving entertainment." But he also exploited his "straight" image to defend his private reality. "Anything that is persecuted, I have a silent urgency to go and assist," he once explained in a Radio 4 interview. "I don't know why." In the case of *Victim*, there is no doubt about his motives, despite the smokescreen he wafted around it to protect his own privacy. "It is extraordinary, in this over-permissive age," he wrote in *Snakes and Ladders*, "to believe that this modest film could ever have been considered courageous, daring or dangerous to make. It was, in its time, all three."[26]

But though Bogarde is the jewel, the setting also plays an important role. Philip Green's score exploits a piano concerto idiom during the main title sequence, usefully complementing the idea of an individual against society: The piano represents the former, on the run, the orchestra embodies the latter, personified on screen by the police. Military snare drums also accompany the arrival of a jet-black police car after the title sequence, emphasizing the sense of threat. This being a blackmail story, part of the tension is created by trying to work out the identity of the blackmailer.

Two red herrings are introduced in the pub frequented by the assembled "inverts." This sinister gay couple, blind P.H. (Hilton Edwards) and Mickey (David Evans), are the gay equivalent of the two equally sinister sisters (played by Hilary Mason and Clelia Matania) who pursue Donald Sutherland and Julie Christie's John and Laura Baxter through Venice streets in Nicolas Roeg's *Don't Look Now* (1973), but who turn out *not* to be the killers we are led to believe. P.H. and Mickey have dialogue that suggests they are behind the blackmail letters but in the end are revealed to be sending mere begging letters under false pretenses. The real blackmailer is Margaret Diamond's Miss Benham, whose name is often made to sound like the rather more appropriate "Miss Venom" by some of the actors. She is the assistant to Norman Bird's homosexual bookseller, Harold Doe, and Miss Benham loathes homo-

Bogarde's barrister, Melville Farr, is outed in *Victim* (dir. Basil Dearden, 1961).

sexuals. "They *disgust* me," she confesses towards the end of the film. Gays make her "physically ill. Someone's got to make them pay for their filthy blasphemy," she raves. Her accomplice Sandy Youth (Derren Nesbitt), a name that is only one letter away from "Randy Youth," calls her "a cross between an avenging angel and a peeping Tom." She also resembles the champion of conventional morality that was Mary Whitehouse, the British social activist and scourge of many a TV producer in the 1960s and '70s, when she ran the National Viewers' and Listeners' Association. Miss Benham's loathing was quite common in the real world. Quentin Crisp, admittedly a very noticeable and extremely effeminate homosexual, describes how "the girls who might be forced to come close enough to me to hand me an envelope were trembling so that they could hardly stand. I never found anything except time that would remove this reaction of stark terror. In order at least to reduce it to a minimum, I cultivated an air of politeness bordering on subservience."[27]

Sandy is eventually revealed to be a homosexual himself, if the significant swerve of the camera onto the print of Michelangelo's David that hangs on the wall of his flat is anything to go by. He and Miss Benham are eventually apprehended by the police, and Melville Farr faces exposure and ruin; but Farr is an honorable man. Having had an affair with Boy Barrett (Peter McEnery), he feels responsible for Barrett's suicide. A photograph of Barret and Farr in each other's arms has been obtained by the blackmailers. Barrett, who has been stealing money to pay his demands, had tried to persuade Farr to help him but, fearing that it is Barrett who is trying to blackmail him, Farr refused. Realizing his mistake, he is determined to put a stop to the blackmailers' reign of terror—for fear, as they say in the film, is the oxygen of blackmail. "It used to be witches," says Barrett's friend Eddy (Donald Churchill), when Barrett is on the run from the police. "At least they don't burn you."

The sympathetic Detective Inspector Harris (John Barrie) has already visited Farr and explained that "as many as 90 percent of all blackmail cases have a homosexual origin." Bogarde's "look," when he is told that Barrett has hanged himself, demonstrates the impact of a remark he had overheard Alan Ladd make in the Pinewood restaurant one afternoon over lunch. "I did a great look," Ladd had said, during a break in filming *The Black Knight* (dir. Tay Garnett, 1954). "If you can do one great look," Bogarde realized, "you're halfway in."[28] The look he gives Farr is indeed a master class in mute communication. Bogarde's decency shines through in this role, and every gesture, every movement counts. "If I hadn't been trying so *bloody* hard to avoid trouble," Farr shouts, "this might never have happened, but it has, and they're not going to get away with it."

Back in the police station, Inspector Harris discusses the case with his less tolerant sergeant, Bridie (John Cairney), in the scene that recasts the "red taffeta skirt" exchange in *Sapphire*:

BRIDIE: But Mr. Farr is married, sir!

HARRIS: Those are famous last words, Bridie. If only these unfortunate devils would come to us in the first place.

BRIDIE: If only they led normal lives, they wouldn't need to come at all.

HARRIS: If the law punished every abnormality, we'd be pretty busy, sergeant.

BRIDIE: Even so, sir, this law was made for a very good reason. If it were changed, other weaknesses would follow.

HARRIS: I can see you're a true puritan, Bridie.

BRIDIE: There's nothing wrong with that.

HARRIS: Of course not. There was a time when that was against the law, you know.

A similar contempt for the gay community is expressed by Frank Pettit's otherwise genial publican, who runs the inverts' favorite watering hole:

They're good for a laugh all right. They're very witty at times, generous too. I hate their bloody guts. It's always excuses. Every paper you pick up, it's excuses. "Environment." "Too much love as kids." "Too little love as kids." "Can't help it." "Part of nature." Well, to my mind, it's a weak rotten part of nature. And if they ever make it legal, they may as well license every other perversion.

Anticipating the tragic stories on the *Man Alive* documentary that followed in 1964, Charles Lloyd-Pack, who plays the traditional role of the gay hairdresser Henry, explains how awful his life as a homosexual has been:

I can't help the way I am, but the law says I'm a criminal. I've been to prison four times. I couldn't go through that again, not at my age. I'm going to Canada. I've made up my mind to be sensible, as the prison doctor used to say. I don't care how lonely, but sensible. I can't stand any more trouble. [...] Nature played me a dirty trick. I'm going to see I get a few years of peace and quiet in return.

Unfortunately, Sandy the blackmailer puts an end to this dream by smashing up Henry's shop, and giving the hairdresser a heart attack in the process. But before that happens, Henry asks Farr to help:

You've got a big position. They'll listen to you. You ought to be able to state our case. Tell them there's no magic cure for how we are—certainly not behind prison bars.

Bogarde had an even "bigger position" than Farr, and it was his standing as Rank's most glittering star that amplified the message more than anything else. Farr concludes, "If I go to court in my own name, I can draw attention to the fault in the existing law," which is what Bogarde did by allowing his name go above the title of the film. The greatest fear of both Bogarde and Farr is that their friends are going to lower their eyes and their enemies are going to say that they always knew. But the way Farr is presented allows him to be identified not only as gay but also as virginal and "uncontaminated." The implication is that nothing of a sexual nature has ever happened—even with the previous lover from university days, whom he told his wife about before they were married. "I may share your feelings," he tells his three establishment friends, who turn out to be gay as well, "but I've always resisted them." Farr is thus made "virtuous" and redeemable, while simultaneously representing the gay cause. "I can't stop loving him," Laura cries, and no doubt Bogarde hoped that his female fans would feel the same, if they ever found out. In fact, by the time of *Victim* he was already getting too old to be a pin-up anyway.

Two years later, Bogarde consolidated his new direction with *The Servant*, and Harold Pinter's multi-layered screenplay for this gave him the opportunity to reveal far more about his own gay identity than the prim and proper Farr had done. Robin Maugham's 1948 novel of the same name, on which Pinter's screenplay was based, had been inspired by an experience Maugham had at the home of Sir Winston Churchill's daughter, Mary—she had invited him for a drink at the home of a friend. The house came with its own manservant, and going down to the kitchen to fetch a lager, Maugham was astonished to find a naked boy in the manservant's room. "I can see you are admiring my young nephew, sahr," the servant smiled. "Would you like me to send him up to you to say good night, sahr?" "At that moment," Coldstream reports, "Maugham could see himself caught in the mesh of a smooth-voiced blackmailer."[29]

An immediate connection with *Victim* is the fact that Bogarde's character in *The Servant* is called Barrett—not "Boy" Barrett, but the rather more sinister-sounding Hugo Barrett. As a name, "Hugo" carries certain connotations as well. Its etymological meaning is "intelligence," which Barrett certainly has (so did the similarly named, distinctly sinister ventriloquist's puppet in the final story of Ealing's chiller *Dead of Night* [dir. Alberto Cavalcanti, 1945]). Barrett knows all about the gay reality beneath the philandering activities of his employer, Tony, who coincidentally (or perhaps not) shares the same name as Bogarde's real-life partner. In the film, Tony is played by James Fox, who, with his golden hair, "grace and breeding," also had, according to Bogarde himself, "a muted quality of corruptibility. This young man could spoil like peaches: he could be led to the abyss."[30] There is also something aristocratic about the name Hugo, which is at odds with Barrett's lowly social position and Manchester accent. Fox understood the dynamic completely: "The beauty of *The Servant*," he explained "was that the domineering one, Barrett, was not the one with the most class."[31]

On a political level, Barrett is a kind of Mephistopheles, out to disrupt the status quo. On a personal level, he is an Iago figure, impelled by the "motiveless malignancy" that had driven Alfie Rawlins in *The Boys in Brown*. On a psychological level, Barrett is very obviously gay and conforms to certain gay stereotypes. During his initial interview for the job of manservant at Tony's bachelor pad, he points out that "cooking is something in which I take a great deal of pride." His soufflé has apparently been much admired. He is also adept at interior design, recommending "Mandarin red and fuchsia" as being "a very chic combination this year." All those interviewers who expressed mild surprise that Bogarde should live in elegant and luxurious surroundings might also have picked up on Barrett's belief that "it makes all the difference in life" to have "tasteful and pleasant surroundings." When the decorators move in, Barrett fussily snaps, "You mind that paintwork!" He whistles a melody from Liszt's Hungarian Sixth Hungarian Rhapsody, which Bogarde would have become familiar with when filming *Song Without End*, and manages to make it sound quietly menacing.

He also knows all about wine vintages—far more so than his employer. "Just a Beaujolais, sir," he explains, "but a good bottler," a phrase neither Tony nor his upper-crust girlfriend, Susan (Wendy Craig), seem to understand. Neither does Tony understand that he is himself gay. He seduces women, but *needs* Barrett to look after him with salt footbaths, "nice hot drinks," cooking and tidying up. He also needs him emotionally, for Barrett understands him far better than any of Tony's women. Losey himself drew attention to this by claiming he didn't want the film "to be simply a study of a little homosexual affair." It isn't *only* about that, but it is largely about the repression of a homosexual affair. Forwood was certainly concerned about Bogarde appearing in another film with a homosexual subtext so soon after *Victim*. As David Caute explains, "Bogarde remembers asking a rather inebriated Losey and Pinter whether *The Servant* was to be a homosexual picture—neither answered. 'I saw nothing homosexual in it,' Bogarde adds."[32]

Susan calls Barrett "a peeping Tom." "He's a vampire too on his days off," Tony replies, again loosely connecting *The Servant* to the horror genre. Indeed, it has much in common with Roman Polanski's first horror film, *Repulsion* (1965), another sexual drama also set largely within the confines of a single flat; and the mention of vampires also raises Losey's symbolic use of mirrors. Vampires, as Hammer films demonstrated around the same time that Losey was making *The Servant*, cast no reflection. There is nothing quite

Bogarde as Barrett (left) with James Fox as Tony in *The Servant* (dir. Joseph Losey, 1963).

so melodramatic going on in Tony's flat, but there are a great many mirrors, and Losey is keen to exploit them to pair opposites and to symbolize Barrett's mission to colonize Tony's flat and his way of life. John Lash, in his book on doubles, has pointed out that to be "taken over or united with the double is fatal," and that "there is a universal consensus that the sighting of the double is warning of imminent death." With regard to vampires, Lash adds:

> As a member of the "living dead," a vampire is the double of a once-living person, but now the original of the double had been totally eliminated: as when, upon losing an original document, we are left with the Xerox copy. Since the double (completely separated from its original) can have no double, the vampire has no reflection.[33]

Though Barrett keeps his reflection, he is indeed a kind of vampire. He attaches himself to Tony like a parasite, and gradually corrupts him, sucking away his fragile dignity and authority, and ultimately destroying him, usurping Tony's position and taking over his establishment. The way in which Barrett often appears in mirrors subliminally suggests the vampire lore associated with them. As soon as Tony makes his comment about Barrett being a vampire, Barrett appears in his bedroom and it is his reflection in the mirror that we see first. One might even extend the parallel to Bram Stoker's Dracula, who not only serves Harker "old Tokay"[34] (which was no doubt just as good a bottler as Barrett's Beaujolais), but also performs the role of devouring domestic servant. Harker records in his diary,

> I went cautiously to my own room and found him making the bed. This was odd, but only confirmed what I had all along thought—that there were no servants in the house. When later I saw him through the chink of the hinges of the door laying the table in the dining-room, I was assured of it; for he does himself all these menial offices, surely it is proof that there is no one else to do them.[35]

When Dracula later appears in Harker's rooms in Piccadilly, while Harker and his friends are deactivating the vampire's coffins, the count's rage is only a little more melodramatic than Barrett's later outburst in which he accuses Tony of being "no gentleman."

> You think to baffle me, you—with your pale faces all in a row, like sheep in a butcher's. You shall be sorry yet, each one of you! You think you have left me without a place to rest; but I have more. My revenge is just begun![36]

Dracula's "contemptuous sneer," which concludes this diatribe, is directly comparable to Barrett's. Barrett has not only made Tony's flat a very suitable "place to rest," but is also only just beginning his own revenge on the upper classes; and there is also Stoker's curious suggestion that Dracula himself might be gay: "How dare you touch him, any of you?" he shouts to his vampire brides as they are about to kiss Harker. "How dare you cast eyes on him when I had forbidden it? Back, I tell you all! This man belongs to me!"[37] It is certainly the case that Tony increasingly belongs to Barrett.

It is not only vampires that *The Servant* has in common with Hammer films. Wendy Craig went on to co-star in Hammer's *The Nanny* (dir. Seth Holt) two years later, and both films are really very similar, each being set almost entirely within the confines of a claustrophobic flat (*The Servant* even more so than *The Nanny*). Losey uses his space to articulate the power struggle between Barrett and Tony, positioning them above, below or on the stairs to reflect the changing dynamic between them. There are no stairs in the flat in *The Nanny*, but Holt is similarly concerned to use the restricted space and the black-and-white photography that both films also share to articulate the psychological action. *The Nanny* concerns a psychopathic child-carer (Bette

Davis) who terrorizes a young boy called Joey (William Dix). Joey knows Nanny's terrible secret: She was accidentally responsible for the death of Joey's tiny sister, who drowned in the bath. The game of cat-and-mouse that plays out between them is very much an echo of Barrett's victimization of Tony, who is largely a child himself: naive, trusting, dependent, lazy, etc. Barrett nannies him until the nannying turns into bullying and finally brutal humiliation. Davis' Nanny, a live-in servant just like Barrett, similarly pretends to be looking after Joey while actually trying to poison him, smother him to death and finally drown him, all of which disasters he manages to escape (unlike poor Tony, who is utterly crushed by Barrett in the end). "You mustn't make things difficult for Nanny," this evil Mary Poppins threatens, pillow under her arm, in the film's climax. One can easily imagine Barrett saying the same thing.

Despite all Barrett's passive aggression, Tony is at first defensive about Barrett, shouting at Susan, "I do wish you'd stop yapping at Barrett." But Susan instinctively distrusts and grows to despise this interloping servant. The feeling is mutual. Indeed, Barrett hates all women, as his insult to a group of girls waiting for him to finish a call in a telephone box demonstrates quite clearly. To him, they are all "bitches," and he spends the film thinking up ways of demolishing them, using them like Don Giovanni, while simultaneously feeling nothing but contempt for them. Brooding in the kitchen, picking his teeth, he really does resemble Iago thinking up ways of incriminating Desdemona and destroying Othello. Tellingly, he had been known as "Basher Barrett" in the army, where he had been apparently very good at drilling raw recruits. Tony has also been in the army, as an officer of course, and towards the end of the film we see a photograph of him in full-dress uniform. The military past shared by both men recapitulates the sublimated homoeroticism discussed earlier. Tony's house, which Barrett has furnished for him, is decorated with a variety of masculine images. Nineteenth-century prints of soldiers in uniform hang on the walls. Model canons adorn the mantelpiece. There are also military figurines, but also much more extreme images of male nudes such as the larger bronze statuette of an athlete with clearly exposed genitalia (male nudes are much less common than female nudes, so this is obviously a deliberate placing). A bodybuilder pin-up can also be seen in Tony's bedroom, and pencil sketches of naked men in provocative poses, again with exposed genitalia, are reflected in the living room mirror. Tony's books are also revealing. Among the titles on display are Vladimir Nabokov's *Pale Fire*, which Edmund White has called "the great gay comic novel, an equally funny and sometimes tender portrait of a homosexual madman."[38] (I will address the matter of Nabokov's personal homophobia in a later chapter.)

Bogarde as Barrett (standing) with James Fox as Tony in *The Servant* (dir. Joseph Losey, 1963.

There is also a copy of a book about Rugby League Football, no doubt of interest to an admirer of the male body, along with an Enid Blyton children's volume, perhaps meant to indicate Tony's fundamental immaturity. His artistic pretensions are implied by a copy of Michael Levey's *From Giotto to Cezanne,* and his social class is represented by bound copies of *Pall Mall Magazine.*

Barrett's sadism is suggested by the sinister leather gloves he wears. Indeed, Barrett is the embryo of the character Bogarde would later develop in Cavani's *The Night Porter.* Here, the sadism takes a less graphic form, but it's just as psychologically destructive, as Barrett fully intends it to be. His malignancy is perhaps less motiveless than Iago's, driven, as it is, by class conflict, misogyny and the desire to expose Tony's gay reality. By ingratiating himself into Tony's house, he achieves the first of these motivations. He triumphs with the second by unnerving Susan. "What do you want from this house?" she asks him, suspecting his gayness with such lines as, "Do you think you go well with the color scheme?" Barrett then sets up a trap into which Tony falls. He arranges for his "sister," Vera (Sarah Miles), to visit him at Tony's flat and then seduce his employer, a seduction that is played out as though both are naughty children misbehaving behind Daddy's back. Significantly, Losey shows us a *reflection* of Tony and Vera kissing, suggesting that this illicit affair is the mirror image of Tony's relationship with Susan. When Susan discovers what has been going on between them, in the most humiliating scene in the film, she walks out without another word.

That scene begins when Tony and Susan return home late one night to find Barrett and Vera together in Tony's bedroom. Barrett's shadow (another kind of double) then appears and hovers menacingly over the stairs. So powerful is the image that he hardly needs to appear in person, but when he does, both he and Vera are shown as reflections, with Tony and Susan flanking the mirror, thus nicely symbolizing the opposing duality of both couples. Barrett explains, with another sly smile: "She's not my sister, sir, so, if I might say so, we're both rather in the same boat." He adds that Vera is his fiancée, but Losey is careful subtly to suggest that she is really just a girl he has hired for the part. He and Pinter imply conversations between them behind doors and show us the knowing glances of one to the other. At the end of the film, in a somewhat Fellini-esque orgy scene, Barrett invites a group of dubious women to the house, all of whom sit in statuesque, mute poses before they are sent packing. When Barrett kisses Susan in this degrading dénouement, we see a reflection of Vera in the mirror behind them, emphasizing, once again, that Vera is Susan's double.

Before that, and after the revelation about Vera, Tony sends Barrett packing, but he is now lost without him. Order in the flat falls to pieces. The flowers Susan brought stand withered and black in the vase under which Barrett so carefully arranged a magazine, to avoid marking the surface. Newspapers lie scattered on the floor and everywhere is untidy. Like the aristocrats in *Gosford Park* (dir. Robert Altman, 2002), Tony is quite unable to look after himself. ("I can't do it!" Maggie Smith's Constant Trenham says in that film, having forced her servant out of the carriage into the rain to open a thermos flask.) Later, Tony meets Barrett in a pub and agrees to give him a second chance; but Barrett lies about not knowing what Vera was up to. "I was so happy there with you," he pleads. "It was like bliss."

Now dressed like a cat burglar in a black polo neck sweater and black trousers, Barrett comes into his own. So does Bogarde, for whom Barrett is indeed a kind of alter ego. All of Bogarde's "Orderly Man" characteristics are on open display here, as Barrett tidies up around Tony, who only wants him to help him with his crossword puzzle. "Look at all this muck and slime!" Barrett fusses. "It makes you feel sick!"

"Well, do something about it," Tony replies like a henpecked husband. "You're supposed to the bloody servant."

"You expect me to cope with all this muck and filth everywhere. All your leavings all over the place."

The dialogue becomes even more "queer": "As soon as I get the Hoover going, you're straight up it." Barrett moans. "You're in everybody's way!" Losey significantly films this interchange in full view of the statuette of the nude athlete. "Here I am scraping and skimping, trying to make ends meet. [...] You're no bloody help either," Barrett continues, Bogarde's own reality giving Pinter's lines even more veracity. It is the perfect portrait of a particular kind of gay couple, who bitch viciously about one another, Barrett the dominant partner, Tony the subservient one.

But this domestic "bliss" soon begins to turn sour. Bad weather keeps the boys indoors and arguments ferment. Laughing in Tony's face, Barrett says, "I'm a gentleman's gentleman and you're no gentleman!" They play ball games on the stairs, the shadows of the banister rails brilliantly filmed by Losey to suggest the bars of the prison they have created for themselves. Barrett keeps threatening to leave. Tony pleads for him to stay, despite the constant humiliations. "I know all about you," Barrett sneers. "I don't know what I'd do without you," Tony whimpers. Then, over a dinner, for which Tony obsequiously compliments Barrett and which they eat together, Barrett confesses, "Sometimes, I get the feeling we're old pals." Tony agrees. They also compare notes that they have both had the same feeling before in the army, at which moment, it is hard not to recall the scene in *The Wind Cannot Read* in which Bogarde and Forwood performed their only scene together, dressed in military uniform.

During a game of hide and seek, Barrett is at his most sinister and knowing. He taunts the terrified Tony, who is hiding in the showers, with a line that must have been profoundly cathartic for Bogarde to say out loud: "You've got a guilty secret!" "But you'll be caught," he continues. "I'm coming to get you." The final orgy scene is intended to suggest the hell from which Barrett's Mephisto has come. It also completes Barrett's social revolution with Tony's final humiliation, but Tanitch quite rightly observed that this "felt gratis [...]. The story was already over."[39] Barrett sends the women packing and locks the door. There is no escape for Tony now.

A counterpart to *Victim* followed in 1968: John Frankenheimer's *The Fixer*. Here, the social injustice is not homophobia but anti–Semitism, which is not so very different in the way it has been punished over the years. After all, Jews and homosexuals rubbed emaciated shoulders against one another in Nazi concentration camps,. In *The Fixer*, Alan Bates (a bisexual himself, if not a Jewish one) plays Yakov Bok, a victim of Russian anti–Semitism in early twentieth-century Tsarist Russia. Frankenheimer's adaptation of

Bernard Malamud's novel is compelling, if somewhat exhausting in the compassion fatigue it induces, the cumulative effect of Bok's sufferings being largely what the film is concerned about.

Bogarde plays a liberal lawyer who does what he can to help, but is killed for his pains. This character, Bibikov, exudes decency, and Bogarde, who looks as though he has been preparing for a role in a Chekhov play, looks splendid. He was not over-enamored of his role, even though it did bring in a rewarding fee, but he did admire his "smashing" costumes. Writing to Joseph Losey, he described them: "A pony skin coat to the floor with otter collar and cuffs and a great hat ... and pince-nez and a beard ... and a lousy part. Aw fuck. This is a dreary letter."[40] The film's message can be summed up in one line, which Bates hurls at the sadistically precise fanatic Grubeshov (Ian Holm), who wants him to confess to a crime he didn't commit. Asked if he knows the meaning of the word "respect," Bates replies, "Respect is something you've got to have in order to get it."

Amid this nasty world of masculine brutality, with soldiers beating and berating the poor Jew in his prison confines, Bogarde's Bibikov appears like a ministering angel: educated (he reads Spinoza, as does Bok), enlightened

Bogarde as Bibikov (left) on a visit to the prison cell of Alan Bates' Yakov Bok in *The Fixer* **(dir. John Frankenheimer, 1969).**

and compassionate. All of Bogarde's charm and sensitivity are brought to bear in his creation of this unfortunate man, who is himself persecuted for attacking the system and sympathizing with the underdog. If the film's central message is contained in a single scene, it is during Bibikov's meeting with the Russian Minister of Justice, Count Odoevsky (David Warner, who had originally hoped to play Bibikov). Their suave conversation amid the Imperial splendors of Odoevsky's palace, contrasts starkly with their first meeting in a Budapest hotel. Warner was feeling ill at the time and was sick on Bogarde's shoe. Apologizing in a letter the next day, he began, "Dear Puked-on," to which Bogarde replied, signing himself "Puked upon."[41]

The dialogue between Odoevsky and Bibikov is a brilliant analysis of the status quo:

ODOEVSKY: How can we keep a man in prison for nine months as a ritual murderer, and then indict him for the misdemeanor of illegal residence?
BIBIKOV: In my view, he shouldn't have been indicted at all.
ODOEVSKY: I'm inclined to agree with you. However, by now the affair has attracted so much attention that the reputation of the government is at stake. I will tell you confidentially that the Tsar himself is convinced of the man's guilt. He receives weekly reports on the case. He is especially impressed with the expert religious testimony of Father Anastasy.
BIBIKOV: Father Anastasy is a defrocked fanatic. He has no religion and no hurrah but his own.
ODOEVSKY: I'm aware of that.
BIBIKOV: Why don't you tell the tsar that his religious expert is a charlatan?
ODOEVSKY: On the day that you inform his majesty that the monk Rasputin is a charlatan, which he is, I will be delighted to say the same of Father Anastasy.
BIBIKOV: In this second decade of the twentieth century, does your Excellency seriously mean to indict a man for ritual murder?
ODOEVSKY: Do you think I'm such an idiot to believe all these stories about the Jews? Of course not! There's no Jewish problem in Russia, nor anywhere else for that matter. There's only the problem of human nature.
BIBIKOV: And is it an extension of human nature to prosecute an innocent man?
ODOEVSKY: Possibly. It's human nature to be discontented. It's also human nature to react to that discontent with passion rather than wisdom.
BIBIKOV: But your Excellency...
ODOEVSKY: Please! To govern men, you must govern their passions. To

unite them, you must unify their passions. Since hate is far stronger than love, it follows that men are best unified by hate and best moved to action by desire to kill what they hate. If our workers and peasants begin to hate the Tsar, as I fear they do, ultimately they will kill him. Far better that they hate and kill the Jew. In fact, it is the only patriotic alternative.

The themes of *The Fixer* are as relevant now as they have ever been, particularly in twenty-first century Russia, where homophobia and anti–Semitism are still social problems, punished in much the same thuggish and unenlightened manner.

Bogarde's penultimate feature film *Despair* (dir. Rainer Werner Fassbinder, 1978), based on Nabokov's novel, recapitulated on the theme of doubles previously explored in *Libel* (dir. Anthony Asquith, 1959). Bogarde plays Hermann, a failed chocolate manufacturer. He encounters a man called Felix, whom he erroneously believes to be his physical double. He tricks Felix into wearing his own clothes, murders him, makes it look like suicide, and Hermann's wife then claims his life insurance. Hermann's plan is to assume Felix's identity and then arrange to be reunited with his wife, but things to do not go according to plan.

Despair also summed up Bogarde's gay dilemma: the double life he had been forced to live due both to the law and social convention. Though Hermann is ostensibly straight, Nabokov himself floats the possibility of a homosexual interpretation of his novel, on which this film is based, by having his protagonist suggest that French readers might "discern mirages of sodomy in my partiality for a vagabond."[42] Hermann's vacuous wife is also another of those obscure objects of desire in Bogarde's films, which are quite possible to read as projections of his own narcissistic eroticism. As Hermann puts it in the novel, "I paced the rooms and surveyed myself in all the mirrors. At that time, I was still on admirable terms with mirrors."[43] Bogarde believed you could have a love affair "without carnality," and Hermann uses the same word to express the opposite with regard to his wife: "Intelligence would take the bloom off your carnality." (Nabokov also uses the word "carnally" in the novel.[44]) The fact that Hermann selects a very masculine man to be his "double" (even though the man in question bears no resemblance to him whatsoever) is also significant, especially as Hermann admires him while he is bathing. Hermann is always dressed in very self-consciously narcissistic attire (immaculate suits and dressing gowns), and his mannerisms are amplifications of Bogarde's by now familiar camp style.

The name of Hermann's double, Felix, means "happy" or "fortunate," which, in comparison with Hermann's negative self-image, he certainly is. In many ways, Felix is not only all that Hermann wants to be but also resembles Bogarde's true self. Nabokov describes him as enjoying gardening and bird-watching, not least pursuing his own personal freedom. He also longs for a friend, just as Hermann longs for a "double." When he first comes across Felix, Hermann thinks he is a corpse, but this is because he regards *himself* as a corpse. The physical dissimilarity is really irrelevant. Hermann has repressed all that Felix liberates. Hermann hates himself, and in killing Felix, he is really killing that hated self, while absorbing Felix into what he misguidedly believes will be his new self. He fails, of course: It is impossible to reject oneself and become someone else, just as an actor, no matter how many roles he performs, must return to himself after the curtain drops or the camera is switched off.

Bogarde (right) with director Rainer Werner Fassdinber on the set of *Despair* (1978).

Hermann also "pretends" to be a movie star, as Bogarde did. "I 'became' a film star," Bogarde once said in a characteristically detached manner, as though it had somehow been a freak accident, unplanned—almost irrelevant. He didn't much care for making movies and admitted that he was not a dedicated actor in the sense of one who lives to act or has a passion for the stage, like Gielgud. Bogarde acted to give himself the money to live in splendid isolation. He did not live to act. Like Franz Liszt, whom he played in *Song Without End,* he was also something of a split personality, seeking solitude but unable to resist the allure of fame.

All actors attempt to kill themselves to be other people, but in fact they can only amplify or excavate what they already are. Bogarde recalled that the role of Hermann in *Despair* "was the nearest thing to a complete mental and physical takeover that I had endured since von Aschenbach had eased silently into my existence: it is an extraordinary experience in every way."

> The actor has to empty himself of *self,* completely, and then encourage the stranger he is to be into the vacuum created. It is not easy. But once caught, and it takes a time to do the catching, one's whole personality alters, and it is not at all understandable to "civilians," as I call non-players, to comprehend. It is more of a mental alteration than a physical one, but sometimes in a bar, in a shop, at the reception desk of a hotel, even talking to Forwood at a meal, I would find that I was speaking, and more than that, behaving, exactly as my alter ego would have done. This is not affectation: it is possession. But it is a curious experience for outsiders to observe.[45]

Bogarde may not have killed his own personality quite as thoroughly as he liked to imagine, but he certainly attempted to kill his gayness in public, and against this we might draw an inverse comparison with Nabokov himself. Though notoriously homophobic and heterosexual in life, he included many homosexuals in his fiction, and genuinely loved, while disapproving of, his sidelined brother Sergei, whose homosexuality led to him dying in a Nazi concentration camp in 1945. Nabokov may well also have been a victim of sexual abuse by one of his two gay uncles. Author Lev Grossman believes that these factors not only help to explain Nabokov's homophobia but also his fascination with *Döppelgangers.* Grossman argues, "Sergei is a crucially important figure in his brother's work, a presence with whom Nabokov grappled, in different ways and with different degrees of success, throughout his lengthy oeuvre."

> Nabokov was fascinated by doubles, and his work is full of them—mirrors, twins, reflections, chance resemblances. Sergei was his brother's double, a "shadow in the background," as Nabokov put it. All his life Vladimir would be the golden wordsmith, the master of language; Sergei was afflicted with an atrocious stutter that would only get worse as he got older. He idolized Napoleon and slept with a bronze bust of him in his bed. He also loved music, particularly Richard Wagner, and he studied the piano

seriously. Vladimir, by contrast, was almost pathologically insensitive to music, which he once described as "an arbitrary succession of more or less irritating sounds." He would creep up behind Sergei while he was practicing and poke him in the ribs— something he remembered with bitter remorse in later life. "They were never friends when they were children," says [Nabokov's sister, Elena] Sikorski. "There was always a sort of aversion."[46]

Nabokov tried to disown, while simultaneously loving his sibling "double," whom he wanted to believe was completely different from him, but who wasn't. Conversely, Hermann thinks his double looks just like him and isn't, while Bogarde thought all the parts he played were completely different from him, and they weren't. Hermann lies to others and to himself. He says he plays the cello, which he doesn't, and that he is a movie actor, which he isn't. Bogarde similarly believed his personal fantasies. And Hermann's confusion when making love to his wife is surely something that Bogarde, with his own narcissistic preferences involving motorbikes, leather trousers and a huge mirror, could have identified with. Early in the film, Hermann sees his double watching him make love, and in these two shots of his Hermann's twin selves, Bogarde gives another master class in Alan Ladd's "great look." As Wladimir Troubetzkoy described this moment in the original novel:

> The reader at first believes that mad Hermann's imagined self is the watching one, the one who is standing naked, resting his hand on a chair, or sitting in the parlour, away from the bed, where his original self is making love to Lydia: but in fact, this watching self is the real one, it is the fancied one who is making love to Lydia. As many times as he can, Hermann Karlovich makes the reader believe in the illusion rather than in reality, then he shows us that we have been fooled (cf. the first pages of his narrative, when he lies constantly and enjoys confessing it).[47]

In cinema, we have all been fooled. The final lines of *Despair* therefore have a personal resonance for Bogarde: "Good people. We are making a film here. In a moment, I will be *coming out*. I'm a film actor, coming out; but don't look at the camera. I'm *coming out*." Though he never officially came out as a gay man, there was really no need to by the end. As he said, all you had to do was read between the lines.

Chapter Six

"Champagne! Champagne!"

Bogarde's restrained performance in *Victim* was only one extreme of his gay range. He was also adept at camp. The earliest indication of this appeared in *Libel,* in which he played three types: a suave aristocrat, a waspish actor who looks just like the aristo, and a mute disfigured man, whose makeup oddly resembles that of Christopher Lee's Creature in Hammer's *The Curse of Frankenstein,* released two years earlier. (The mute man, known as "Number 15," is indeed described as "a living corpse.")

However, unlike Alec Guinness in *Kind Hearts and Coronets* (dir. Robert Hamer, 1949), in which Sir Alec portrayed wildly differing members of the same family, Bogarde really plays two versions of his narcissistic self: the charming host and the waspish thespian. This latter resurfaced years later, in modified form, in *Providence* (dir. Alain Resnais, 1977), in which Bogarde similarly played two different interpretations of a single character. One of them, an effete lawyer with a lashing tongue, was nominally straight, but we can't be so sure about the camp actor in *Libel.*

The story of *Libel* is simple: During the war, aristocrat Sir Mark Lodden (Bogarde) encounters a lookalike, actor Frank Welney. Welney, a failure in everything, decides to kill Mark, assume his identity and live a lavish lifestyle after the war. In the struggle, Mark fights back and disfigures him, damaging both Frank's face and his brain. When a fellow prisoner (Paul Massie) accuses Mark of actually being Welney, a libel trail is instigated at which the mysterious "Number 15" (so named because that was the number of his bed in a psychiatric hospital) turns out indeed to *be* Welney. Mark is exonerated and all ends happily ever after, apart from "Number 15," who disappears from view after a short court appearance.

Some clever camerawork has Mark actually walk in front of Welney while in the prison camp, and in many ways, this dual role was tailor-made for an actor who liked to stare at his own photograph while astride a Harley Davidson motorbike to help stimulate his private thrills. Also, the heavily disguised "Number 15" carries other connotations—not merely of that ultimate outsider, Frankenstein's Creature, but also of the lifelong disguise Bogarde himself wore with regard to his true nature. Bogarde's entire life was lived incognito, while simultaneously in the public eye.

His mission to get closer to the truth of that situation by starring in *Victim* had actually been anticipated, earlier the same year as *Victim*'s release, in *The Singer Not the Song* (dir. Roy Ward Baker). He plays Anacleto Comachi, an immaculate, atheistical Mexican bandit with a very British accent, which contrasts absurdly with the cod–Spanish accents of his rough and dusty henchmen. Anacleto wears tight leather trousers and is attracted to a Roman Catholic priest (John Mills), in whom he thinks he

Bogarde as "Number Fifteen" (aka Frank Welney) in *Libel* (dir. Anthony Asquith, 1959).

can identify a truly "good" man, unlike his own bad self. If anyone was in any doubt about Bogarde's own personality, this film should have set the record straight, and it is quite reasonable to interpret his performance here as a kind of warm-up for *Victim*: Under the cover of "a role," here was an opportunity for Bogarde to reveal his gay reality for all the world to see. In fact, the film failed at the time, when camp self-irony was not expected, still less fully understood by Bogarde's fan base. Arms akimbo, in *contrapposto*, leather trousers glistening in the sun, his black leather gloves stroking a cat like a Bond villain, and saying "Good morning!" caricaturing the matinée idol he had become, Bogarde self-evidently sent up both himself and his role in this film. Philip Green's frenetically melodramatic score invests every exit, entrance, scene-change and glance with camp *angst*.

Bogarde, being both gay *and* an atheist (his apparent experience of Belsen having put paid to any idea of God as a possibility), could no doubt find many things to identify with here. He was also an outsider who was simultaneously "the king of Pinewood," and in this respect, too, was not unlike Anacleto—another outsider who runs the town in his own way. The casting of John Mills as the priest infuriated Bogarde, quite rightly, as Mills was hardly Marlon Brando, and it is hard to imagine Mills and Bogarde get-

Bogarde as Anacleto in *The Singer Not the Song* (dir. Roy Baker, 1961).

ting together for a cup of tea let alone anything more intimate. The priest is oblivious of Anacleto's attraction to him, and unaware that a young woman, Locha de Cortinez (Mylène Demongeot), is also in love with him, but already engaged to someone else. We are meant to be concerned about the girl: At first, we're led to think that she loves Anacleto, but then we realize it is the priest who is the real object of her affections, and that her prospective husband is actually irrelevant. But Bogarde, though he delivers his lines professionally, was having none of this, and his sidelong smirks soon suggest that the reason why the priest has been unaware of Locha's love is because he has been nurturing unrequited, indeed repressed longings for the bandit. Mills fails completely to convey this aspect, which Bogarde no doubt realized he would. There is also the theological aspect to consider: the conflict between the priest's faith and determination to defeat Anacleto's tyranny and impercipience.

But Bogarde made his relationship with the priest the central issue for those who wanted to see. The priest is meant to be all the more desirable because he is chaste, like Ambrosio in Matthew Lewis' famous eighteenth-century Gothic shocker *The Monk*. God also seems to be on his side, as he survives Anacleto's various attempts at doing away with him: his prayer book, rather like Alfred's Love Manual in *The Fearless Vampire Killers,* prevents a knife attack, and a passing-space on a winding mountain road provides him with an escape route in the nick of time when, because the brake cables of his car have been sabotaged, he nearly plunges to his death.

These "accidents" were arranged by Anacleto, whom we see fondling the duck-headed shaft of a whip as he issues his orders. One feels that only Anacleto would own such a quaint object. "It's a pity," he muses, having sent off his assassins. "I liked him." "You like this priest too much," one of his henchmen observes later. Another of them sings, "No woman weeps as a man can weep," while strumming his guitar. Laurence Naismith, a venerable British actor forced, unlike Bogarde, to assume a fake Mexican accent in his role as "Old Uncle," also knows all about the love of one man for another: "You love this priest so much," he says to Anacleto, "you'd put yourself between him and me. Ha ha! That's funny, because I love you too." But this doesn't stop Anacleto shooting Old Uncle when the latter tries to kill the priest.

None of this is convincing as a Western, but as a camp allegory it speaks volumes. Nigel Balchin's script is full of innuendo, which Bogarde makes almost explicit. To Mylène Demongeot's Locha de Cortinez, he says: "It must be heartbreaking to fall in love with a man you can never have. I understand this." And when the priest's maid suggests they buy a snake to kill rats, the priest very oddly replies, "I couldn't come between a man and his wife's snake."

One wonders if *The Singer Not the Song* is a homosexual version of Michael Powell and Emeric Pressburger's *Black Narcissus* (1947), in which a love-crazed Anglican nun (Kathleen Byron), attracted to the handsome Mr. Dean (David Farrar), tries to kill another nun who has been similarly smitten. *Black Narcissus* is much more spectacular and far more visually interesting than Baker's film, but the sexual tensions and religious context are similar. The priest is unable to persuade Anacleto to become a believer, even when he illegally returns from the exile that the priest eventually manages to force upon him. "All you've done," Anacleto explains, "is to prove to me that while the singer's good, the song is worthless." Anacleto encourages Locha to run away before getting married by the man she loves to a man she doesn't, and then Anacleto is willing to bargain: He'll persuade Locha to return if the priest publicly exonerates Anacleto and thus facilitates his return to running the community on his own terms, rather than those of the church. The priest refuses at the last minute, Anacleto spits on the church and, during a final shoot-out, the two men die together in another kind of *Liebestod*, arm in arm, as Anacleto repeats, "The singer—the singer, not the song."

Baker was not insensitive to gay issues (he went on to direct Britain's first lesbian vampire film, *The Vampire Lovers,* 1970) but without Bogarde's subversive contribution, the gay subtext of *The Singer Not the Song* would not have been anywhere near as observable as it is. In several ways, this film, and particularly Bogarde's performance in it, conform to the criteria identified by Susan Sontag in her "Notes on 'Camp,'" first published in 1964, three years after the film was released. "Camp," she writes, "is art that proposes itself seriously, but cannot be taken altogether seriously because it is 'too much.'"[1] She identifies "camp" as the triumph of epicene style.[2] Camp aims to "dethrone the serious"—it is playful.[3] It is exaggerated[4] and "sees everything in quotation marks."[5] It is also concerned with "seeing the world as an aesthetic phenomenon," and observes that camp's emphasis on *style* is a slight to content.[6]

These criteria are particularly applicable with regard to Bogarde's other great camp performance in Joseph Losey's *Modesty Blaise,* a film in which style ultimately obliterates whatever content it may have had to start with. There is really nothing *but* style in this misguided attempt at satirizing the James Bond idiom, which by then had already become satirical within its own terms of reference.

The Bond films were always playful and "too much," but Losey pressed on regardless. Apart from Richard Macdonald's beguiling production design with its op art and psychedelic references, Bogarde's scenes (which have their fair share of the visual flair) are the most interesting ones. He portrays the epitome of Sontag's observation that "Detachment is the prerogative of an elite; and as the dandy is the 19th century's surrogate for the aristocrat in matters of culture, so Camp is the modern dandyism. Camp is the answer to the problem: how to be a dandy in the age of mass culture."[7] Bogarde's villain, Gabriel, is very obviously a camp homosexual, with a distinct penchant and talent for interior design and elegant clothing. He is also detached from everyone but himself and his style. "Homosexuals," Sontag believed, "have pinned their integration into society on promoting the aesthetic sense."[8]

The wafer-thin plot—Gabriel's plan to steal some diamonds—is really just an excuse for Bogarde to mince around exotic locations in a white wig, shelter under differently colored umbrellas, pass through groovy interiors, wave limp wrists at his henchmen, peer through slit-shaped spectacles or from under a camp peaked cap, drink from an absurdly outsized glass with goldfish swimming in it, and banter often unfunny effete lines, one of which he utters when pinioned in the sand, dying of thirst, when defeated at the end: "Champagne! Champagne!" (Bogarde apparently wrote that line for himself.[9]) He also is also seen regularly crossing his legs, which is apparently a giveaway sign of gayness. His arrival at base camp, so to speak (a location in Sicily, which stood in for Gabriel's fortress), is announced by an organ-playing monk. Gabriel himself wears an immaculately white three-piece suit and reports, "Mama was most amused and very condescending to me." Again, the mother fixation is intended as another "invert alert."

One does wonder if Gabriel's mother is like Fons Rademakers' "Mother" in Harry Kümel's vampire film *Daughters of Darkness* (1971), who is in fact a "sinister" gay man, reclining in his conservatory on lilac-colored cushions beside a lilac lily. (Gabriel also sports a lilac umbrella, drinks lilac liquids and has lilac columns supporting his gazebo.) When "Mother's" lover, Stefan (John Karlen), explains on the phone that he has just married Valerie (Danielle Ouimet), "Mother" quietly replies, "What you did wasn't foolish, Stefan; it was merely unrealistic." Indeed, "Mother" resembles even more Bogarde's grotesque Gustav von Aschenbach, after the latter's visit to a barber in *Death*

Bogarde as super-villain Gabriel in *Modesty Blaise* (dir. Joseph Losey, 1963).

in Venice, made in the same year, 1971. Von Aschenbach's pale white face, obviously dyed black hair and eyebrows is a heterosexual's nightmare vision of homosexuality, combining decadence, depravity, artificiality and, of course, ambiguity. There is also a great deal of quiet threat in the short phone conversation between Stefan and "Mother." Similarly, Gabriel's "only motive" is "malice"—"You know, McWhirter, one of these days I shall have to tell her who I am." Mother has obviously not yet realized the truth about her son.

Fanning himself, as he so often does, before blowing up a plane, Gabriel remarks: "The pilot's got a charming voice. About 35 I should think," but the pilot turns out to be from the prosaic location of Woking and, even worse, is married. "I was very much afraid of that," he says. Though quite happy to blow up planes, this epitome of effete criminality is distressed by the sound of lobsters screaming when they are cooked alive, and, in Gabriel's other celebrated line, he asks over breakfast, "Could it be that this egg is fertilized?"

As David Caute describes it, *Modesty Blaise*

> exploits the *Avengers* culture—cool, amoral, gorged on gadgetry and playfully disguised lethal weapons, with English gentlemen who may not be quite gentlemen in bowler hats, extravagant villains, grotesque settings involving transvestites, masks, clowns, gargoyles. If Losey intended a critique of consumerism, of the new, sleek capitalism peddling marketable decadence, he succeeded only in proving that "post-industrial" capitalism is happy to turn criticism into one more commodity.[10]

All Bogarde had to do was carry on as he had begun in *The Singer Not the Song* and send himself up. It wasn't really that far from the truth anyway. Elegant, urbane, charming and fully aware of his own artificiality … various interviews over the years have revealed the Gabriel within Bogarde. In a Rank interview piece called "Dirk Bogarde in Conversation," filmed in 1961 (five years before *Modesty Blaise*), the interviewer noticed that the bookshelves of Bogarde's "luxurious" and "exquisitely furnished" house contained volumes of Tacitus. He asked if Bogarde read Latin. Bogarde flashed a Cheshire cat smile and explained, "No. I bought them to fill in the bookcase."

Two years later, this camp quality bled into Bogarde's interpretation of the nominally heterosexual Pursewarden in *Justine,* George Cukor's ill-fated 1969 film adaptation of Laurence Durrell's *Alexandria Quartet.* As Bogarde's early whodunit *The Woman in Question* (dir. Anthony Asquith, 1950) had demonstrated, it is quite possible for a film to tell a story as seen from the different points of view of various characters, which is exactly what Durrell's tetralogy does so intriguingly. "'We live' writes Pursewarden somewhere 'lives based upon selected fictions. Our view of reality is conditioned by our position in space and time—not by our personalities as we like to think, thus every interpretation of reality is based upon a unique position'"[11]—but there is too much ground to cover for a single film and, as Tanitch perceptively realized, "take away the elaborate literary structure and the jeweled prose and all you are left with is lust, murder, gun-running, child prostitutes, political intrigue, homosexuality, treachery, male transvestism, incest and Coptic Christians."[12] Consequently, it is not always easy to work out what is going on, and Michael York's voice-over all too obviously guides us through the vast chunks of plot like an operatic recitative on speed. Pursewarden suffers the most, not just because the complexity of his character is so curtailed by the script, but because Bogarde, seemingly unsure what to do with him, "camps it up"—just as Kenneth Williams always did in the *Carry Ons*.

This is not to say that the film is without considerable visual interest. Its sumptuousness seems to anticipate that equally awkward transition from novel to screen that is Guy Green's adaptation of John Fowles' *The Magus,* made the following year (1968). Most sumptuous of all is the carnival scene ("pure mischief is the velvet domino"[13]), its vivid colors echoing the Gothic extravagance of Roger Corman's 1964 Poe feature *The Masque of the Red Death,* with its similarly macabre carnival mood, sadism, sex and immolation. *Justine*'s masque also ends in death: a homosexual called Toto (Cliff Gorman) is killed by a hatpin through the neck while wearing a mask, having been mistaken for the titular heroine, played by the sultry and excellently mysterious Anouk Aimée. (A similar sort of thing happens to Alex Scott's Dr. Hargreaves in the Vincent Price vehicle *The Abominable Dr. Phibes,* directed by Robert Fuest in 1971). As Durrell explains:

> All the best murders ... are the fruit of the yearly carnival; while most love affairs begin or end during these three days and nights during which we are delivered from the thrall of personality, from the bondage of ourselves.... You cannot tell whether you are dancing with a man or a woman. The dark tides of Eros, which demand full secrecy if they are to overflow the human soul, burst out during carnival.[14]

Bogarde as Pursewarden in *Justine* (dir. George Cukor, 1969).

Alas, the film refrains from including the even more decadently Gothic vampire anecdote, set in Venice, which Durrell has Pursewarden relate in *Balthazar,* the second novel in the sequence. This vignette stands so well on its own that Raymond T. McNally included it in his anthology *A Clutch of Vampires,* which is where I first became aware of Durrell's masterwork. But so much of Durrell's *Quartet* had to be deleted to fit into just under two hours of film, and it was an obvious omission. Nonetheless, it would have been a pleasure to have experienced Bogarde relate this story about a rather different kind of death in Venice in which one Carlo Negroponte, a diabolist who "went in for cloaks and shoes with buckles and silver walking sticks," accompanies Pursewarden to the Venice Carnival, "the one time of the year when vampires walk freely abroad, and those who are wise carry a pig of garlic in their pockets to drive them off."

> Next morning I went to my host's room and found him lying pale as death in bed, dressed in the white nightshirt with lace cuffs, with a doctor taking his pulse. When the doctor had gone, he said: "I have met the perfect woman, masked; I went home with her and she proved to be a vampire." Then drawing up his nightshirt he showed me with exhausted pride that his body was covered in great bites, like the marks of a weasel's teeth. He was utterly exhausted but at the same time excited—and frightening to relate, very much in love. "Until you have experienced it," he said, "you have no idea what it is like. To have one's blood sucked in darkness by someone one adores." His voice broke. "De Sade could not begin to describe it…. I am meeting her again tonight by the marble griffin at the Footpads' Bridge. O my friend, be happy for me."[15]

None of this, of course, has anything to do with the novel's overall story of Coptic Christians arming Palestinian Jews in exchange for protection from Muslim animosity on the withdrawal of British rule in Egypt, though it does continue to reference the influence of De Sade's sexual philosophy, which runs like a scarlet thread throughout the *Quartet,* and introduces each of the four novels. One of the two Sadean quotations that open *Balthazar,* would have seemed right at home at the start of *Despair*:

> The mirror sees the man as beautiful, the mirror loves the man; another mirror sees the man as frightful and hates him; and it is always the same being who produces the impressions.[16]

In the film, Justine and her wealthy husband (John Vernon) are gunrunners. Justine is a Mata Hari figure who exploits her various lovers to extract useful information to further the cause. The film is thus a kind of four-sided love triangle with Justine dividing her attention between her husband, a schoolteacher named Darley (Michael York) and Pursewarden. We suspect that Justine actually loves none of them. Sensing something unusual about Pursewarden's sexuality, she asks if he is homosexual. "Just because I refuse to walk through your sexual turnstiles like every other oaf in Alexandria," he replies with venom, "I must be queer. Guilty as charged, your worship," except that he isn't. Pursewarden's sexual tastes are reserved exclusively for his own sister. Of all the many lines Durrell gives Pursewarden in his epic, the screenplay provides him with this particular one, which gives quite the wrong impression, and yet chimes perfectly with Bogarde's distinctly camp delivery. ("When are you going to stop being a sin-cushion into which we have to stick our rusty pins," another line spat at Justine, seems tailor-made for Bogarde at his most waspish, while simultaneously reducing Durrell's overall Sadean subtext to an aside.) He wanders around this studio-bound Alexandria with a limp wrist, and even says "Peekaboo!" to Justine's enigmatic husband. In fact, he verges on Kenneth Williams camp in his drunken petulance, and the whole affair seems to mirror what Bogarde attempted in life: to be gay to those who knew, at least, while attempting to convince those who did not that he was straight.

There are genuine homosexuals among the *dramatis personae*. The belly dancer Melissa, with whom Darley has been having an affair, has several transvestite colleagues. Pursewarden attempts sex with her too, but it doesn't work—not because he is homosexual but because he can't perform with anyone other than his sister. Bogarde furnishes Pursewarden's confession with the same nervous cough he had used in *Victim*: "How lucky children are," he muses regretfully. "They don't know a thing about the great big iron gate of guilt ready to fall." He even calls his sister "my victim. And I'm hers"—a very interesting word in the context of Bogarde's filmography. In the end he commits suicide, that cliché so often shared by unhappy homosexual characters, but in Pursewarden's case it is because he can't cope with the truth about Justine's gunrunning. He bites down on a cyanide capsule, foreshadowing his Hitleresque suicide at the end of *The Damned* the following year.

Bogarde's ability to convey malice was even more useful when it came to filming Alain Resnais' *Providence* (1977), which to some extent echoes Pirandello's famous 1921 absurdist metatheatrical play Six *Characters in*

Bogarde as Claud Latham in *Providence* (dir. Alain Resnais, 1977).

Search of an Author. Once again, Bogarde's character here, Claud Langham, is not technically gay. He is very happily married to Ellen Burstyn's Sonia. But we only discover this at the end of Resnais's surreal account of a dying man's fantasies. Clive Langham, the dying man, is played by John Gielgud, who spends a painful night, thinking up the plot of his final novel, while thrusting suppositories up his backside in attempts to alleviate his terminal pain. This act alone suggests a kind of gay subtext, particularly as it is Gielgud who does it while shouting "Fuck" quite often, which in 1977, when expletives were only just beginning to be socialized, was still quite shocking and not what audiences expected such a grand old man of the theater to say in public. Indeed, Bogarde might have shouted Sir John's line, "You'll not get me, you fucking bastards!" with more conviction. (After all, he prided himself on being a tough nut to crack.)

Clive Langham is a sybaritic, wine-bibbing hedonist who has never understood how his son can be so morally upright, happily married, and content with bourgeois respectability. He consequently imagines him as a priggish, self-centered monster of cutting sarcasm. And that is exactly how Bogarde plays it until, morning having broken and Clive now being out of bed, the family meets up for his birthday and Claud is revealed as a charming, thoughtful and thoroughly delightful man. Both sides of Claud reflected Bogarde, who, on his own admission, could mercilessly lash out with his tongue when necessary. When Russell Harty suggested to him that there was a side to him that could be rather waspish, Bogarde replied:

> I can be taken so far and no further. I don't think that's being waspish. I have lost my temper, I suppose, about five times in my life, and it is *extremely* unpleasant, because I store up all the things I find as false in people and let them have it full in the puss. It's not a very beguiling habit, but it's my way of reasserting, because I'm very often taken for granted because I'm so cuddly and so dear. I ain't. I didn't survive this far by being cuddly and dear. People have to be taught a lesson sometimes, but it's very rare.[17]

For most of *Providence*, Bogarde is intensely waspish in his performance of his fictional father's misguided idea of what Claud is like. He rolls his r's, enunciates each consonant with pedantic precision and raises the general pitch of his voice by several tones throughout. As Tanitch observed, "The waspish wit could hardly have been more theatrical; it out–Webbed Clifton Webb."[18] Because the whole scenario is so artificial, Bogarde's campness reached new heights of unreality, for these figments of fantasy, which are constantly being interrupted by Clive's own confused memories and anxieties, are themselves highly unreal. The film is really a dreamscape, and Resnais is adept at suggesting the environment of the unconscious.

Claud, in both the fantasy and the reality, is a lawyer—a profession towards which Clive is already unsympathetic. "What a tailor's dummy he is," he says in voice-over as we observe the buttoned-up, black-haired, pale-faced, tight-lipped, limp-wristed Claud sip a glass of wine. He has spent the day in court cross-examining David Warner, whom we later learn is playing Claud's brother, Kevin. Kevin is accused of killing a werewolf while in the army, though Kevin insists it was a mercy killing. (He later turns into a werewolf himself, which emphasizes that this horror film motif is a metaphor of social alienation.) In court, Claud, with scornful hauteur, scoffs, "A werewolf! Well, well, well." To which Kevin replies: "Why are you so contemptuous?"

Sonia takes pity on Kevin and invites him to dinner, eventually suggesting that she might have an affair with him. (Clive, in "real life," cannot imagine what she sees in Claud, so having an affair, even if it is with her brother-in-law, seems perfectly reasonable to him.) When he finds out, Claud's fury suggests a camp queen eyeing up an unpromising male prostitute: "He's so frightfully unattractive. It doesn't matter whether you're good enough for my wife, but are you good enough for me? I really don't think so."

Gay resonances return in Oedipal fashion when Clive imagines Claud falling in love with his own mother, Helen (Elaine Stritch). We later learn that Helen killed herself because Clive ignored her, and Clive imagines that Claud has never really forgiven him. This only increases his negative image of him. As Claud and Helen embrace, Clive's voice-over comments, "She looks like his mother. Clearly the boy must have a subconscious mind, like everybody else."

There is also a footballer (Denis Lawson), who was thought up by Clive to be Kevin's fictional brother Dave, but he later decides to recast Kevin as Claud's brother (which he is in fact, though we don't know that yet), and so the footballer finds himself wandering through several scenes with nothing to do, before Clive's authorial voice sends him off stage. In one of these encounters, he is brought face to face with Claud, whose haughty and ironic disdain for the game reflects Bogarde's own lack of interest in competitive sport in general (another gay stereotype to which he strongly conformed): "It's a fine game, football. Beautiful to watch. Well, you know, I mean if the general activity seems meaningless, the form—the pattern—is elegant … choreographic! There's plenty of poetry there."

At this, the footballer promptly punches Claud in the face. Such a thing might well have actually happened to the un-sporty Bogarde when he was a boy. Indeed, Bogarde's lack of interest in competitive sport caused Losey some astonishment when he discovered he couldn't even hit a ball in the game of tennis he was required to play in *Accident*. Losey remarked that Bogarde was a "completely non-physical man. He can't ride a horse, he can't swim, he can barely walk. The only thing he can do is garden."[19]

Chapter Seven

"I don't think you know what the truth is any more."

The spy genre was an appropriate one for an actor who lived a kind of double life with a "guilty secret," as Barrett puts it in *Victim*. Bogarde made six spy movies, including the James Bond satire *Modesty Blaise*. A rather more conventional Bond satire was *Hot Enough for June* (dir. Ralph Thomas, 1964), a comedy of mistaken identity, which nonetheless had its moments of genuine tension. It was set mostly in Communist Prague, while in fact filmed in Padua. Bogarde plays Nicholas Whistler, an unemployed writer offered a job as a spy, though he believes he is employed by a glass manufacturing company. He finds himself being chased by the secret police and desperately tries to gain sanctuary in the British Embassy. His predicament foreshadows that of Susan George in the *Hammer House of Horror* episode "Czech Mate" (dir. John Hough, 1986): Her character is framed by her unscrupulous boyfriend (Patrick Mower) and is eventually locked away in a Communist jail. *Hot Enough for June* also looks forward to the genuine Bond film *The Spy Who Loved Me* (dir. Lewis Gilbert, 1977), in which Roger Moore's Bond falls in love with female Russian agent Barbara Bach. Bogarde's Nicholas Whistler similarly falls in love with Sylva Koscina's Vlasta Simenova, the daughter of Leo McKern's police chief. Whistler is therefore presented as eminently heterosexual, even though the film itself has certain gay references entirely in keeping with the British upper class milieu of spies such as Kim Philby, Guy Burgess and Anthony Blunt.

It begins with a long tracking shot down a corridor, following the measured footsteps of John Le Mesurier's spy, Roger Allsop. Angelo Lavagnino's sinister music suggests that we are about to watch a serious spy drama, but laconic humor soon disabuses us. As Allsop returns the belongings of a recently deceased spy, they are put in a filing cabinet marked 007, implying that it is up to Bogarde's character to replace Bond himself. Later, when he arrives in the offices of his new employer, the layout of the set echoes that of

M's office in Bond films: He enters the lobby of the main office with his rain-coat over one shoulder, and is greeted by Amanda Grinling's secretary much as the various incarnations of Bond are greeted by Lois Maxwell's Miss Moneypenny. A door to the right leads to the office of Robert Morley's Col. Cunliffe, the M to Bogarde's 007. Unlike Bond, however, Whistler confesses that he is a "frightful coward" and hates the military, having avoided his national service.

On the plane that takes Whistler to Prague, he sits next to actor, William Mervyn's fellow passenger, who shows him a newspaper headline reporting the arrest of a British spy. It reads, "I am not a spy—Ralph Thomas," accompanied by a photograph of Ralph Thomas, the director of the film. (This kind of in-joke was also echoed by Hammer in *Blood from the Mummy's Tomb* [dir. Seth Holt, 1971], in which an estate agent's board outside an empty house reads "Neame and Skeggs"—the surnames of the film's production managers Christopher Neame and Roy Skeggs. The Hammer connections continue in

Bogarde (right) with Robert Morley in *Hot Enough for June* (dir. Ralph Thomas, 1964).

Whistler's hotel bedroom in Prague, which features the same elaborately carved headboard of the double bed seen in the hotel bedroom of Don Sharp's *The Kiss of the Vampire,* made the previous year.)

Hot Enough for June's most homosexual moment does not feature Bogarde at all. Instead, this is left to the heterosexual Robert Morley. Another spy has been killed and a replacement is needed. Cunliffe explains to Allsop: "They got poor Caruthers through some woman that he'd taken up with. You might try and find someone who's not quite so susceptible in that direction, will you? On the other hand, don't lean too far in the other direction either," upon which, he sends an air kiss to the somewhat disconcerted Le Mesurier; and when a blind, which conceals a map of secret agents on the wall, keeps rolling up of its own accord, Cunliffe complains to Allsop, "I mean, look at it, dear."

The other suggestion of a gay subtext to all this upper class spying occurs in a gents' lavatory in the Prague hotel. Whistler has encountered a janitor (John Standing) who has responded to his password "Hot enough for June," whereupon he is passed the secret information. Whistler has no idea what's going on, but the janitor explains, "I am a spy. The same as you are."

WHISTLER: Spy? I'm not a spy. I'm nothing to do with a spy. I am here on perfectly legitimate industrial...

JANITOR: Espionage?

WHISTLER: If you want to use that sort of a word, yes; but it's between one firm and another. It's quite common practice in business.

JANITOR: You tell that to the firing squad, my old darling.

(Appropriately, Standing's family in real life had originally owned Bletchley Park before it was requisitioned by the British government as the secret codebreaking establishment during World War II, where the homosexual Alan Turing presided as code-breaker in chief.)

Bogarde has some purposefully erotic close-ups during his love scenes with Koscina, which obviously convinced many of his female fans, but when Whistler is escaping from the police and phone reception for room service from an adjacent hotel room (furnished with the same *Kiss of the Vampire* bed), he uses the camp Mancunian accent he gave to Barrett in *The Servant* the previous year.

Bogarde's other spy films were all serious, some of them more sexually transgressive than others, but all were responses to the political situation of the Cold War in the 1960s, which made this genre so popular. Bogarde regarded the first, *The Mind Benders* (dir. Basil Dearden, 1963), as ahead of its time:

No one knew very much about brainwashing; no one really believed it was possible, nor, apparently, did they wish to. If they had ever heard of Gary Powers, or had known then what they know today about psychiatric treatment of political dissidents, maybe we might have fared a little better; but they didn't, alas, and one headline which blared, "Bogarde Thriller Is Shabby and Nasty" summed up the general reaction.[1]

The film anticipated the '60s much more successful brainwashing spy drama *The Ipcress File* (dir. Sidney J. Furie) by a couple of years, and, given a different treatment, *The Mind Benders* could well have been a horror film. The review to which Bogarde referred, by the *Daily Express* critic Leonard Mosley, was of the opinion that the film belonged "to quote yet another remark from the film, 'strictly to Frankenstein country' and it is a pretty shabby and sordid example of the genre."[2] The film does in fact contain a certain Gothic resonance, with references to "the physics of the soul" and "that horrible tank," which does indeed look like something in a Bernard Robinson design for one of Hammer's Frankenstein laboratories. (It is in this water tank that Bogarde is immersed for hours on end, all sensory impressions annulled.) As well as "Frankenstein country," there is also the line "Z for Zombie"; and the effect of experiments in the isolation tank are described as dissolving a man spiritually until he becomes "a soulless, mindless, wellness thing. Not even man at all. A kind of sea-anemone."

Poster for *The Mind Benders* (dir. Basil Dearden, 1968).

Bogarde gives one of his straightest performances here, convincingly playing a man happily married with children, until he volunteers to undergo submersion in the isolation tank to prove the innocence of a colleague, Prof. Sharpey (Harold Goldblatt). Sharpey had spent time in the isolation tank himself, and later committed suicide, having taken a bribe from an enemy country in exchange for sensitive secrets. To prove that Sharpey had been made susceptible to brainwashing by the isolation process, and that his case should be filed under "Z, for Zombie, rather than T for Traitor," Bogarde's boffin, Dr. Henry Longman, puts himself through the same ordeal. Emerging from the tank, not unlike Frankenstein's reanimated creature, Longman is then subjected to brainwashing. An intelligence officer, Major Hall (John Clements) and Longman's academic colleague, Dr. Tate (Michael Bryant), program him to turn against Oonagh (Mary Ure), the wife he loves. The brainwashing is a success and Sharpey is exonerated, but not before Longman and Oonagh almost divorce. The change in Longman's behavior is subtle. At first nothing seems to have happened, but he gradually becomes cold, stern and distrustful, regarding his wife as "practically a tart," which is exactly what he has been conditioned to say.

All this re-programing has a great deal in common with the kind of aversion therapy Bogarde himself is claimed to have undergone as a "cure" for his homosexuality. Various techniques have been used over the years to achieve this, the most common being the projection of erotic imagery coupled with electric shocks, sometimes delivered directly to the genitals, but castration, lobotomies, torture and drug "therapy" have all also been used. If *The Mind Benders* was ahead of its time as a movie, the issues it raised had been practiced for many years before. By the time Antony Burgess used aversion therapy as a "cure" for the troubled Alex in *A Clockwork Orange* in 1962, the subject was much more timely, especially when it was filmed by Stanley Kubrick in 1971. Alex is forced to watch imagery of increasingly grotesque violence accompanied by the music of Beethoven, which he loves. "You're not cured yet," says the doctor in charge of the process. "There's still a lot to be done. Only when your body reacts promptly and violently to violence, as to a snake, without further help from us, without medication, only then…"[3]

Longman is similarly "repulsed" by his wife, who reveals that he even put her on display in a prostitute's window in Amsterdam. Bogarde handles the transformation subtly, but the effect is just as unnerving as the physical transformation of Fredric March's Dr. Jekyll into the simian Mr. Hyde in Rouben Mamoulian's 1931 film. *The Mind Benders* is indeed a kind of Jekyll and Hyde movie: one man, two personalities, and is also a kind of secularized version of A.C. Benson's posthumously published short story "Basil Netherby,"

in which a composer is possessed by another man's spirit. Netherby is transformed from "a pale, rather haggard youth, loose-limbed and untidy" into "a
strongly built and firmly knit man, with a ruddy color and bronzed cheek,"
both "cheerful and amusing."[4] Bogarde's Longman, once casually dressed,
now appears with a tie, scholarly spectacles and a practiced coldness.

Reunited with his wife, having broken through the barrage of his brainwashing, he assists her to give birth, in a recapitulation of the scene at the
end of his first *Doctor* film, which melted a million hearts as he helped bring
a baby into the world on a snowbound Christmas Eve. There was nothing
camp, effete or "selfish" here, proving that gay people are not necessarily any
of those things. Bogarde's ability to present a completely straight, serious,
committed and compassionate character ably demonstrates that it is always
the person and not his sexuality that really matters.

Bogarde played a different kind of academic boffin in *Sebastian* (dir.
David Greene, 1968). Although he claimed to have had no idea what the film
was about ("I just did as I was told"), it is hardly a difficult story to understand.
Bogarde plays a mathematics boffin, an Oxford academic recruited into government intelligence to crack Russian codes in swinging '60s London. What
makes the film an attractive proposition for an actor who wanted to hide his
own reality is that Bogarde's character, Sebastian, is in charge of what Michael
Caine's Alfie would have called a bevy of beautiful birds. All his code-breakers
are young women with long legs (on which the director, David Greene, lingers
lasciviously). They screech like schoolgirls from St. Trinian's in a Bingo hall
when they break their codes: "I've got a word!" shouts one, and everyone else
throws their papers in the air like celebratory confetti. All this was obviously
very much more Greene's private fantasy than Bogarde's, as was the idea of
his having an affair with Susannah York, who plays Sebastian's favored code-
breaker Rebecca Howard, with whom he even has a baby son. But amid all
these heterosexual trappings are a variety of gay signals—those things that
Bogarde always asked the readers of his autobiographies to read between the
lines to discover.

Significantly, the most famous British code-breaker, on whom Sebastian
is undoubtedly based (if only loosely), was the homosexual Alan Turing.
Despite his subsequent affair with York's Rebecca, Sebastian isn't really interested in the girls under his authority. Dizzyingly brilliant blondes they may
be (with a fair share of equally brilliant brunettes and blacks), but all Sebastian
wants them to do is break their codes, which they dutifully do to Jerry Gold-
smith's jazzed-up baroque score, while Sebastian retreats to his office. This
latter, with its large louver screen over a picture window (which, when
opened, gives a full panorama of the number-crunching "crumpet" below),

was obviously a dream come true for David Greene. But Sebastian's attitude to the girls is distinctly patronizing: "Right, my lovely children. [...] Switch your gorgeous minds to overdrive. This is really quite important." Later, after a sabbatical, he returns to work and is even more like a heartthrob headmaster at a girls' finishing school: "I see before me a lot of new faces. Well, those of you who don't know me will be told by those who do that I am a reasonable man."

Sebastian's superior, Gen. Philips (Nigel Davenport), tells the head of intelligence (John Gielgud) that Sebastian "plays about with a little rubber ball," which Sebastian does indeed use as an aid to concentration. It is rather an odd thing for Phillips to isolate without some kind of Freudian implication. In another scene, Rebecca says, "I wonder if Sebastian's married. He's so impregnable." He is, indeed, almost as tough a nut to crack as Bogarde was himself, and she doesn't break him open until he has humiliated her by cracking a code she has invented—a code she thought so impregnable that he would never discover its message: "Sebastian is a pompous idiot."

There are many shots of Sebastian walking on his own through London. Obviously a bachelor, he seems completely isolated but in fact maintains a

Bogarde with Lilli Palmer in *Sebastian* (dir. David Greene, 1968).

casual liaison with feather-brained pop singer Carol Fancy (Janet Munro). Otherwise, he spends his spare time at an all-male gentlemen's club. Rebecca pursues him even there, pulling him away from his game of chess with an old boy (Charles Lloyd-Pack) in a scene that might have been a deliberate in-joke. (Seven years previously, Pack played the gay barber in *Victim*.) Pack is given just one shot in the entire film, his own attempt as the Alan Ladd "great look," and he does indeed give one great look of utter disbelief when Rebecca drags Sebastian away. The look screams disbelief (as if to say, "Sebastian—with a *girl?*"). It is hard not to associate that look with Lloyd-Pack's previous role in *Victim,* and this is backed up in the next scene set in the revolving restaurant high atop the Post Office Tower in London. "Are you scared of women?" Rebecca asks. Sebastian assures her he is not, but later seems bored when forced to watch her trying on clothes in a trendy boutique. Again, it seems that the director is much more engaged with what is going on than Sebastian, who looks equally uncommitted when he later dances cheek to cheek with Rebecca. When they end up back in Sebastian's flat, Rebecca is horrified to discover that it is illuminated by soulless fluorescent strip lighting and decorated with the world's most hideous gray wallpaper.

Sebastian's grim approach to interior design starkly contrasts with Russell Harty's description of Bogarde's own house in Provence as "a house of exquisite taste," with a "kind of unity." Harty "wondered if you had created it together [with Forwood]," to which Bogarde testily responded, "If you're inferring that we might sit down knitting and pulling rugs, forget it. That doesn't happen."[5] No admission of his emotional relationship with Forwood was forthcoming. Sebastian, by contrast, lives alone, and his flat, appointed in quite the opposite fashion, is obviously meant to reflect the personality of an entirely undomesticated academic and heterosexual bachelor.

"I could so easily love you," Rebecca insists.

"Well, I shouldn't rupture yourself," Sebastian replies—or is it really Bogarde, despite the wallpaper against which he says it? Again resonating with what we now know about Bogarde, Rebecca shouts, "You are coated in the old careless charm like bloody icing sugar." This leads to a kiss, but in a later scene with equally gay Gielgud, whose character knows that Sebastian is "escorting" Rebecca, Sebastian replies with typical Bogarde defensiveness, "Generally speaking, I consider my private life to be my own concern."

"Well, yes, of course it is," Gielgud replies, "but then again, of course, it isn't," which is true both in terms of the film and of Bogarde himself. In the context of Bogarde's secrecy, largely forced upon him by social prejudice, lines such as those below, again addressed to Rebecca as they lie together in bed after decorously off-screen intercourse, take on another meaning: "I fill my life with patterns of mistrust.... I'm a kind of septic tank for all the world's ugly secrets, all the news that's unfit to print."

As Rebeca rips off Sebastian's hideous wallpaper, she shouts, "You just go lying there feeling bitter." No doubt Bogarde himself was often bitter—with good reason. When shipping his furniture to France, it was deliberately vandalized, and, to add insult to injury, customs officials unnecessarily strip-searched his car before allowing it on the ferry as a kind of punishment not only for leaving England, but also for being "queer." The same thing happened when Bogarde returned to England with his belongings:

> Every pallet, the large chipboard containers in which all one's goods are packed, opened up to reveal heartbreak upon heartbreak. It was an exact repeat of the trip that they had made out to France. Even worse. [...] One piece of ruined furniture followed another, as one broken frame, smashed mirror, torn and legless chair, splintered piece of rosewood, or canvas landscape through by a marble lamp base made its appearance [...] Someone had unwrapped every individual piece and dumped the lot: hence the white armchairs, now covered in oil stains, and the terrace table plus four or five of its small tin chairs, being used by the firm's employees as a restful set-up for a game of poker and a few cans of Heineken.[6]

Coldstream writes, "The adjective most commonly used by his acquaintances to describe Dirk [after Forwood's death] is 'bitter.'"

> He had further reason to be so when the biggest-selling Sunday newspaper stated that Tony had died in St. Stephen's, which, it slaveringly pointed out, was the leading hospital in the treatment of AIDS, and that Dirk had become a "tragic recluse."[7]

Back in Sebastian's grotesque flat, Rebecca's wallpaper-stripping soon reveals a surveillance bug, which has been listening in to Sebastian's private conversations in the name of national security. This also has a curious resonance with an event Bogarde described in his autobiography *Cleared for Take-Off.* Summoned unexpectedly to the British Consul in Nice, he suddenly found himself under suspicion:

> I sat, the chair creaked, the man from the FO (foreign office) had a fixed smile as he sorted some papers. [...] Suddenly the man from the FO, to whom I had never been introduced and who did not offer me a name, said with a burst of boyish enthusiasm how much both he and his wife had enjoyed *Death in Venice.*[8]

He was then shown a series of photographs "mug shots of a selection of Slavs,"[9] and asked if he recognized any of them. He did not. "Very well. I see," the official said.

> "Now, just because you have left us in the U.K., don't, for one moment, think that we still don't keep a friendly ... eye on you. We still look after you. We are concerned for your well-being at all times." He had a small watery smile now. I felt suffocated with futile anger. "I would suggest that if you are put in the position, through your work,

for example, of going across to the East that you inform us immediately. Don't ever make *any* move in that direction without informing us in the U.K. All right?"[10]

Bogarde's memoirs are notoriously unreliable. Coldstream insists that "he spun elaborate, mischievous, sometimes cruel tales to a point where he convinced himself they were true,"[11] and it is tempting to regard this episode as another figment of an imagination, concocted from memories of his own films, *Sebastian* in particular. The implication of this supposed interrogation was that as a gay man, and a famous one at that, he was a security risk, which was how Alan Turing had been regarded after the war. The official verdict on Turing's death is that he took his own life, but it is quite possible that he was killed by British security, which made his death look like suicide. In *Breaking the Code,* Herbert Wise's 1996 BBC television adaptation of Hugh Whitemore's play, Derek Jacobi plays Turing. Prunella Scales, as Turing's mother, says,

> Let me tell you something about my son. His first day at Sherborne was the first day of the General Strike. He bicycled all the way from Southampton to Sherborne—60 miles—so he would be sure of getting to school on time. It was reported in the local newspaper. A boy who would do that would never take his own life. And he was still young. He had everything to live for. Everything.

Sebastian is also politically unreliable, having previously had a relationship with the left-wing Elsa Shahn (Lilli Palmer). After she is dismissed for leaking information, Sebastian sends her affectionately away with a curious variant of a line from the traditional Socialist *Internationale.* Rather than keep the *red* flag flying, Sebastian chose, "Keep the pink flag flying free." Of course, a "pinko" is well-known slang for a socialist, but that color also has gay associations, certainly since the Nazis forced homosexuals to wear pink triangles in concentration camps. Sebastian's line resonates even more in the wake of Elsa's reply, "You ought to get married or something."

When, around the middle of the film, Sebastian resigns, Gielgud's intelligence officer extends a hand. "I expect we'll meet again." "I doubt it," Sebastian replies, walking out. "Oh, I expect we shall," Gielgud muses, as indeed they do later in the film—and they were also to meet again in their professional lives when reunited in Alain Resnais' *Providence.*

The Serpent (dir. Henri Verneuil, 1974) also featured subtly gay implications. Bogarde played the intelligence "mole" of the title, Philip Boyle; he was obviously based on Guy Burgess rather more than Kim Philby. Arthur Thirkell, writing in *The Daily Mirror,* was of the opinion that the role "calls for no more animation than a tailor's dummy,"[12] and it is certainly the case that Bogarde was hardly being stretched: The "camp" mannerisms were already well-honed. Boyle, head of MI6, eventually reveals that he has been a Marxist since he was 19, but his louch, upper-crust ways suggest more a rebellious public schoolboy than a committed idealist. Indeed, a less likely Marxist than Bogarde would be hard to find, and one can't help thinking of his own disbelief of Visconti's Communism when watching him perform here. In *Snakes and Ladders,* Bogarde wrote:

> [Visconti] claimed to be Communist but I found it hard to accept the fact among the palaces, Picassos, footmen and cooks and the splendour and abundance of his living style. So I placed him vaguely Left, which irritated him constantly and made him promise that one day he would explain it all to me.[13]

Bogarde's Boyle similarly haunts chandelier-festooned gentlemen's clubs, is immaculately dressed at all times, smokes cigarettes drawn from a personalized cigarette case emblazoned with a silver serpent device, and arranges to have troublesome individuals assassinated. Critic Russell Davies observed that Bogarde "droops urbanely through his scenes, shifting inside his suit, rolling his tongue from cheek to cheek—offering, in short, all the shrugs, pouts and minute disclaimers that usually indicate he has been given nothing to occupy his mind,"[14] but which also indicate the mute pink elephant in the room. Yul Brunner, as a high-ranking KGB officer who defects to the West, was a much more convincing Communist, but even though Boyle is not subjected to interrogation from the CIA about his sexual preferences, as the (heterosexual) KGB officer is. Bogarde's performance, with its mannerisms, and the use of what Tanitch usefully calls a "camp 'old dear' manner,"[15] leaves one in no doubt that Boyle is a homosexual. He does address one of his colleagues as "old dear."

Permission to Kill (dir. Cyril Frankel, 1975) is much more interesting, mainly because Bogarde's character, Alan Curtis, is less obviously homosexual, though we are given plenty of clues. The film opens with a topless shot of Nicole Calfan as a secret agent Melissa Lascade, walking towards the camera to open a door, behind which Curtis stands. Curtis is entirely impervious to this sight, makes use of the patronizing epithet "my dear," when addressing her, and the misogynistic tag of "your tiny little head" when advising her not to get any ideas about defending herself as he has brought an armed guard with him. He then engages in a businesslike conversation with this spy, whom he intends to employ as an assassin.

The target is Bekim Fehmiu's Alexander Diakim, exiled leader of a dissident political party, and the hit will be made should Diakim insist on returning to his homeland before Curtis thinks the time is right. In an attempt to persuade Diakim to stay away from this unspecified country, Curtis blackmails a group of Diakim's former friends and even his mistress (Ava Gardner) to intercede on his behalf. Should that fail, the assassin's bullet will do the

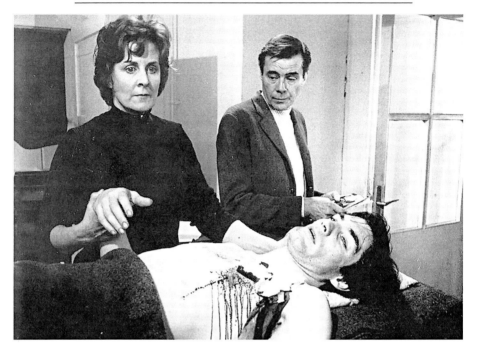

Bogarde with Peggy Sinclair and a wounded Timothy Dalton in *Permission to Kill* (dir. Cyril Frankel, 1975).

trick. In the event, Curtis has to blow up Diakim with a contingency "device" before being shot himself.

Bogarde excels in conveying the moral vacuum Curtis inhabits, along with the schizophrenic nature of his lifestyle. Melissa says they are both "schizos." In phone calls home, Curtis reveals that he can be a caring, quite cuddly husband to a wife who thinks he is abroad on a European Union farming conference. But the real Curtis is a ruthless power-broker. Murder is nothing to him, nor the suffering of those he exploits, demonstrating again how good Bogarde would have been in more traditionally Gothic horror films. *Permission to Kill* has certain things in common with Hammer's *The Satanic Rites of Dracula* (dir. Alan Gibson, 1973), made two years earlier. Curtis presides over a slideshow of the five "subjects" he intends to blackmail into cooperation, much as William Franklin's Torrence, in *Satanic Rites,* projects images of the five people spotted by Maurice O'Connell's agent, Hanson, at Pelham House, where Black Masses are performed and Dracula's bid to destroy the world by means of a plague bacillus are being hatched. Dracula, being a vampire, doesn't appear in the fifth slide, but all five of Curtis' "subjects" do. A later scene is also very much like the early moments of *Satanic Rites* during

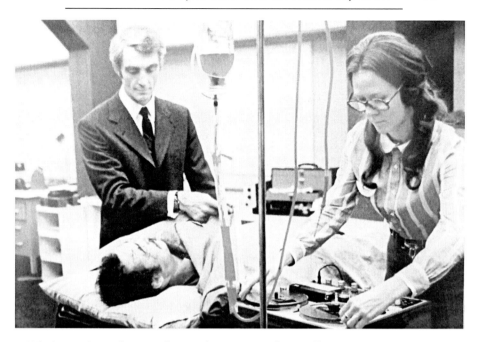

Valerie van Ost and Peter Adair tend to Maurice O'Connell's wounds in *The Satanic Rites of Dracula* (dir. Alan Gibson, 1973).

which Hanson, who has been severely beaten, lies in the secret government office where he is being debriefed while slowly dying under the care of Peter Adair's world-weary doctor.

Similarly, in *Permission to Kill,* Timothy Dalton, as politician Charles Lord, is observed lying in Curtis' secret headquarters, having been shot in a previous scene. He is nursed by a dismayed female assistant (Peggy Sinclair), while Curtis goes about his business completely unmoved by the presence of a dying man. The way both scenes are shot is also strikingly similar.

Dalton's character is the openly gay one. Ironically, Lord is trapped much as Melville Farr in *Victim* was by means of an incriminating photograph. While Lord is in bed with his current boyfriend Cliff Williams, Curtis bursts in with a group of paparazzi and flashbulbs. In 1975, it was still unusual to see two men in bed together on the big screen, and the ensuing gay badinage was also daring for its time, even if somewhat stereotypical. The photos having been taken, Lord argues: "People don't get fired for this kind of thing any more. Haven't you heard of the term 'consenting adults'?" He adds that half the jobs in the government would be vacant if all the gays were removed.

"Yes, but you've not been exactly careful, have you?" Curtis replies, "or particular. Rough trade, that's the term—all of them undesirable contacts from the point of view of the foreign office. You can do what you like where you like, but you mustn't frighten the horses."

Cliff Williams has, of course, been conveniently "planted" by Curtis for just this occasion, which Lord now realizes: "Do tell me," he sneers, "I'm absolutely fascinated. How does a nice, clean upstanding copper like you get to know a pretty little piece of bait like young Cliff? Personal research, as it were?"

Curtis merely returns a languid smile at this, but that is all we need from Bogarde to signal that Lord has made contact with the truth. Lord continues to taunt Curtis throughout the film:

"Oh, it's you," he pouts, when Curtis appears in the hotel room in Austria where he is awaiting his instructions. "I was beginning to think you didn't fancy me any more."

"Just dropped in to see if you're all right," Curtis replies.

"How *darling* of you."

"Anything you want?"

"Well, I could do with something a tiny but more amusing than old Ethel here [the burly bodyguard who shadows him], but I suppose you keep all the pretty ones to yourself."

Again, a knowing smirk is Curtis' only response. Later, when "Ethel" follows him into a bar, Lord snaps, "Do stop creeping around like Dracula's Daughter," another telling Gothic reference. "It's all right," says Lord. "I'm not going to pounce on you. You're not my type." Later, he jokes that he has seduced "Ethel" (actually "Jennings" [Anthony Dutton]): "Now he's running around town in a blonde wig and pearls." When Jennings is replaced, having been knocked out by Lord, Lord beams with studied irony, "Oh goody! Beef-cake at last."

Bogarde's private life once more comes to mind when Lord accuses Curtis of "creating false impressions and doing conjuring tricks. I don't think you know what the truth is any more." Curtis' reply is even more telling, given that it is Bogarde who speaks it:

"The truth is what I make it," he insists. Bogarde's eight autobiographies are evidence of that, all of them being unreliable from a factual point of view.

A later discussion about homosexuality is also remarkably enlightened, given that this was 1975, long before civil partnerships between gay people were legal—let alone marriage:

"These photographs will be following me around for the rest of my life," Lord complains to journalist Scott Allison (Frederic Forrest).

"Oh, Charlie, for God's sake, nobody gives a damn any more. I mean, so you prefer men. I happen to like women. Some guys even go for sheep!"

"Well, I don't think sheep would go down too well at the foreign office."

We never find out more about the private life of Curtis, and when he is dispatched at the end, we are left wondering what his wife will be told. The marriage is obviously a sham, as is the apparently caring husband he pretends to be. Perhaps Curtis has been so corrupted by his own lies that he no longer knows whether he is gay or not. Bogarde's performance suggests that he might be, though his own comments made at the time suggest ambivalence: *Permission to Kill* "got me out of that awful rut after *Death in Venice* and *The Night Porter*," he told film critic Margaret Hinxman in *The Daily Mail*, "when most of the scripts I was offered featured aging queers and perverts." But in his way, Curtis might well have been both.

Chapter Eight

"I don't believe in morality."

Bogarde played musicians three times (four, if one counts his piano-playing lawyer in *Libel)* and an artist twice, first in *So Long at the Fair* in 1950 and second, rather more rewardingly, in Anthony Asquith's adaptation of George Bernard Shaw's *The Doctor's Dilemma* (1958). His first foray into musical terrain came at the beginning of his career in "The Alien Corn" (dir. Harold French, 1948) one of the four segments of *Quartet,* based on stories by W. Somerset Maugham. In this, he played George Bland, heir to a grand estate. His parents hope he will lead a normal life as a country squire, conservative politician and cricketer, but George has different ideas: He wants to be a professional pianist. His cousin Paula (Honor Blackman) persuades George's father to allow him two years to study hard and then submit himself to judgment. If he fails to pass the test, he will agree to give up the piano, marry her and assume his humdrum aristocratic duties. Alas, the expert musical opinion is negative and, his life no longer seeming to be worth living, young George promptly shoots himself. The title references both a chapter from "Ruth" in the Bible and Keats' "Ode to a Nightingale," which quotes from it: "the sad heart of Ruth when, sick for home, She stood in tears amid the alien corn."[1]

George is equally an alien in his own home. He doesn't fit in, his ambitions are unorthodox, and his talent is inadequate to measure up to the world outside. Maugham increases this sense of alienation by making the Blands Jewish. "We're all Jews, the whole gang of us, and everyone knows it and what the hell's the good of pretending we're not?" George asks.[2] He is thus an outsider within a group of outsiders. When he goes to Germany for his intensive study, he becomes self-consciously bohemian:

> He had grown very fat. His hair was extremely long, it curled all over his head in picturesque confusion; and he had certainly not shaved for three days. He wore a grimy pair of Oxford bags, a tennis shirt and slippers. He was not very clean and his fingernails were rimmed with black. It was a startling change from the spruce, slim youth so elegantly dressed in such beautiful clothes that I had last seen.[3]

Bogarde approximates this description, bar the increased weight. In every other respect, he is perfectly cast. Clearly, George's bohemianism is an affectation, and his piano-playing merely an "accomplishment." With his usual ruthlessness, Maugham demolishes his pretensions in the final verdict of Lea Makart, the professional genius who judges him:

> "What is it you want me to tell you?" she asked.
> They looked into one another's eyes.
> "I want you to tell me whether I have any chance of becoming in time a pianist in the first rank."
> "Not in a thousand years."[4]

Played in the film with devastating *sangfroid* by Françoise Rosay, her winged bonnet giving her the authority of the Valkyrie, Brünnhilde, announcing to Siegmund that he must die in battle, Makart continues Maugham's lines almost word for word:

> "If I thought you had in you the makings of an artist I shouldn't hesitate to beseech you to give up everything for art's sake. Art is the only thing that matters. In comparison with art, wealth and rank and power are not worth a straw." She gave us a look so sincere that it was void of insolence. "We are the only people who count. We give the world significance. You are only our raw material."[5]

As well as including Maugham's observation, "In art the difference between the amateur and the professional is immeasurable," Rosay's Makart adds, "I can see that you have worked very hard. You have acquired technique and brilliance; but you lack the magic—the quality that is a combination of soul and fire without which no artist can reach the heights. I'm sorry. You're playing is square." Receiving this unwelcome news stoically, George asks one final favor: Would Miss Makart play for him, which she does, removing her rings first and launching into a *bravura* performance of Schubert's A-flat Impromptu. Maugham has her play Bach instead, as well as having her ask if George would like her to play for him, but the effect is the same, and Bogarde, so early in his career, gives a superb example of what he later heard Alan Ladd say about his day's work in the Pinewood refectory, except that here, he does several "great looks," encompassing defeat, admiration, recognition, despair and esthetic rapture.

His suicide follows soon afterwards, the subsequent inquest kindly offering a verdict of accidental death rather than suicide, as, in the words of James Hayter's foreman: "He must have been cleaning his gun, not knowing he'd left it loaded from the end of last season. As for that business about the music, sir, we don't attach much importance to that. A young gentleman of Master George's position, sir, would never shoot hisself just because he couldn't play the piano good." But this is the whole point—and the reason why Bogarde was cast in the role. He lent to it, as he lent to his later robbers and spivs, a neurotic quality, which had always popularly been associated with a particular kind of homosexual. Indeed, in *Victim,* Bogarde's character has had an affair with just such a type, called Stainer. "He was a neurotic and an hysteric," he explains. "'Deny me or I'll kill myself!' He was always crying wolf. He was clever and amusing but quite unstable and possessive. One night he telephoned and said he was going to kill himself. I didn't believe him before, but apparently, this time he meant it."

From the talented amateur in "The Alien Corn," Bogarde graduated into playing one of the greatest pianists of all time in the Liszt biopic *Song Without End* (1960); but he warmed up for all that the year before with Shaw's epic artist-scoundrel, Louis Dubedat, in *The Doctor's Dilemma,* which turned out to be a much more rewarding role. The dilemma of the title is stark but morally complicated: Should a doctor sacrifice the life of a good but unexceptionable man to save a genius who has no sense of morality or decency? Shaw was no doubt thinking of Liszt's son-in-law, Richard Wagner, the ultimate Romantic genius, when conceiving the impecunious, supremely selfish but marvelously inspired Dubedat. ("You mean you'd want the money back again?" he asks the doctor. "I presume people sometimes have that in view when they lend money," the doctor replies.[6]) Dubedat's death speech ("I believe in Michael Angelo, Velasquez and Rembrandt; in the might of design, the mystery of colour, the redemption all things by Beauty everlasting"[7]) deliberately echoes Wagner's short story "An End in Paris," which ends with a similar deathbed credo: "I believe in God, Mozart and Beethoven, and likewise their disciples and apostles;–I believe in the Holy Spirit and the truth of the one, indivisible Art."[8] Wagner's appalling personal behavior, his pernicious anti–Semitism, his greed, dishonesty and exploitation of friends and supporters were far more shocking than Dubedat's, just as Wagner's towering musical genius was far greater than anything Dubedat could ever have painted, but the idea was the thing.

As Shaw's Ridgeon describes him, Dubedat, "King of men, was the most entire and perfect scoundrel, the most miraculously mean rascal, the most callously selfish blackguard that ever made a wife miserable."[9] He fully recognizes Dubedat's genius ("Yes: this is the real thing," he gasps, admiring one of his drawings), but Ridgeon is forced to limit his patients. "You are asking me to kill another man for his sake," he explains to Dubedat's wife; "for as surely as I undertake another case, I shall have to hand back one of the old ones to the ordinary treatment. Well, I don't shrink from that. I have had to do it before; and I will do it again if you can convince me that his life is more important than the worst life I am now saving. But you must convince me first."[10]

Bogarde was ideal for Dubedat, as he had all the required charm, all the selfishness and urbanity, and also (as *The Servant* and *The Night Porter* later confirmed) the ability to be remarkably cruel. He also happened to be an accomplished amateur artist himself. Bogarde received much praise for his *Doctor's Dilemma* performance and he regarded it as an important land-

Bogarde with Leslie Caron in *The Doctor's Dilemma* (dir. Anthony Asquith, 1958).

mark, giving him a real character with which to grapple. It also (unwittingly) laid the foundations for those aspects of *Death in Venice* in which, as we shall see later, Thomas Mann equated artists with criminals. Dubedat's commitment to Beauty necessarily required his amorality. "I don't believe in morality," he claims with Nietzschean conviction, ("I'm a disciple of Bernard Shaw … the most advanced man now living," he adds in Shaw's original text, which was sadly much cut down to fit cinematic proportions.) "I haven't the ridiculous vanity to set up to be exactly a Superman," Dubedat insists, "but still, it's an ideal that I strive towards just as any other man strives towards his ideal.… I don't believe there's such thing as sin."[11] Dubedat is not gay, but might just as well have been for such an inspiring lack of respect for convention, and Bogarde's private reality usefully informs Dubedat's outsider status here. Coldstream also records a revealing anecdote Bogarde told about the filming: "My doctor on my right was Robert Morley. On the word 'Action' I turned to Robert … only to hear him say to me: 'Dubedat! What did Oscar Wilde do?'" The take was in ruins.[12]

Doctor's Dilemma's Wagnerian echoes should have been of assistance to Bogarde when playing Liszt, but *Song Without End* was hardly worthy of its subject. Bogarde was fully aware of the film's deficiencies. Filming it was "a grinding and profoundly unhappy experience."[13] Forced to learn how to play the piano like the world's greatest virtuoso in a mere 12 weeks (or at least give a good impression of playing like Liszt), he also found himself choking to death on the dialogue, though George Cukor, who took over when Charles Vidor died from a heart attack three weeks into shooting, "was even able to make me realize that a line like 'Pray for me, Mother!' was possible if you managed to believe it."[14] The best line is Lyndon Brook's as Richard Wagner, piqued that Liszt, who is now enthusiastic for his *Rienzi* overture, had once ignored him. Liszt asks if there is anything he can do to help him, to which Wagner haughtily replies that if he ever writes anything for the piano requiring great technical skill, he might send it to him.

The film is absurd, with Chopin and George Sand arriving unannounced at Liszt's Chamonix hideaway and promptly being taken on a pub-crawl by the great virtuoso. Given Liszt's own tendency to embroider stories around music, he might even have approved. *New York Times* music critic Harold Schonberg recounted Liszt's "program" for Chopin's F minor Fantasy in similar terms:

> Chopin had been playing the piano and was in a depressed mood. A low knocking on his door suggested the first two bars of the Fantasy, and the third and fourth bars suggest his invitation to enter. The doors swing open and admit George Sand, Camille Pleyel, Liszt and others. They take up positions around Chopin, who plays agitated triplets. Sand, with whom he had quarreled, falls on her knees and begs forgiveness. At the final march the visitors go out, leaving Chopin to complete his work.[15]

For all the script's nonsense, the basic facts are in place: Liszt did have three illegitimate children with Countess Marie d'Agoult, who left her husband to encourage and support Liszt in his quest to become a serious composer. Liszt did jilt her in favor of the Russian Princess Carolyn Sayn-Wittgenstein, and their attempts at marriage were indeed foiled by the Catholic Church, who refused at the last minute to allow Carolyn to divorce her husband. But

Bogarde and Capucine in *Song Without End* (dir. Charles Vidor and George Cukor, 1960).

Capucine, who plays Carolyn, was far too conventionally beautiful and glamorous for this cigar-smoking intellectual, who was, according to Liszt's biographer Alan Walker, "exceedingly plain."[16] Geneviève Page as Marie d'Agoult is blonde, whereas the real Marie was dark-haired; and, as mentioned earlier, Bogarde looked much more like Cliff Richard than Liszt. Vidor apparently thought differently, as Bogarde recalled years later:

> "You look cute," he said and patted my knee absent-mindedly.
> "I feel ridiculous personally."
> "You look great, kid. Great. I like the hair. You look just like him ... like the pictures we got up in the office ... you seen them? You look just like him. Claude-Pierre said so too and he should know. Claude-Pierre is French from France and he's done all your costooms and he *knows*."[17]

In fact, the only person who looks remotely like the person they were supposed to be playing was Lyndon Brook.

On being shown his dressing room in Hollywood, Bogarde was promptly informed that he had not been the first choice for the lead, being "a Limey with a British accent ... so you just gotta be careful and keep your nose nice and clean?"

> "You ain't gay, are you?" I shook my head. He patted his crotch. "Just thought I'd ask, that's all, most everyone is in this town ... but we'll get on fine."[18]

It is a revealing reminiscence, Bogarde once again protesting too much, but Liszt was very definitely not gay, his serial womanizing, despite having taken holy orders, even causing disapproval from Richard Wagner (who was guilty of much worse). But *Song Without End* gave Bogarde a perfect opportunity to pretend to be straight, despite the often outrageously camp virtuosity of Liszt's keyboard style. Bogarde accordingly resists camp gestures and manages to channel the response of genius to insensitive aristocrats into wounded pride rather than waspish petulance. Though he is nothing like Liszt to look at, he did offer the female fans (who would desert him a year later, after the release of *Victim*) with the dream that he was eligible. And there were numerous opportunities for him passionately to kiss Capucine, who was billed as "the most beautiful woman in Paris." Their fantasy love affair on screen, as we have seen, became a kind of fantasy love affair in Bogarde's private life, which he then projected back onto reality, whatever reality actually was in Bogarde's opinion. He even claimed that marriage had been proposed between them and that Columbia wanted their engagement to be announced at the film's London press reception.[19] This failed to materialize, and Capucine seems to have realized why when he described to her his feelings that *Victim* was a "bit of a problem."

"What's the problem?"

"The passion is another bloke."

"I don't see the problem," said Capucine. "My God! You English. You think that nothing happens to you below your necks."[20]

Capucine was a regular houseguest of Bogarde and Forwood, and was involved in a curious incident when playwrights Willis Hall and Keith Waterhouse were invited to lunch. The meal was greatly delayed, with much to-ing and fro-ing of Bogarde from the kitchen to the dining room, with raised voices behind the scenes. Around 2:30, "Capucine swept in, bearing a large silver salver. She slammed it onto the table. 'There you are, cunt,' she said conversationally, and swept out. We all looked curiously at the covered dish. Dirk raised an eyebrow, that half-smile again, then leaned forward and lifted the cover. Lunch was revealed: Heinz Spaghetti in tomato sauce. And in some quantity. Dirk was in no way fazed."[21]

Much as Bogarde enjoyed having her around, Capucine's function was really little more than that of a disguise, as Helena Bonham Carter realized when she spent time at the Bogarde establishment: "He would always make out that he was a macho heterosexual. He talked about Capucine. He said that Ava Gardner had the most beautiful feet in the world. But why bother with *me*? He was conscious of keeping the mystery, weaving webs. But he was really a hunk of self-denial."[22]

It is hard to understand how film critic Alexander Walker could seriously have called Bogarde's performance as Liszt "as near a portrait of genius as any actor probably can get,"[23] but the many shots of him at the keyboard are certainly a demonstration of his sheer application and professional determination to do his best. Fortunately, a rather more interesting portrait of musical genius was to follow ten years later with *Death in Venice*.

Chapter Nine

"You cannot reach the spirit through the senses!"

Visconti's *The Damned* was only the first part of a trilogy about the decline of German Romanticism and the origins of the Third Reich, which Thomas Mann, in a radio speech during the war, defined as German Idealism gone wrong. Visconti's approach was retrogressive, beginning with the end and then working back through the Late Romantic period of Mahler, Mann and Nietzsche in *Death in Venice* before finally arriving at the foundation in the relationship between Ludwig II of Bavaria and Richard Wagner in *Ludwig* (1973). Having appeared in *The Damned,* it was logical that Bogarde should star in *Death in Venice,* as Gustav von Aschenbach (whose name had been deliberately echoed by the Aschenbach of Helmut Griem in *The Damned,* signaling a continuity between these two eras). Responding to Mann's admission that Mahler had been in his thoughts when writing the novella, Visconti transformed Aschenbach from a writer into a composer, music being, after all, *the* preeminent organ of the German Romantic movement. He also conflated aspects of Mann's other great novel about German idealism gone wrong, *Doctor Faustus,* to emphasize the importance of Nietzsche's philosophy on both "Death in Venice" and the tragedy of twentieth-century German history. However, Bogarde's makeup resembled neither Mahler nor Nietzsche, instead suggesting Thomas Mann himself. Originally, the intention was to suggest the composer, with a false nose that did apparently make him look "very like Mahler himself,"[1] but the nose kept falling off. In desperation, Forwood rummaged around and found a mustache.

> He handed me one at random. I stuck it on; it was bushy, grayish, Kipling. In another box of buttons, safety pins, hair grips and some scattered glass beads he disentangled a pair of rather bent pince-nez with a thin gold chain dangling. I placed the hat back on my head, wrapped a long beige woolen scarf about my neck, took up a walking stick from a bundle of others which lay in a pile, and borrowing a walk from my paternal grandfather, heavily back on the heels, no knee caps, I started to walk slowly round

and round the room emptying myself of myself, thinking of pain and loneliness, bewilderment and age, fear and the terror of dying in solitude. [...] From a long way away [I] suddenly heard Visconti's voice break the almost unbearable stillness. "Bravo! Bravo!" it cried. "Look, look, all of you! Look! Here is my Thomas Mann!"[2]

While Mahler was not a homosexual, both Nietzsche and Mann, to varying degrees, were, and Visconti obviously realized that Bogarde's presence would help link *Death in Venice* to *The Damned*. His leading man was ideally suited to understand the story's homosexual context, particularly as it concerned the artistic sublimation of the libido. Bogarde's Achenbach is presented as a widower. Midway through the film we are shown a flashback where his younger self is enjoying Alpine scenery with his wife and child, both of whom we are meant to assume have died (perhaps echoing the death of Mahler's own daughter at the time he was composing his *Kindertotenlieder*). Mann was also married when he conceived his story, which in terms of its external action was heavily drawn from life. He had always wrestled with his own latent homosexuality, as his diaries frequently record:

Friday, September 20, 1918

These mornings mere adolescents of young soldiers are drilling in the park again. Yesterday they were doing so under the command of an exceedingly bourgeois middle-aged lieutenant. So far they continue to obey, executing as one man the procedures prescribed by the system. The execution of the "Order Arms!" is charming, with the *delicate* return of their rifle butts to the ground as the third maneuver.[3]

Sunday, March 30, 1919

In my exhaustion, forgot to note that yesterday the Hermes-like young dandy who made an impression on me several weeks ago attended my reading. In conjunction with his slight, youthful figure, his face has a prettiness and foolishness that amounts to a nearly classical "godlike" look.[4]

Monday, July 5, 1920

Yesterday began a long letter about *Death in Venice* and my relationship to homo-eroticism to the poet C.M. Weber (Olaf).[5]

Wednesday, July 14, 1920

It can scarcely be a question of actual impotence, but more likely the customary confusion and unreliability of my "sex life." Doubtless this stimulation failure can be accounted for the presence of desire that are directed the other way. How would it be if a young man were "at my disposal"?[6]

Sunday, July 25, 1920

Am enraptured with Eissi, terribly handsome in his swimming trunks. Find it quite natural that I should fall in love with my son.[7]

During the visit to Venice, which inspired his novella, Mann had been fascinated by and attracted to a young boy, who eventually formed the basis of

Tadzio, Aschenbach's beautiful muse. The real-life model of Tadzio was a Polish boy called Władysław Moes, who recalled later in life that an "old man" had been watching him throughout the Venetian holiday he had taken with his aristocratic family in 1905.[8] Visconti refers to this by having the Polish family in the film also called Moes.

In terms of simple action, Aschenbach's pursuit of Tadzio is largely all that happens, but to interpret the film merely as a veiled "confession" of Mann's homosexual impulses—not to mention those of Visconti and Bogarde—one would be guilty of the kind of shameless superficiality of the American film producer who described it as being "about an old man chasing a kid's ass."[9] Homosexuality is obviously part of what the story is about, but the story is also a platform for a much more profound discussion about the nature of inspiration, creativity, the power of beauty and the sublimation of the erotic drive.

Notwithstanding, the context for this discussion is indeed profoundly homoerotic, more so in the novella than the film. Visconti's adaptation accurately recreates the external events of the novella, sumptuously conjuring the vanished *fin-de-siècle* world so beloved by the director, but fails successfully to address the complex philosophical elements in Mann's text. The film is certainly a sensual parade of images, and Björn Andrésen's Tadzio is knowing and flirtatious. (Visconti explicitly connects him to the prostitute whom Aschenbach had visited in his youth, just as had Nietzsche, and Adrian Leverkühn, the fictional composer largely based on that philosopher in Mann's *Doctor Faustus*. The scene in which the comparison is made explicit in Visconti's *Death in Venice* is directly drawn from *Doctor Faustus*; but Mann's sensual imagery is far more graphic and disturbing, as we shall see.)

The philosophical basis of Mann's story is markedly Nietzschean. Nietzsche believed that a successful life is that which reconciles the opposing Apollonian and Dionysian impulses. Nietzsche characterizes the former as symbolizing "measured restraint, that freedom from the wilder emotions, that calm of the sculptor god."[10] The Dionysian impulse, on the

Bogarde as Gustav von Aschenbach in *Death in Venice* (dir. Luchino Visconti, 1970).

contrary, is the personification of intoxication, under the influence of which "everything subjective vanishes into complete self-forgetfulness. In the German Middle Ages, too, singing and dancing crowds, ever increasing in number, whirled themselves from place to place under this same Dionysian impulse."[11]

> In song and in dance, man expresses himself as a member of a higher community; he has forgotten how to walk and speak and is on the way toward flying into the air, dancing. His very gestures express enchantment. Just as the animals now talk, and the earth yields milk and honey, supernatural sounds emanate from him, too: he feels himself a god, he himself now walks about enchanted, in ecstasy, like the gods he saw walking in his dreams. He is no longer an artist, he has become a work of art.[12]

It was the function of Nietzsche's *Übermensch* to contain the Dionysian within the self-discipline of Apollonian restraint, to acknowledge and master the Dionysian and sublimate it into the art of living. Only by confronting the terrifying ecstasy of what is Dionysian in nature can we hope to channel its ambivalent force into culture, which alone can redeem humanity from the horror of the phenomenal world. It is Aschenbach's tragedy that he has neglected the Dionysian in his nature, favoring instead the relentless pursuit of Apollonian form. His personal motto is *"Durchhalten"*—"Hold fast," his ideal hero displays "an intellectual and virginal manliness, which clenches its teeth and stands in modest defiance of the swords and spears that pierce its side."[13]

When Aschenbach is drawn to Venice in all its corrupting glamor and death-drenched decadence, he is quite unable to withstand the powers of Dionysus, represented by *La Serenissma* in general and Tadzio in particular. He undergoes moral collapse, courting a transfigurative death by remaining in the cholera-infested city, lured by the ideal beauty of the boy, and transformed into a parody of himself by a barber in a grotesque attempt to recapture his lost youth.

The terrible dream of overwhelming sensual violence, which Aschenbach experiences one night as he sleeps in his hotel bedroom, represents the Dionysian dilemma he faces. He is simply not strong enough to withstand the erotic power of long-neglected drives:

> His heart throbbed to the drums, his brain reeled, a blind rage seized him, a whirling lust, he craved with all his soul to join the ring that formed about the obscene symbol of the godhead, which they were unveiling and elevating, monstrous and wooden, while from their full throats they yelled their rallying-cry. Foam dripped from their lips, they drove each other on with lewd gesturing and beckoning hands. They laughed, they howled, they thrust their pointed staves into each other's flesh and licked the blood as it ran down. But now the dreamer was in them and of them, the stranger god was his own. Yes, it was he who was flinging himself upon the animals, who bit and tore and swallowed smoking gobbets of flesh—while on the trampled moss there now

began the rites in honour of the god, an orgy of promiscuous embraces—and in his very soul he tasted the bestial degradation of his fall.[14]

None of this dream forms part of Visconti's vision, which he attempts to approximate naturalistically by having one of Aschenbach's symphonies booed at its première, causing him to have a heart attack. The catcalls and whistling of an unsympathetic audience are quite insufficient to suggest the Dionysian nightmare in Mann's original. Visconti admitted his difficulty with this crucial element:

> "At first," he said, "I did think of shooting the nightmare *Blow Up* style, in a Munich nightclub like a kind of eighth circle of Dante's *Inferno,* with an orchestra from *The Damned,* into which I'd have propelled Aschenbach, skipping over half a century.
> "Finally I gave it up because I realized that this would have broken the tone, [violated] the taste in the film.... For the nightmare which, in the book, is the point of deepest depression and foretells [Aschenbach's] death, I substituted the concert fiasco, which fulfills the same function in the film and represents the despair that heralds the end."[15]

Visconti also conflates the complex esthetic and philosophical arguments of the novella into one succinct scene between Aschenbach and his friend Alfred, played by Mark Burns. Here, Aschenbach's quest for Apollonian beauty at the expense of Dionysian inspiration is attacked by his critically ruthless but realistic comrade:

> ASCHENBACH: You know, sometimes I think that artists are rather like hunters aiming in the dark. They don't know what their target is, and they don't know if they've hit it. But you can't expect life to illuminate the target and steady your aim. The creation of beauty and purity is a spiritual act.
> ALFRED: No, Gustav, no. Beauty belongs to the senses. Only to the senses.

Aschenbach insists, "You cannot reach the spirit through the senses. You cannot! It's only by complete domination of the senses that you can ever achieve wisdom, truth and human dignity." Alfred throws Aschenbach's Apollonian ideals back in his face: "Truth? Justice? Human dignity? What good are they?" he asks, with contemptuous impatience.

If the pursuit of beauty is one's only goal, the answer is, presumably, "not very much," though we should never lose sight of Nietzsche's aim at the *synthesis* of Apollonian and Dionysian. It is balance and acceptance that Aschenbach lacks, and we are drawn to the overriding reality that his image of beauty is image *male,* not female. Thus, his denial is not just sexual but specifically homosexual, a denial Mann fully understood, because he had also repressed this aspect of his own personality. The story may use Dionysian metaphors to explore a wider psychological theme applicable to all orientations, but the fact that it is here homosexual adds a further layer of meaning, and as such "Death in Venice" can be interpreted as what we would now call a "gay text," a plea for acknowledgment, acceptance and equality. Mann later argued that this aspect of the story was arbitrary.[16]

This, however, seems disingenuous after the fact, and suggests that he is attempting to distance himself from the confessional aspect of the story. After all, if everything that happened in the story actually happened to Mann, as he claimed, the homoerotic element *also* surely played a very real role. Richard Winston has observed that Mann never openly admitted to "what he felt to be a defect in his nature ... except in the deep privacy of his diaries. Yet he nursed this secret as a source of pleasure, of interest, of creative power." Mann even admitted that his long essay *Betrachtungen eines Unpolitischen*, written during the First World War, was "an expression of my sexual inversion."[17] He regarded his close friendship with Paul Ehrenberg as "a purgative, as a cleanser and solvent of sexuality,"[18] which reminds one strongly of Bogarde's Platonic partnership with Tony Forwood. In a May 6, 1934, diary entry, he reminisces about his time with Ehrenberg: "certain utterances among the notes of the P.E. period, this 'I love you. My God, I love you!'"[19] And these are the words he gives Aschenbach to say to Tadzio in "Death in Venice":

> "How dare you smile like that! No one is allowed to smile like that!" He flung himself on a bench, his composure gone to the winds, and breathed in the nocturnal fragrance of the garden. He leaned back, with hanging arms, quivering from head to foot, and quite unmanned he whispered the hackneyed phrase of love and longing—impossible in these circumstances, absurd, abject, ridiculous enough, yet sacred room and not unworthy of honour even here: "I love you!"[20]

Ronald Hayman identifies several of the many homoerotic elements in Mann's diaries: his enjoyment at watching "a very handsome young man," "14-year-old boy twins ... who interest me because of their charming symmetry," "great pleasure and emotion on observing a young man stripped to the waist,"[21] and so forth. It is therefore a waste of time to argue that "Death in Venice" is not "about" homosexuality. Of course it is—as well as being about a great deal more besides. But it was the distinctly homoerotic aspect that attracted Visconti to it, and at the same time, coincidentally, composer Benjamin Britten, whose opera on the subject delved somewhat deeper into the story's philosophical aspects.

Visconti's personal commitment to Mann's novella was very much connected with his own feelings of sexual guilt. His biographer Laurence Schifano explains:

> Visconti could not contemplate pleasure or even beauty—as in *Death in Venice*—without pain and punishment, without a ritual death. Although he occasionally brought a

frivolous, resolved atmosphere to life, it was always tinted with nostalgia, with the autumnal colours of eighteenth-century fantasy bathing a paradise lost forever. For him, as for Wilde and Proust, love was always guilty; no matter how lucid he was, no matter how free he fancied himself, he had to overcome obstacles and taboos to love, had to pay for the terrible pleasure of transgression in money and/or pain.[22]

Schifano also observes that lines by the nineteenth-century homosexual poet, August von Platen-Hallermünde, informed his entire approach to the film: "He who has contemplated beauty with his own eyes is already dedicated to death."[23] One might argue that this Dionysian dilemma could apply equally well to a story in which homosexuality played no part—think of *Tristan und Isolde*, for example. But the dedication to death of which von Platen speaks is an expression of what was then regarded as the transgressive guilt of homosexuality, a payment for indulging in the "forbidden," not "merely" infidelity. *Death in Venice* simply would not be convincing if Aschenbach had been attracted to a pretty 20-year old woman. (For him to be attracted to a little girl would have simply turned him into a sexual predator, like Martin in *The Damned*.) Aschenbach's tragedy is that the realization of his sexual orientation has arrived too late. "You never possessed chastity," Alfred informs him in the film. "Chastity is the gift of purity, not the painful result of old age and you are *old*, Gustav." Aschenbach's grotesque transformation at the hands of a Venetian barber only emphasizes the fact.

"The degree and kind of a man's sexuality reaches up into the topmost summit of his spirit," wrote Nietzsche in the 75th aphorism of *Beyond Good and Evil*. Similarly, to underplay the homoeroticism of *Death in Venice* is to misunderstand it. Needless to say, it is about far more than "an old man chasing a kid's ass," but that is a good place to begin with when attempting to analyze what is actually going on. The film is about the pursuit of beauty, a quest for which Bogarde was admirably well suited. As Sylvia Syms recalled, Bogarde displayed all the characteristics of the celibate, but was "capable of great love" and, as Coldstream paraphrases, "he certainly loved great beauty, at a cerebral but uncomplicated level [...], and when Sylvia Syms lost the baby she was carrying at the time she made *Victim*, and was extremely unwell, her hospital room was a riot of exquisite blooms carefully chosen by Dirk."[24] Dirk also drew on his own experience when creating the persona of Aschenbach, particularly his three unhappy childhood years when he stayed with relatives in Scotland:

I assembled a rag bag of trinkets into which I am still able to rummage. Aunt Teenie's dreadful twitch on her poor scarred face became the twitch on von Aschenbach's face at moments of stress, in *Death in Venice* for example; my own shyness and diffidence and loneliness at those Tennis Parties or Tea Parties became his when he arrived, alone, at the Grand Hotel des Bain. The games I played then, and the things I stole, gleaned, collected, observed, have remained with me, vividly, for the rest of my life.[25]

However, the kind of beauty, intellectual or not, that is being pursued in Visconti's *Death in Venice* is not of the female variety, other than the maternal yearnings represented by Silvana Magnano, who plays Tadzio's mother. She was in fact an avatar of Visconti's own, much-adored mother, from whom he inherited his fascination with clothes, and which led to his collaboration with the meticulous costume designer Piero Tosi. The entire film presents a particularly gay point of view, reflecting Visconti's own agenda as much as Mann's. Just as Visconti almost religiously positioned photographs of his own parents in his various homes, so Bogarde's Aschenbach places photographs of his wife and daughter in his hotel room on the Lido. Visconti's own memories of opulent *fin de siècle* furnishings are lovingly recreated in the various environments through which Aschenbach walks and watches. And, not least, Visconti equates Venice with his own homosexuality, for, as Schifano puts it, Venice became "a meeting place for homosexuals who here, more completely than anywhere else, escaped society's condemnation of the 'accursed race,' strolling, said Paul Morand, 'ringed and cooing like the pigeons in St. Mark's Square.'"[26] The ship that brings Aschenbach to the city is called *Esmeralda*, the name of the prostitute whom Leverkühn visits in *Doctor Faustus* and from whom he contracts the syphilis that will not only enhance his genius but also ultimately destroy him. Visconti's equation of Tadzio with this prostitute in the flashback scene, which begins with Tadzio playing "Für Elise" on the piano, emphasizes this equation. The pursuit of beauty leads to death unless one is strong enough to become truly "Dionysian" in the Nietzschean sense of having faced up to and been absorbed into an Apollonian whole, those potentially destructive forces of ecstasy and violence, beauty and intoxication. Aschenbach is not equipped to survive. Mann suggests why this is the case by emphasizing his discipline, solitude and a tenacious, even sacred commitment to work:

> He began his day with a cold shower over chest and back; then, setting a pair of tall wax candles in silver holders at the head of his manuscript, he sacrificed to art, in two or three hours of almost religious fervour, the powers he had assembled in sleep.[27]

Bogarde conveys this overly Apollonian aspect of Aschenbach's personality by details of behavior, such as the precise way he eats the strawberries that infect him with cholera, and in the fastidious way he dresses; we see Aschenbach actually at work only once in Visconti's film, when he is shown composing his ultimate masterpiece under the influence of Tadzio's beauty on the Lido. Visconti uses the fourth movement of Mahler's 3rd Symphony as

Aschenbach's composition, with its setting of Nietzsche's words, "O Mensch! Gib acht!" from *Thus Spake Zarathustra*:

> O Man! Attend!
> What does deep midnight's voice contend?
> "I slept my sleep,
> "And now awake at dreaming's end:
> "The world is deep,
> "Deeper than day can comprehend.
> "Deep is its woe,
> "Joy—deeper than heart's agony:
> "Woe says: Fade! Go!
> "But all joy wants eternity,
> "—wants deep, deep eternity."[28]

It is (deliberately) ironic that Aschenbach should set these lines inspired by the beauty that will ultimately destroy him, as Nietzsche's poem expresses his theory of "Eternal Recurrence"—that need of the *Übermensch* to withstand the onslaught of Dionysian wisdom—its woe and its even deeper joy—and to develop the strength to say "Yes" to life come what may.

> Did you ever say Yes to one joy? O my friends, then you said Yes to *all* woe as well. All things are chained and entwined together, all things are in love;
>
> If ever you wanted one moment twice, if ever you said: "You please me, happiness, instant, moment! then you wanted *everything* to return!
>
> You wanted everything anew, everything eternal, everything chained, entwined together, everything in love, O that is how you *loved* the world,
>
> You everlasting men, loved it eternally and for all time: and you say even to woe: 'Go, but return!'" *For all joy wants—eternity!*[29]

This, in essence, is Nietzsche's argument *against* Christianity and all other forms of pessimism:

> Everything hitherto called "truth" is recognized as the most harmful, malicious, most subterranean form of a lie; the holy pretext of "improving" mankind as the cunning to *suck out* life itself and to make it anaemic. Morality as *vampirism.*... He who unmasks morality has therewith unmasked the valuelessness of all values which are or have been believed in; he no longer sees in the most revered even *canonized* types of man anything venerable, he sees in them the most fateful kind of abortion, fateful *because they exercise fascination.*... The concept "God" invented as the antithetical concept to life—everything harmful, noxious, slanderous, the whole mortal enmity against life brought into one terrible unity! The concept "the Beyond," "real world" invented so as to deprive of value the *only* world which exists—so as to leave over no goal, no reason, no task for our earthly reality! The concept "soul," "spirit," finally even "immortal soul," invented so as to despise the body, so as to me it sick—"holy"—so as to bring to all the things in life which deserve serious attention, the questions of nutriment, residence, cleanliness, weather, a horrifying frivolity![30]

Bogarde would have been sympathetic to these arguments, the possibility of God having been destroyed forever by his experiences in the Second World War. Whether he actually visited Belsen or not, the reality of the Holocaust was enough to make God an impossibility for him. "God was invented by man for those who lose faith in living." he insisted. "I believe in another force—the force that helps plants to grow."[31] A supporter of euthanasia, he was eventually cremated. He had no belief in survival after death, but he did believe in living for the pleasure of living rather than the single-minded pursuit of any artistic ideals. He did not regard himself as a dedicated actor with a passion for acting, like John Gielgud. "I don't like it very much," he famously insisted. Acting was "merely" a "way of earning my living." "I simply like to be on my own. I like the silence. I couldn't live in a city"[32]—sentiments that seem to be fully in sympathy with the passage by Nietzsche:

> I have found strength where one does not look for it: in simple, mild, and pleasant people, without the least desire to rule—and, conversely, the desire to rule has often appeared to me a sign of inward weakness: they fear their own slave soul and shroud it in a royal cloak (in the end, they still become the slaves of their followers, their fame, etc.). The powerful natures *dominate*, it is a necessity, they need not lift one finger. Even if during their life time, they bury themselves in a garden house.[33]

"I detested the commercial vulgarity of the cinema," Bogarde confessed, "much as I detest the commercial vulgarity of television, which gives you every degree to play down to the lowest common denominator, and does not lift anybody up but takes everybody down to the lowest thought that they can have. That I think is fatal and wrong, and that's why I didn't like the cinema."[34]

Chapter Ten

"No women!"

The trilogy of "Doctor" films transformed Bogarde into a major star. Comedy was never particularly his specialism, however, and neither was he required to be particularly comic in these films, Dr. Simon Sparrow being in fact the straight man and really only a foil to the comedy going on around him. The first film's biggest laugh came when Sparrow replied to Dr. Lancelot's question regarding blood coagulation ("You, what's the bleeding time?") with, "Ten past ten, sir." What made Bogarde so popular in these films was his vulnerability, and what he called "the little boy looking for God." He had practiced this image in an earlier comedy, *Penny Princess* (dir. Val Guest, 1952), in which he found himself wandering around for much of the film in nothing but his pajamas. A more vulnerable little boy looking for God, it would be hard to imagine, though in this instance he was actually looking for Yolanda Donlan who plays a dumb blonde and the unlikely ruler of the Ruritanian country of Lampidorra, which had previously been bought by a distant relative. Having inherited it, she travels there to take up her duties and falls in love with Bogarde's cheese salesman, Tony Craig. The plot is wafer-thin and the comedy distinctly forced, the whole enterprise depending almost entirely on Bogarde's boyish charm.

This charm was itself dependent, in the eye of his female fans at least, on Bogarde's sexually non-threatening image, in a way that the equally homosexual Kenneth Williams' image was not. Williams had actually seen Bogarde in Venice, two years after the first "Doctor" film. ("They're all here," he wrote in his famous diary on June 18, 1963. "It's a disgrace."[1]) Williams had also been to see him in *Victim* when it first appeared. He regarded that film as "all v. slick, same team as *Sapphire* (Relphs) and like that, superficial and never knocking the real issues. Never touching on what Kenneth Walker once described as 'playing out the tragedy of the heart, alone, with no one knowing of their troubles…'"[2]

Years later, Williams had this observation to make when watching Bogarde being interviewed on television by Russell Harty in 1981:

153

We saw Russell Harty interviewing Dirk Bogarde & v. squirmy it was! The anecdotes were tag-less and badly told & the appearance discouraging!—awful black-dyed hair which threw the lined face into relief & the mannerisms were extraordinarily camp but *not* funny. D.B. said he deplored the deterioration in "English manners" and went on about the decline of moral standards, but since he's living abroad (in France) I don't think he's much of an authority on English standards anyway. It was all rather tatty and sad.[3]

Williams was, as usual, well informed and perceptive. This is really a very astute analysis of that particular TV appearance, in which Bogarde was obviously feeling very vulnerable and did himself no favors. In *Cleared for Take-Off*, Bogarde describes a different occasion, but one with perhaps the same emotions:

I was seeking invisibility, pulling back into my shell, like the hermit crab I'd often thought I might resemble. It didn't work, of course. You *can't* just suddenly dissolve in the middle of the King's Road (or a square off it). Anyway, the kind of hermit crab I was pretending to be, or wishing to be, was usually naked and seeking an empty shell. You can't pull into an empty shell and hide if you are tarted up in your one best Aquascutum single-button two-piece.[4]

After reading Bogarde's *An Orderly Man,* Williams observed, "[H]e writes very well & there are moments of extraordinary poignance," adding,

Not a vein of comedy but lots of ironies & a good feel for atmosphere. There is quite a lot devoted to belittling the early film work & a dismissal of chat shows as rubbish etc. but the former brought him fame & the latter brought him a publisher.... Men of 60 don't have jet-black hair: his looks as if it's covered in boot polish. I suppose vanity forbids that he says it. He's certainly frank about the later pictures being commercial flops. That's the real truth I suppose: he worked profitably in superficial stuff but wanted to be in "great artistic" pieces. Why? A sort of snobbery really & an inability to accept certain fundamental truths.[5]

One presumes that that last phrase refers as much, if not more to Bogarde's sexuality as his career.

In his performances, Williams was far more aggressive and outrageous than Bogarde. His camp persona left no room for sexual ambivalence, and it is instructive to compare his own Dr. Tinkle in *Carry on Doctor* (dir. Gerald Thomas, 1967) with Bogarde's Dr. Sparrow. His name notwithstanding, Tinkle, like Sparrow, is, structurally, a serious role, his function being to feed lines to comic partners such as Frankie Howerd and Sid James. There is even a reference to the big joke of *Doctor in the House:* "No bleeding, good," says Dr. Tinkle, examining the backside of Howerd's Mr. Bigger. "Just like the service round here," Bigger replies. True, Tinkle does take pills when overexcited and washes them down with water from a vase of flowers, and he does have a powerful one-liner himself when arranging a dinner date with

Hattie Jacques's Matron ("Young chickens may be soft and tender," she says, "but the older birds have more on them." "True," Tinkle agrees, "and take a lot more stuffing"). But most of his lines are purely functional, like Sparrow's. The major difference is that Williams' performance is alive with his habitual highly camp mannerisms, grotesque facial expressions and extreme vocal inflections. He was not as conventionally good-looking as Bogarde either, and it is the combination of all these in his performance rather than the lines that provides most of the comedy. By contrast, Sparrow has few comic lines and is never physically grotesque. Both Tinkle and Sparrow are nominally heterosexual, but despite the difference in their performances, Bogarde and Williams had more in common personally. As Coldstream reports, Sylvia Syms was fully aware of this:

> She believes [Dirk] had the characteristics of the celibate, of one who, like Kenneth Williams, "loves to watch, to tell dirty stories, but who does not like the messiness, the untidiness of sex." Certainly, the monastic simplicity with which Dirk always furnished his bedrooms would tend to bear out the theory, at least in part.[6]

In the first of the series, *Doctor in the House* (dir. Ralph Thomas, 1954), the other medical students (played by Donald Sinden, Donald Houston and Kenneth More) are all unquestionably conventional fellows. Sinden (as Tony Benskin) is a lothario, Houston ("Taffy" Evans) plays rugby, and More (Richard Grimsdyke) has a steady girlfriend. Bogarde's Simon Sparrow, by contrast, is very polite, diffident, shy, boyish and, perhaps most significantly, confused. He admits to playing wing three-quarters in rugby matches at school, and his skill at the game later saves him from being expelled from medical college, but this is hardly convincing, especially in the light of comments by Dennis Rendell, a fellow pupil at Bogarde's prep school, who recalled, "Derek [Dirk] wasn't very good at games. He didn't like soccer. He was slightly effeminate on the field, and didn't like barging into people."[7]

Sparrow (a suitably diminutive name) is troubled by the forward behavior of his landlady's daughter (played by future Bond girl Shirley Eaton). She wants him to examine her foot and, later, other parts of her anatomy, so he moves out into his chum's digs, which at first dismays him not only because the place is in very manly disorder, but also because the chum's girlfriend asks him to help her fasten her clothing. Simon's single status causes his chum Richard to worry that he is "harboring a mother fixation." A trial run is arranged with a gauche nurse, played by future Carry On star Joan Sims, who munches an apple throughout Simon's unsuccessful seduction. "Why can't you let that boy be celibate if he wants to be?" Taffy asks. Simon protests that he doesn't want to be celibate, but a great deal of Bogarde's attraction to female fans was he that he was indeed sexually "safe." There was nothing of the lothario about him or about Simon Sparrow.

Bogarde, star though he was, was never "one of the lads," as revealingly demonstrated in an anecdote reported by Coldstream. Richard Gordon, the author of the books on which the Doctor films were based, felt that Bogarde was much more reserved than the other actors. The camera crew referred to him as "Ginger," i.e. "Ginger Beer," Cockney rhyming slang for "queer." Sinden was very much aware of Bogarde's distance (which was really shyness and social insecurity). While out on location, Sinden and the others would have their lunch on the steps of a fountain at University College London, but Bogarde preferred to retreat to the privacy of his Rolls-Royce. "It was very much the chaps together, and the feeling came around that he was the only homosexual among us,"[8] Sinden concluded, but it was Bogarde's sensitivity and softness, combined with such vulnerable good looks made the films a tremendous success. Sparrow faints on his first day in the operating theater, and when he delivers his first baby, the mother looks up at him and says, "You were so kind."

Bogarde and Brigitte Bardot in *Doctor at Sea* (dir. Ralph Thomas, 1955).

In *Doctor at Sea* (dir. Ralph Thomas, 1955), Dr. Sparrow is again presented as delicate (susceptible to sea sickness), young (of course), prettier and better dressed than his fellow actors, and therefore motherable, which is exactly what all his female fans wanted to do, if they weren't dreaming of more erotic encounters. *Doctor at Sea,* however, is a remarkably misogynistic film, with lines such as, "The patients might feel better with a woman in the background, but I don't." Joan Sims, soon to be condemned to a life in Carry On films, plays the gawky daughter of Sparrow's employer, and when he finds himself forced to accompany her to the cinema, he decides to run away to sea. The ship he chooses is called the *Lotus,* distantly echoing the company of men who sail away with Odysseus to the land of the Lotus Eaters. It "carried no passengers, and that meant no women!"

"You're not married are you?" James Robertson Justice's ship's captain asks one of his crew.

"No," the officer replies.

"You keep it that way. Wives and waves don't mix, old boy."

The captain "doesn't approve of women," adding, with perhaps an intentional double entendre, "they are un-seaman-like." There are other curious observations, such as the story of a former officer who "thought he was Cleopatra when they were in the Nile delta." Sparrow's predecessor is called "Flowerday," and is implied to have been gay. Sparrow is at the least chaste. He doesn't indulge in the company of loose women when ashore, like the others. He does get drunk, though. When he can't find the money to pay the bill, he finds himself in jail with his shipmates. A policeman is discovered wearing a dress, and the captain and Mr. Archer (Hubert Gregg) waltz together to the consternation of observers. There are, however, plenty of women in the film—most famously Brigitte Bardot in her first screen role (she had been selected out of many hopefuls by Bogarde himself). But this is a woman's picture only in the sense that it was designed to appeal to Bogarde's female fan base.

Doctor at Large (dir. Ralph Thomas, 1957) continued the mixture as before. For *Daily Sketch,* critic Harold Conway perceptively identified Bogarde's "unforced charm" as the most important ingredient of this winning formula. *Doctor in Distress* followed in 1963, again directed by Ralph Thomas, with James Robertson Justice's Sir Lancelot finding himself in love with his own physiotherapist. Bogarde agreed to appear in this movie meringue strictly as a business proposition after *The Mind Benders* and *The Servant* had failed to generate much income, and Sir Launcelot's conversion to feminine company signaled the end of Bogarde's involvement in the series. It continued to practice without him, however, and eventually became a long-running TV series.

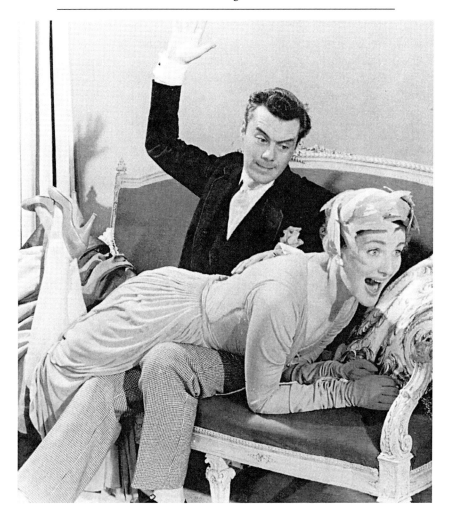

Bogarde and Barbara Murray in *Doctor at Large* (dir. Ralph Thomas, 1957).

It is profoundly ironic that these ostensible heterosexual romps were so immensely popular due to their exploitation of Bogarde's "gay" charm. Women in particular were smitten by the image of a compassionate and vulnerable, though in fact eminently capable young Dr. Sparrow delivering a baby on a snowy Christmas Eve. Placing Biblical resonances aside, this scene epitomizes what the film producers believed every 1950s British woman wanted: a gentle, sensitive, heterosexual man. As many women subsequently discovered, when a gay man provides only the first two categories, it is not enough to make a marriage work; but the fantasy persists.

Bogarde went to sea again in 1962 with Sir Alec Guinness in *H.M.S. Defiant* (aka *Damn the Defiant!*, dir. Lewis Gilbert). A ship crewed entirely by men is an obvious place to start if one wishes to play out homosexual issues, not that Gilbert intentionally had that in mind in this adaptation of Frank Tilsley's 1958 novel *Mutiny*, but it is perhaps significantly given to Bogarde to shout through a loud-hailer, "Get those wretched women off the ship!" as the female followers and wives of the crew are winched away in a huge net just before the warship sets sail. We are reminded of James Robertson Justice's "No women!" in *Doctor at Sea*, especially when the next shot shows live pigs being winched on board.

Bogarde's character, Lt. Scott-Padget, is not meant to be gay, but Scott-Padget's sadism does rather suggest that he enjoys watching men being whipped, and Bogarde's general manner, his looks and his hairstyle, despite the handsome eighteenth-century naval uniform, are exactly what Guinness himself felt was wrong about Bogarde's performance: "He bears no resemblance to any naval officer and is totally un-period in manner and looks. He's gay and amusing but pretty silly." As Coldstream, who also quoted Guinness, observed, "Dirk seemed to enjoy himself far more with the cracking whip and the quiet exercise of domination than he ever did in the films where he had to attempt a love scene, no matter how delightful the object of his attention." And Gilbert, while interested in Bogarde's "sinister" qualities, realized that Bogarde would never "have made James Bond," being essentially "kind of feminine."[9]

The film has much in common, thematically at least, with Herman Melville's posthumously published novel *Billy Budd* (1929), which is equally concerned with mutiny aboard a Royal Navy warship in precisely the same year as the action of *H.M.S. Defiant* takes place, 1797. Benjamin Britten was attracted to the story in 1951, collaborating with Eric Crozier and E.M. Forster on his operatic adaptation. The story lent itself to Britten's lifelong interest in the corruption of innocence in the shape of young boys by ruthless men. Though Crozier was not gay, Forster was, and it was he who drew Britten's attention to the story in which the eponymous impressed young sailor attracts the unwelcome attention of a similarly sadistic master-at-arms, John Claggart, who is envious of Billy's good looks, innocence and popularity with the crew.

Claggart falsely charges Billy with attempting to foment mutiny. When Billy is summoned to the captain to defend himself, his stammer causes him so much frustration that he strikes Claggart and unintentionally kills him, which, of course seals his fate. Here, virtually on a plate, were all of Britten's homosexual themes: a beautiful young boy destroyed by an older man, who

Bogarde's Lt. Scott-Padget (right) encounters Murray Melvin's Wagstaffe (left) onboard ship in _H. M. S. Defiant_ (dir. Lewis Gilbert, 1962).

envies and probably desires him too; a company composed exclusively of men; innocence and corruption; punishment and salvation. _H.M.S. Defiant_ is really no more than a superficial re-working of this scenario. Bogarde's Scott-Padgett is the equivalent of Claggart, while Crawford's own son, Harvey, played by David Robinson, who is hardly more than a boy, is one of the two Billy Budds aboard the _Defiant_. Harvey is originally wide-eyed and idealistic about life at sea; his rude awakening takes the form of being victimized by Scott-Padgett as a way of revenging himself on the captain. The fine-featured Murray Melville as the appropriately named and elegantly dressed Wagstaffe, though caught by the pressgang while in the arms of a serving wench, is pretty obviously the other of the film's Billy Budd equivalents. Wagstaffe is pushed against Scott-Padgett by a shipmate and though he escapes a flogging, a less fortunate member of the crew who incurs Scott-Padgett's displeasure does not. During practice firing, this fellow, "on an impulse of anger," puts up his fists at the touchy lieutenant, which is quite enough for him to receive 20 lashes, duly administered with drum rolls and full martial ceremony. Scott-Padgett had hoped for 60 lashes, but is overruled by Guinness's lenient Capt. Crawford, a very similar kind of man to *Billy Budd's* Capt. Vere. Bogarde's leer of delight as the punishment is delivered is almost of onanistic pleasure. *H.M.S. Defiant* was the only film Bogarde made with Sir Alec, who did nonetheless encounter him again in 1995 after the former's return to London. The ironic tone perhaps reflects his feelings on working with him:

> Bumped into Dirk Bogarde in Fry's splendid vegetable shop in Cale Street. He was fingering oddly shaped tomatoes with a knowledgeable air. He rejected them and cast a dark eye over some frivolous greenery. He finally settled for a big, shiny yellow pepper. I was envious of his concentrated marketing skill.[10]

Bogarde's only film for John Schlesinger, *Darling,* appeared in 1965 at the height of the swinging phoniness it satirized. Julie Christie's "darling," a ruthlessly selfish *arriviste* called Diana Scott, claws her way to the top of the fashion-media world. She is obviously very feminine, but it is quite possible, and indeed revealing, to compare Darling's relationship with Bogarde's journalist Robert Gold, with the fatal attraction of Bosie for Oscar Wilde. Wilde, after all, was an author like Robert, equally as generous, and just as foolishly infatuated; Darling is just as manipulative and even more superficial than Bosie, destroying Robert's marriage, spreading chaos and unhappiness wherever her voracious ego goes. "How could anybody as trivial and as shallow as you cause so much pain as you do?" Robert asks during their big break-up scene. "Your idea of fidelity is not having more than one man in the bed at the same time. You're a whore, baby, that's all. Just a whore."

To be fair, Robert is hardly a model of fidelity himself, leaving his wife and family for this empty-headed mannequin. "I was always easily seduced," he admits at the end, after Darling has abandoned the lavish lifestyle she has achieved. She has been driven to distraction by loneliness and boredom, wandering around a vast mansion like Charles Foster Kane in Xanadu, and now has hopes that she and Robert will be reunited like old times, a dream of which Robert, with a ruthlessness fully the equal of her own, soon disabuses her. We might easily compare this situation to that of Wilde, who, in *De Profundis,* complains about the way in which Bosie dragged him down:

> I blame myself again for having allowed you to bring me to utter and discreditable financial ruin. I remember one morning in the early October of '92 sitting in the yellowing woods at Bracknall with your mother. At that time I knew very little of your real nature. I had stayed from a Saturday to Monday with you at Oxford. You had stayed with me at Cromer for ten days and played golf. The conversation turned on you, and your mother began to speak to me about your being, as she termed it, "*all wrong about money.*" I have a distinct recollection of how I laughed. I had no idea that the first would bring me to prison, and the second to bankruptcy. I thought vanity a sort of graceful flower for a young man to wear.[11]

Like Robert and Darling, Bosie also joined Wilde in Paris after the latter's release from prison, though Wilde wasn't quite as abrupt as Robert in finishing the affair.

Christie's Darling could easily have been the kind of superficial and selfish gay man epitomized by Bosie. Her mother admires her when playing the Virgin Mary in a school nativity play. "She'll go a long way," she murmurs admiringly, unaware of the irony in which the film rejoices. Like Wilde— who was equally unfaithful to his wife, Constance, when "feasting with panthers" as he termed his homosexual escapades—Robert and Darling meet in secret. "I hate this furtiveness," Robert complains. "It's so corny." At which point a phallic train hurtles symbolically over a bridge. Like any ambitious social climber, the climbing matters to Darling, not the view from the top. She feels "madly 'in'" when accompanying Robert on his interviews. "I don't remember much anyone said," she admits. "That wasn't really he thing. The thing is, they accepted me."

It is easy to be critical of Darling Diana, but it is necessary to contextualize her actions. In many ways, women were just as repressed and victimized as gay men. Julie Christie explained:

> Here was a woman who didn't want to get married, didn't want to have children like those other kitchen-sink heroines; no, Darling wanted to have *everything*. Of course, at the time, this was seen as greedy promiscuity and she had to be punished for it. But there was an element of possibility for women, of a new way of living, which is why the film was such a success.

Robert Murphy quotes this passage in his own study of the cinematic history of the period: "Diana's life might be empty, superficial and ultimately sad, but it still seems more fun than working in Woolworths. She is manipulative but transparently so, ambitious and selfish but by no means as inhuman and unscrupulous as many of the people who surround her."[12] Accusations of irresponsibility, promiscuity and superficiality have also been leveled at the gay community, and as if to resonate the gay parallel here, *Darling* contains several overt homosexual references. Two black men share a flat above Darling and Robert's, and at a charity event at which Darling draws a raffle for rich socialites, a man called Alex says to the event's host, "I like your black boys, John. I suppose I can't wrap one up and take him?" Also, one of Darling's other relationships is with a gay photographer (Ronald Curram) who eventually goes off with another man, destroying their platonic affair.

Bogarde's gay reality went on to underpin one of his most heterosexual roles in Losey's *Accident*. He claimed that Losey and Harold Pinter, who adapted Nicholas Mosley's original novel, had originally wanted someone else for the part. In fact, it had been the producer Sam Spiegel who had hoped for Richard Burton.[13] Bogarde might not have seemed the obvious choice to play a pipe-smoking Oxford philosophy don, married with two children, who, suffering a mid-life crisis, falls hopelessly in lust with a beautiful German student (Jacqueline Sassard). This woman, Anna, is also pursued by a rival don, Charley (played by Stanley Baker), and Stephen's young student William (Michael York).

Bogarde, as one would expect, gives a brilliant performance. It also manages to suggest a possible gay reading of his role as Stephen. As Tanitch observed, "There was always the feeling, unwarranted perhaps, that the tutor might also be in love with the undergraduate."[14] And though Bogarde regarded this film as his *Hamlet,* in that he thought there was no trace of his own personality in that of Stephen,[15] he was wrong. Bogarde's persona is written just as large over this film as any other in which he appeared, despite the contrasting character he plays. For a start, there are familiar gestures: in the central scene, a drunken dinner party during which Stephen and Charley play out their animosities, Bogarde points at Baker from the head of the table just as he did in *The Damned,* in which the weak man he plays attempts to impose his will on others, with unsuccessful petulance. Bogarde's portrayal of a lonely, guilt-ridden middle-aged man, who is aware that he is becoming old, is not so far removed from his Aschenbach in *Death in Venice.* Both are in pursuit of obscure objects of desire. In *Accident,* that object happens to be female, but it could so easily have been male in the golden-haired, blue-eyed form of Michael York. (The guilty expressions of Bogarde's Stephen as he rescues

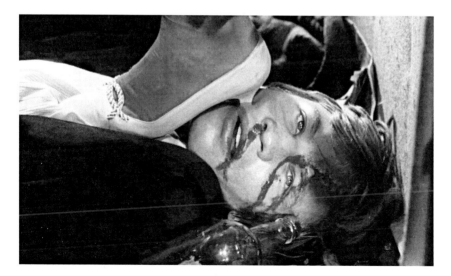

Michael York in *Accident* (dir. Joseph Losey, 1967).

Anna from the car crash at the opening of the film could so easily reflect a gay man's fear of being found out.) Bogarde's inherent vulnerability is perfect for Stephen, who is definitely number three in this trio of lustful men. Baker is very much the alpha male, and indeed he even seduces Anna in Stephen's house when Stephen is out, which gives Bogarde an opportunity to convey bottled-up, seething anger while cooking himself an omelet, which has never been bettered. Bogarde does lose his temper in *The Damned,* but he is less convincing there than his restrained fury is in *Accident.*

The film begins with a somewhat surreal shot of Stephen's house, reminiscent in mood of Magritte's unnerving painting *The Empire of Lights.* We hear the noise of a plane overhead, which gradually recedes, having established a sense of unease. The camera then eerily zooms closer as we begin to hear a car engine, which gradually grows louder before the smash and crunch on crashing. This is the central metaphor of the film: the emotional lives of all the characters are similarly destructive and catastrophic. Stephen appears at the door and Losey's camera picks out bluebells in the verge followed by the startling profile of an equally startled white horse. Bogarde always claimed to have had a car accident himself while serving in the army in India. According to his own account, several people were killed. "We drove home in torrential rain and struck a group of soldiers somewhere along the Barrackpore road. We turned over twice I seem to recall…. I have never driven since."[16] So he may have brought personal experience to bear, though in fact there is no evidence that such an accident ever took place.

Stephen runs to the scene, and another metaphor of the callous way in which everyone is going to treat each other occurs when he helps Anna out of the wreckage. William is dead, but she nonetheless steps on his face. We soon learn, however, that this is in fact the end of the story, the rest of the film being a flashback, so it is a while before we realize the sequence of events that have led up to the opening accident.

Accident is a study in lust and guilt, and it really makes very little material difference if the object of that lust is a man or a woman. Personally, Bogarde was far more interested in love than lust ("You can have a love affair without carnality"), but knew full well that lust is really more about the person who is lusting than the interchangeable object of desire. A gay sensibility is no obstacle when it comes to conveying that. Nicholas Mosley was originally concerned that it might have been:

> I thought that Dirk can act this, he can act that, but I didn't really see how he could
> smolder with lust for this young girl—or indeed for the older played by Delphine
> Seyrig, in the middle of the film. But he did the scene with her very well; I don't

know that he really put over Stephen's intense frustration, his longing for the girl and his frustration with his pregnant wife; but I don't think anybody could have done it better.[17]

What Bogarde does convey in the scene when Stephen for a moment believes that it is Anna rather than his wife Rosalind (Vivienne Merchant) is lying in his bed, is exactly what a gay man might feel when realizing that he is trapped in a heterosexual marriage and finds himself obsessed with someone else of his own sex. Stephen lies down next to Rosalind and with great tenderness says, "I love you," before falling back on the pillows in anguish with a silent scream.

It is quite possible that Losey was aware of these gay undercurrents, as he was apparently not immune to the attraction of other men. The only evidence we have of any actual homosexual activity comes from one of his screenwriters, Evan Jones, who called Losey "a promiscuous bisexual" who had made advances to him, which he declined. Bogarde, as one would perhaps expect, dismissed the possibility, but other women have variously claimed him to be "lightly oriented towards pederasty" (Charlotte Aillaud), and to have gained a "sort of pleasure" in looking at men like Stanley Baker and Alain Delon (Florence Malraux).[18]

Pipe smoking, *à la* Tolkein or C.S Lewis, suited Bogarde much less than cigarettes, and the image does little to enhance Stephen's conventional "masculinity." But the affectionate relationship he has with his children is much more convincing. Here, Bogarde's apparently longstanding desire for children of his own, together with his experience with Jon Whiteley and the children in *Our Mother's House,* lends great warmth and charm to these scenes. University dons then lived in a largely all-male world of the kind that was epitomized by the dictum of "No Women!" in *Doctor at Sea.* Gathered together in the university library, Stephen and other faculty members, along with Alexander Knox's Provost, listen as Charley reads out a paper on sexual intercourse among students. Earlier, Stephen had hypocritically warned William that he "won't countenance male lust against any of my female students." But the subsequent boating scene in which Stephen finds himself pressed up close and personal against Anna within the narrow confines of a punt makes his feelings abundantly plain. Losey dwells on Anna's legs as John Dankworth's languid sax and harp accompaniment accompanies the plangent ripples, the elegant swan and William's distinctly phallic thrusts of the punt pole into the riverbed beneath. Embarrassed and bewildered by this close proximity with the object of his desires, Stephen folds his arms as Losey shows us lovers embracing on the riverbank. He even films Stephen and Anna from between William's legs. As a montage of "that obscure object of desire," not even Buñuel could have done better. As if to parody the wet dream that Stephen is having, he promptly falls into the river—an accident that presages the fatal car accident to come.

Stephen complains of feeling old—that his muscles are no longer in control, hence his tumble, but William, who represents the youth Stephen laments loosing, attempts to reassure him: "I wouldn't say you looked old. I'd say you still have a pretty good figure." That he casts this judgment while the bare-chested Stephen is changing his wet clothes in his college rooms, suggests how easily this film could be a drama about a gay attraction rather than a straight one. The brilliant images by which Losey symbolizes the film's emotional undercurrents could easily apply to either; the steaming kettle that is about to boil over, the hands that nearly touch while resting on a gate when Stephen and Anna go for a walk together after Sunday lunch, not to mention the car crash itself.

On the night before that tragedy, Stephen has attended an upper crust reception with William. It was filmed at Syon House with its full-size spectacular reproduction of that epitome of Classical male beauty, the Apollo Belvedere. Johann Joachim Winckelmann described this statue as having smooth muscles "like molten glass blown into scarce visible waves,"[19] the homosexual implication of which is made clear by his belief that "supreme beauty is rather male than female."[20] It is between both the Apollo and the equally masculine bronze of the Dying Gaul at the other end of the hall, that the young men, dressed in bow ties and dress shirts, play a rough-and-tumble game much like rugby. Bogarde's Stephen looks as dismayed as he would have done on the school playing field when William tells him he has to defend the goal: "Only the old men watch—and the ladies," he adds, when Stephen demurs. And indeed, Losey shows us two young debutantes enjoying from the sidelines the erotic rough and tumble of this unruly scrum, which ends with Stephen wrestling with William—another opportunity for the story to reach the same destination by means of an alternative route, so to speak. "He really is a magnificent athlete, that boy," says the Provost in the later cricket match, at which Bogarde looks equally out of place, though this time bored rather than terrified.

The film's most drastic departure from the novel is truly shocking: Stephen, having rescued Anna from the wreckage of the accident, still smarting from his humiliations and failure to have her, takes this opportunity to rape her. David Caute usefully included the critic Raymond Durgnat's opinion of Stephen as "a 'can't quite' man": He "can't quite declare himself to Anna, he can't quite get Charley's TV job, he can't quite be honest, and in a fury of despair he concludes with a near-rape."[21] "It won't be 90 minutes of Doris Day," Bogarde confided to film critic Dilys Powell. There is, of course, nothing gay about the near rape of a female student by a middle-aged don, but the sense of desperation would have applied even more if William had been Stephen's real object of desire.

Conclusion

Towards the very end of his performing career, Bogarde appeared in two television films, which again addressed the subject of homosexuality. The first, screened in 1986, was Bogarde's own adaptation of Graham Greene's comedy of manners *May We Borrow Your Husband?*, in which Bogarde plays an author who observes two gay interior decorators seduce the husband of newlywed bride Charlotte Attenborough. Bogarde falls in love with her despite one of the decorators (David Yelland) suggesting that he knows full well that Bogarde's character is as gay as he is. This, beyond what Tanitch describes as a raised eyebrow, was far as Bogarde was willing to take his character, but the moment is telling and clearly intended as one of the many lines he had always asked the curious to read between. The idea of appearing in an adaptation of this story had been proposed before by Losey because of its thematic continuity with *The Servant,* and it was, in Coldstream's words, "precisely *because* of those echoes"[1] that Bogarde wasn't interested at the time; but in the end it was Bogarde's nephew, Brock, who persuaded him, introducing him to the director Bob Mahoney, who offered Bogarde the alluring incentive of writing the screenplay himself.

The other TV drama, screened two years later, was *The Vision,* directed by Norman Stone. Bogarde played a celebrated television presenter, James Marriner ("Gentle Jim"), who finds himself being seduced by a right-wing evangelical Christian played by Lee Remick. Her evangelical "People's Channel" goes against everything in which the genial and liberal Gentle Jim had previously believed. Jim is tempted, because his career has sunk to the low level of appearing in margarine commercials, which strangely echoes the humiliating conversation Bogarde reports in *Cleared for Take-Off,* between himself and a newspaper journalist, whose opening gambit was, "I suppose things must be *difficult* for you now? Working for the BBC. You *must* be broke? They don't pay a fortune, do they? And *no* car? Have you a car in dirty old London? … No car! … We have come down in the world!"[2] The story of *The Vision* is prescient of fake news, cultish commercialism, and all the sin-

168

ister media manipulation of Donald Trump and Rupert Murdoch in the twenty-first century. Lee Remick plays Grace Gardner, the wonderfully hate-able, power-dressed head of "The People's Channel." This is the satellite TV organ of a right-wing evangelical organization called "The Vision," which aims to prepare the world for a Third World War, out of the ruins of which it will gain control of the entire world. It does this by subliminal brainwashing: dumbing down, BBC-bashing and the erosion of democracy and freedom by capitalism masquerading as "family values,"

To help sell their message, the channel hires Bogarde's James Marriner, a faded TV presenter from a more liberal age, whose essential decency is to sugarcoat the bitter pill of "The Vision"'s agenda. Grace immediately identifies in Jim what so many had identified before in Bogarde: "professional vulner-ability." "You have so much charm," she continues. Her own charm is some-what steelier. In fact, having played the mother of Damien Thorn in *The Omen*, Lee Remick had had ample opportunities to observe what playing an Antichrist required, and this is largely her role here. Several of Jim's lines also have a telling resonance: "People think sex is the only temptation, the only betrayal," he says, "but there are others." To his daughter, played by Helena Bonham-Carter, he confesses, "There are some things I don't do very well." "Like being a husband?" the daughter suggests.

Jim's wife (Eileen Atkins) observes, "You're like a child, aren't you? You think nobody hurts until you feel the pain." The pain is caused by "The Vision's" exposure of the affair Jim has been having with another woman. Grace uses this in an attempt to control the man she wants to promote her new network, but Jim insists on resigning, only realizing what kind of organization he has joined when it's too late. Bogarde knew all about Jim's fear of scandal, even though Jim's was of the heterosexual variety, and the shots of him sitting on his own, desperately unhappy and isolated, are just how one imagines Bogarde in his London flat after the death of Forwood. ("The air was still," Bogarde wrote in *A Short Walk from Harrods*. "Dense as fluff. I could hear the cistern filling up in one of the bathrooms. [...] I was short of everything. Direction mainly. What on earth to do? It was the suitcase metaphor again. Pieces scat-tered everywhere, bits lying around. Unconnected. Unfamiliar suddenly. And I had not the least notion of how to start repacking."[3])

While homosexual resonance was kept at bay in this production, it does appear during one of the best scenes: Jim's wife invites the waiting press inside the family home and spins them a lurid story to outdo (and expose) the crass-ness of the headlines already printed:

> This isn't easy for me, but now the whole horrible business has come out into the open, I think it's time that the real truth is told. I knew there was something wrong when

life—our married life—came to an end. That sort of thing happens. I suppose I thought there might be a girlfriend tucked away somewhere, but it wasn't a girlfriend. There never was a girl friend. [...] Jim met him in a bar in East Berlin. He's an East German. He's some sort of policeman.

The journalist asks, "Mrs. Marriner, if I've got this right, you're telling us your husband is a secret homosexual who is having an affair with a Communist spy? Forgive me, but are you having us on?" In fact, regarding Bogarde, this wasn't so far from the truth. Bogarde had never had an affair with a German spy, but the possibility had, after all, been floated by the man from MI5 (if we are to believe Bogarde's account).

"You mean you can tell the difference between truth and lies?" Jim's wife replies. "And you prefer the truth to the lies? [...] I had no idea. I thought you just wanted a story."

"We do like it to be true as well," the journalist smiles.

"Then what's all this doing in the papers, then?" she spits, shaking the newspaper in front of him. "Just doing your job, are you? Just obeying orders. [...] Dirt and lies and broken lives."

Appropriately, this journalist, while besieging Jim's house outside, had been reading one of the titles in the *Dennis Wheatley Library of the Occult*, suggesting a taste for the lurid and sensational, but also subliminally enforcing the Satanic, cultish mood of this story as a whole, in which the channel's president is depicted as a white-suited Aleister Crowley figure (played by Bruce Boa). The People's Channel also holds sinister prayer meetings, during which all the entire staff members bow their heads. Grace presides at a presidential lectern, in a manner that now seems chillingly prescient of Donald Trump's equally evangelical, right-wing administration in the U.S. (Prayer meetings accompanied Trump's election campaign.) The idea of a Satanic organization masquerading as evangelical Christians had already been exploited by Hammer in the company's very free adaptation of Wheatley's *To the Devil ... A Daughter* (dir. Peter Sykes, 1976). But in the case of *The Vision*, the emphasis is on the power of television rather than telepathy. "We're going to rebuild the will of a continent. With television," Grace says. "In America, it is television that can forge the will of the people."

"You believe it's been prophesied!" Jim realizes. "The End Time. The Last Battle. Armageddon!" Thus are further links with the *Omen* films forged, in particular *Omen III: The Final Conflict* (dir. Graham Baker, 1981), where much the same agenda is explored in more traditionally genre-specific parameters. Jim's last-ditch attempt to expose The Vision for what it is fails. Thinking he's speaking live, he finds out that his act of sabotage has been anticipated, and it wasn't live after all:

The People's Channel is a front. There's some kind of movement behind it. It's called "The Vision." I don't know what's going on, but it's bigger than television. It's about politics. It's about elections. I don't know how they do it. They use information—not just here but from all over Europe. They're getting us ready for war. It's *about* war.... This network will lie to you. First they'll give you what you want, then they'll give you what *they* want, and by that time it will be too late.

The Vision anticipated the erosion of Western liberalism and democracy, which we now see all too disturbingly in today's increasingly right-wing and almost terminally capitalistic convulsions, and one of the freedoms so hard-won, which is now once again so vulnerable to attack by this authoritarian agenda, is gay rights. The Vision's emphasis on "family values" would surely have included homophobia as well. The battle against prejudice obviously still has a long way to go. Homosexuals are still very much the object of hate crimes, legislation and "aversion therapy." We live in a world where it is still possible in some countries to have your hand chopped off merely for being homosexual. Gay people are still mocked and made fun of, they are still bullied and discriminated against. The situation in Britain and America has immensely improved since the 1950s, but vigilance is still required. Until we stop identifying people as "gay people" rather than simply "people," as Quentin Crisp argued, it always will be.

So what relevance has Bogarde and his films to the contemporary world? As we hurtle ever more recklessly towards a fractured and populist society, bringing in its wake a concomitant resurgence of right-wing ideology, Bogarde's films, *Victim* in particular, far from seeming old-fashioned, might come to be seen as increasingly bold and challenging. It is a curious irony that gay freedoms should be so indebted to a film star who never openly admitted to being gay; but, as Bogarde explained, the space between the lines contains the secret. In fact, the power of the message is increased fourfold by its understatement, which prevents the danger of being counterproductive, as in the case of Liberace and the "Cassandra" scandal. Bogarde's quiet championing of his identity is an advantage to the ultimate aim of integration and acceptance. To be gay is to be different from straight, certainly, but it should be so in no more socially significant manner than in being blue—rather than brown-eyed. If we can ignore the color of a person's eyes, we should be able to ignore the color of their skin and the nature of their sexuality, while simultaneously celebrating the qualities and diversity these bring.

As I have attempted to explain, gayness is present throughout all of Bogarde's performances, even if only by its significant omission. Like a pink thread, it weaves its way through a variety of roles, which were always, in the final analysis, aspects of Bogarde's own personality. He was that kind of actor.

The parts he took became him, rather than the other way around, despite his feeling of "possession." He possessed the roles, and by so doing, he found a way to explore a personality he was reluctant to reveal otherwise, but surely only because of the way in which the times and moral structures in which he lived had dictated. The result was very possibly as exhilarating for him as it was for me watching him. For that, he has my endless gratitude and admiration.

Filmography

Year	Film	Role	Director
1939	*Carry On George*	Extra	Anthony Kimmins
1947	*Dancing with Crime*	Policeman	John Paddy Carstairs
1948	*Esther Waters*	William Latch	Ian Dalrymple & Peter Proud
	Quartet	George Bland	Harold French
	Once a Jolly Swagman	Bill Fox	Jack Lee
1949	*Dear Mr. Prohack*	Charles Prohack	Thornton Freeland
	Boys in Brown	Alfie Rawlings	Montgomery Tully
1950	*The Blue Lamp*	Tom Riley	Basil Dearden
	So Long at the Fair	George Hathaway	Terence Fisher and Anthony Darnborough
	The Woman in Question	Bob Baker	Anthony Asquith
1951	*Blackmailed*	Stephen Mundy	Marc Allegret
1952	*Hunted*	Chris Lloyd	Charles Crichton
	Penny Princess	Tony Craig	Val Guest
	The Gentle Gunman	Matt	Basil Dearden
1953	*Appointment in London*	Wing Commander Tim Mason	Philip Leacock
	Desperate Moment	Simon van Halder	Compton Bennett
1954	*They Who Dare*	Lt. Graham	Lewis Milestone
	Doctor in the House	Simon Sparrow	Compton Bennett
	The Sleeping Tiger	Frank Clements	Joseph Losey
	For Better for Worse	Tony Howard	J. Lee Thompson
	The Sea Shall Not Have Them	Flight Sgt. Mackay	Lewis Gilbert
1955	*Simba*	Alan Howard	Brian Desmond Hurst
	Doctor at Sea	Dr. Simon Sparrow	Ralph Thomas
	Cast a Dark Shadow	Edward Bare	Lewis Gilbert
1956	*The Spanish Gardener*	José	Philip Leacock
1957	*Ill Met by Moonlight*	Major Patrick Leigh Fermor	Michael Powell & Emeric Pressburger
	Doctor at Large	Dr. Simon Sparrow	Ralph Thomas
	Campbell's Kingdom	Bruce Campbell	Ralph Thomas
1958	*A Tale of Two Cities*	Sydney Carton	Ralph Thomas
	The Wind Cannot Read	Flight Lt. Michael Quinn	Ralph Thomas
1959	*The Doctor's Dilemma*	Louis Dubedat	Anthony Asquith
	Libel	Sir Mark Lodden/Frank Welney/Number Fifteen	Anthony Asquith
1960	*Song Without End*	Franz Liszt	Charles Vidor & George Cukor

Year	Film	Role	Director
1961	*The Singer Not the Song*	Anacleto	Roy Baker
	The Angel Wore Red	Arturo Carrera	Nunnally Johnson
	Victim	Melville Farr	Basil Dearden
1962	*H.M.S. Defiant*	Lt. Scott-Padget	Lewis Gilbert
	The Password Is Courage	Sergeant-Major Charles Coward	Andrew L. Stone
	We Joined the Navy	Dr. Simon Sparrow	Wendy Toye
1963	*The Mind Benders*	Dr. Henry Longman	Basil Dearden
	I Could Go on Singing	David Donne	Ronald Neame
	Doctor in Distress	Dr. Simon Sparrow	Ralph Thomas
	The Servant	Barrett	Joseph Losey
1964	*Hot Enough for June*	Nicholas Whistler	Ralph Thomas
	King & Country	Capt. Hargreaves	Joseph Losey
1965	*The High Bright Sun*	Major McGuire	Ralph Thomas
	Darling	Robert Gold	John Schlesinger
1966	*Modesty Blaise*	Gabriel	Joseph Losey
1967	*Accident*	Stephen	Joseph Losey
	Our Mother's House	Charlie Hook	Jack Clayton
1968	*Sebastian*	Sebastian	David Greene
1969	*The Fixer*	Bibikov	John Frankenheimer
	Justine	Pursewarden	George Cukor
	Oh! What a Lovely War	Stephen Attenborough	Richard
	Return to Lochabar	Commentary	Don Kelly
1970	*The Damned*	Friedrich Bruckmann	Luchino Visconti
1971	*Death in Venice*	Gustav von Aschenbach	Luchino Visconti
1974	*The Serpent*	Philip Boyle	Henri Verneuil
	The Night Porter	Max	Liliana Cavani
1975	*Permission to Kill*	Alan Curtis	Cyril Frankel
1975	*Providence*	Claud Langham	Alain Resnais
1977	*A Bridge Too Far*	Lt Gen. Browning	Richard Attenborough
1978	*Despair*	Hermann Fassbinder	Rainer Werner
1990	*Daddy Nostalgie*	Daddy	Bertrand Tavernier

Year	Television	Role	Director
1947	*Rope*	Charles Granillo	Stephen Harrison
	Power Without Glory	Cliff	Joel O'Brien
	The Case of Helvig Delbo	Underground Man	Robert Barr
1965	*Blithe Spirit*	Charles	George Schaeffer
	The Epic That Never Was	Commentary	Bill Duncan
1966	*Little Moon of Alban*	George Schaeffer	
1969	*Upon This Rock*	Bonnie	Stanley Abrams
1981	*The Patricia Neal Story*	Roald Dahl	Anthony Hervey & Anthony Page
1986	*May We Borrow Your Husband?*	William	Bob Mahoney
1988	*The Vision*	James Marriner	Norman Stone

Chapter Notes

Introduction

1. John Coldstream, *Dirk Bogarde—The Authorized Biography* (London: Weidenfeld & Nicolson, 2004), 13.
2. *Dirk Bogarde—Above the Title* (Yorkshire Television, dir. Nick Gray, 1986).
3. Dirk Bogarde, *A Particular Friendship* (London: Penguin Viking, 1989), 55.
4. *Dirk Bogarde—Above the Title* (dir. Nick Gray, 1986).
5. Bogarde, *A Particular Friendship*, 2.
6. *Desert Island Discs* (BBC Radio 4), first broadcast 24 October 1993.
7. Coldstream, *Dirk Bogarde*, 278.
8. *Last Laugh in Vegas*, Episode 3 (ITV, dir. Iain Thompson, 2018).
9. *Dirk Bogarde—Above the Title* (Yorkshire Television, dir. Nick Gray, 1986).
10. John Ruskin, *Sesame and Lilies* (London: George Allen, 1902), 164.
11. Dirk Bogarde, *An Orderly Man* (London: Chatto & Windus/The Hogarth Press, 1983), 1.
12. Antony Easthope, *What a Man's Gotta Do—The Masculine Myth in Popular Culture* (London: Palladin/Grafton Books, 1986), 96–97.
13. *Ibid.*, 39–40.
14. *Ibid.*, 166.
15. *Dirk Bogarde—Above the Title* (Yorkshire Television, dir. Nick Gray, 1986).
16. Robert Tanitch, *Dirk Bogarde—The Complete Career Illustrated* (London: Ebury Press, 1988), 6.
17. *Dirk Bogarde—By Myself* (Lucinda Production, dir. Paul Joyce, 1992).
18. Bogarde, *A Particular Friendship*, 22.

Chapter One

1. Boze Hadleigh, *The Lavender Screen: The Gay and Lesbian Films—Their Stars, Makers,* *Characters, and Critics* (rev. ed.) (New York: Citadel Press, 2001), 23.
2. H. Montgomery Hyde (ed.), *Notable British Trials—The Trials of Oscar Wilde* (London: William Hodge, 1948), 236.
3. Colin Wilson, *The Outsider* (London: Victor Gollancz, 1956), 58–59.
4. *Ibid.*, 59.
5. Hermann Hesse, *Steppanwolf* (Harmondsworth: Penguin, 1965), 54.
6. Christopher Lee, *Tall, Dark and Gruesome* (London: Victor Gollancz, 1997), 189.
7. Carlos Clarens, *Horror Movies—An Illustrated Survey* (London: Secker & Warburg, 1967), 11.
8. *Ibid.*, 14.
9. Gary D. Rhodes, *Tod Browning's Dracula* (Sheffield: Tomahawk Press, 2014), 163.
10. Ellis Hanson, *Out Takes: Essays on Queer Theory and Film* (Durham: Duke University Press, 1999), 198–199.
11. Dirk Bogarde, *A Short Walk from Harrods* (London: Penguin Viking, 1993), 271.
12. Dirk Bogarde, *Cleared for Take-Off* (London: Penguin Viking, 1995), 156.
13. John Coldstream, *Dirk Bogarde—A Biography* (London: Weidenfeld & Nicolson, 2004), 543.
14. Bogarde, *Cleared for Take-Off*, 166.

Chapter Two

1. Virginia Woolf (ed. Anne Oliver Bell), *A Moment's Liberty—The Shorter Diary of Virginia Woolf* (London: The Hogarth Press, 1990), 451–452 (Entry for Thursday, 30 March 1939).
2. Hugh Walpole, *Four Fantastic Tales* (London: Macmillan, 1932), 516–518 ("The Prelude to Adventure").
3. Hugh Walpole, *Rogue Herries* (London: Macmillan, 1935), 29.

4. Hugh Walpole, *Wintersmoon* (London: Macmillan, 1933), 135.

5. *Arena:* "The Private Dirk Bogarde" (BBC, dir. Adam Low, 2001).

6. Humphrey Carpenter, *Benjamin Britten—A Biography* (London: Faber & Faber, 1992), 578.

7. John Coldstream, *Dirk Bogarde—The Authorized Biography* (London: Weidenfeld & Nicolson, 2004), 511.

8. *Ibid.*, 207.

9. Carpenter, *Benjamin Britten*, 80.

10. Coldstream, *Dirk Bogarde*, 325.

11. *Ibid.*, 194.

12. *Ibid.*, 220.

13. Carpenter, *Benjamin Britten*, 366–367.

14. *Ibid.*, 98.

15. Coldstream, *Dirk Bogarde*, 491.

16. *Ibid.*, 498.

17. Michael Kennedy, *The Dent Master Musicians—Britten* (London: Dent, 1993), 59.

18. Coldstream, *Dirk Bogarde*, 342.

19. *Ibid.*, 294.

20. *Ibid.*, 462.

21. *Ibid.*, 429.

22. Frederic Raphael, *Somerset Maugham and His World* (London: Thames and Hudson, 1976), 45.

23. Rupert Hart-Davies, *Hugh Walpole—A Biography* (London: Macmillan, 1952), 311.

24. Raphael, *Somerset Maugham*, 56.

25. Coldstream, *Dirk Bogarde*, 317.

26. Raphael, *Somerset Maugham*, 94.

27. Coldstream, *Dirk Bogarde*, 531.

28. Dirk Bogarde, *For the Time Being* (London: Penguin Viking, 1998), 64.

29. Dirk Bogarde, *A Short Walk from Harrod's* (London: Penguin Viking, 1993), 236.

Chapter Three

1. *Dirk Bogarde—By Myself* (Lucinda Productions, dir. Paul Joyce, 1992).

2. Christine Geraghty, *British Cinema in the Fifties—Gender, Genre and the "New Look"* (London: Routledge, 2000), 124.

3. *Ibid.*

4. Dirk Bogarde, *Snakes and Ladders* (London: Chatto & Windus, 1978), 252.

5. *Ibid.*, 125.

6. Thomas Mann, "Tonio Kröger" in *Stories of Three Decades*, 85–132 (London: Martin Secker & Warburg, 1946), 105.

7. John Coldstream, *Dirk Bogarde—The Authorized Biography* (London: Weidenfeld & Nicolson, 2004), 183.

8. *Ibid.*, 181.

9. Samuel Taylor Coleridge (ed. Stephen Potter), *Select Poetry & Prose* (London: Nonesuch Press, 1971), 388.

10. Robert Tanitch, *Dirk Bogarde—The Complete Career Illustrated* (London: Ebury Press, 1988), 27.

11. Sigmund Freud (trans. James Strachey), *The Interpretation of Dreams* (Harmondsworth: Penguin, 1983), 364–365.

12. Bogarde, *Snakes and Ladders*, 223.

13. David Caute, *Joseph Losey—A Revenge on Life* (London: Faber and Faber, 1994), 121.

14. Coldstream, *Dirk Bogarde*, 323.

15. Laurence Schifano, *Luchino Visconti—The Flames of Passion* (London: Collins, 1990), 370.

16. *Ibid.*, 371.

17. *Ibid.*, 373.

18. *Ibid.*, 327.

19. Richard Davenport-Hines, *Gothic—Four Hundred Years of Excess, Horror, Evil and Ruin* (London: Fourth Estate, 1998), 8.

20. Dirk Bogarde, *An Orderly Man* (London: Chatto & Windus/The Hogarth Press, 1983), 164–165.

21. Michael Burleigh, *The Third Reich: A New History* (New York: Farrar, Straus and Giroux, 2001), 192.

22. Susan Sontag "Fascinating Fascism" in *The Nazification of Art—Art, Design, Music, Architecture & Film in the Third Reich*, ed. Brandon Taylor and Wilfried van der Will, 204–218 (Winchester: The Winchester Press, 1990), 216.

23. Adolf Hitler (trans. Ralph Manheim), *Mein Kampf* (London: Hutchinson, 1980), 432.

24. Sontag: "Fascinating Fascism" in *The Nazification of Art*, ed. Taylor & van der Will, 217.

25. *Ibid.*, 217–218.

26. Bogarde, *An Orderly Man*, 171.

27. Thomas Carlyle, *Sartor Resartus* (London: Dent, 1940), 45–46.

28. Sontag: "Fascinating Fascism" in *The Nazification of Art*, ed. Taylor & van der Will, 217.

29. http://www.theobtusegoose.co.uk/men-crossing-their-legs-definitely-still-gay/.

30. Tanitch, *Dirk Bogarde*, 170.

31. Bogarde, *An Orderly Man*, 187.

32. Oscar Wilde, "The Picture of Dorian Gray" in *Complete Works of Oscar Wilde*, with an introduction by Vivian Holland, 17–167 (London: Collins, 1977), 17.

33. The Marquis de Sade (trans. Meredith X), *Philosophy in the Boudoir* (London: Creation Books, 1995), 79–80.

34. Friedrich Nietzsche (trans. Josefine

Nauckhoff), *The Gay Science* (Cambridge: Cambridge University Press, 2001), 110.

35. Lothar Machtan (trans. John Brownjohn), *The Hidden Hitler* (Oxford: The Perseus Press, 2001), 321.

36. Peter Conradi, *Hitler's Piano Player—The Rise and Fall of Ernst Hanfstaengl, Confidant of Hitler, Ally of FDR* (London: Duckworth, 2006), 73.

37. *Ibid.*, 264.

38. Antony Easthope, *What a Man's Gotta Do—The Masculine Myth in Popular Culture* (London: Palladin/Grafton Books, 1986), 107.

39. Bogarde, *An Orderly Man*, 183.

40. *Ibid.*, 190.

Chapter Four

1. *Dirk Bogarde—Above the Title* (Yorkshire Television, dir. Nick Gray, 1986).

2. A. A. Gill, *A A Gill Is Away* (New York: Simon & Schuster, 2007), 283.

3. Anatole France (trans. Alfred Allinson), *The Merrie Tales of Jacques Tournebroche* (London: John Lane, 1910), 114.

4. Rainer Maria Rilke (trans. Stanley Appelbaum), "Der Knabe" in *Selected Poems* (New York: Dover, 2011), 50–51.

5. John Buchan, "Greenmantle" in *The Four Adventures of Richard Hannay*, with an introduction by Robin W. Winks, 81–254 (Boston: David R. Godine, 1988), 129.

6. Dennis Wheatley, *The Satanist* (London: Heron, 1972), 64.

7. T. E. Lawrence, *Seven Pillars of Wisdom* (London: Penguin, 2000), 23.

8. *Ibid.*, 28.

9. Michael Herr, *Dispatches* (London: Pan Macmillan, 1978), 135.

10. *Ibid.*, 159.

11. Anthony Swofford, *Jarhead: A Marine's Chronicle of the Gulf War and Other Battles* (New York: Scribner, 2003), 6–7.

12. Modris Eksteins, *Rites of Spring—The Great War and the Birth of the Modern Age* (London: Papermac, 2000), 91.

13. Quentin Crisp, *The Naked Civil Servant*, (London: Penguin, 2006), 98.

14. *Dirk Bogarde—Above the Title* (Yorkshire Television, dir. Nick Gray, 1986).

15. *Afternoon Plus* (Thames Television, 1981).

16. John Coldstream, *Dirk Bogarde—The Authorized Biography* (London: Weidenfeld & Nicolson, 2004), 91–92.

17. *Ibid.*, 122.

18. *Ibid.*, 122–123.

19. *Dirk Bogarde—By Myself* (Lucinda Productions, dir. Paul Joyce, 1992).

20. Martin Esslin, *The Age of Television* (London: Routledge, 2017), 30.

21. Adam Nicolson, *The Mighty Dead—Why Homer Matters* (London: William Collins, 2014), 136–137

22. Antony Easthope, *What a Man's Gotta Do—The Masculine Myth in Popular Culture* (London: Palladin/Grafton Books, 1986), 66.

23. *Ibid.*

24. Peter Adam, *The Arts of the Third Reich* (London: Thames and Hudson, 1992), 203.

25. Robert Tanitch, *Dirk Bogarde—The Complete Career Illustrated* (London: Ebury Press, 1988), 131.

26. Christine Geraghty, *British Cinema in the Fifties—Gender, Genre and the "New Look"* (London: Routledge, 2000), 123.

27. Tanitch, *Dirk Bogarde*, 131.

28. *Daily Telegraph* (London), 4 January 2014, https://www.telegraph.co.uk/news/10548303/Michael-Gove-criticises-Blackadder-myths-about-First-World-War.html.

29. Coldstream, *Dirk Bogarde*, 395.

30. Tanitch, *Dirk Bogarde*, 178.

31. Coldstream, *Dirk Bogarde*, 395.

32. *Ibid.*, 397–398.

33. *Ibid.* 399.

34. *Ibid.*, 401.

35. Herr, *Dispatches*, 62.

36. *Ibid.*, 198.

37. *Ibid.*, 73.

38. Edmund Burke, *A Philosophical Enquiry into the Origin of Our Ideas of the Sublime and Beautiful* (Oxford: Oxford University Press, 1990), 35.

39. *Ibid.*, 36–37.

40. *Hammer—The Studio that Dripped Blood* (BBC, dir. David Thompson, 1987).

41. Geraghty, *British Cinema in the Fifties*, 122.

42. *Ibid.*, 124.

43. Tanitch, *Dirk Bogarde*, 74.

Chapter Five

1. *Man Alive:* "Consenting Adults: The Men" (BBC, prod. Tom Conway, 1967).

2. *Dirk Bogarde—Above the Title* (Yorkshire Television, dir. Nick Gray, 1986).

3. *Arena:* "The Private Life of Dirk Bogarde" (BBC, dir. Adam Low, 2001).

4. *Dirk Bogarde—Above the Title* (dir. Nick Gray, 1986).

5. "Cassandra," "Crying All the Way to the Bank…," *Daily Mirror*, 26 September 1956.

6. Quentin Crisp, *The Naked Civil Servant* (London: Penguin, 2006), 87.

7. *Dirk Bogarde—By Myself* (Lucinda Productions, dir. Paul Joyce, 1992).

8. *Afternoon Plus* (Thames Television, 1981) https://ru-clip.net/video/i1kT9RZi-ZU/dirk-bogarde-interview-thames-tv-1981.html.

9. Coldstream, *Dirk Bogarde*, 545–546.

10. Crisp, *The Naked Civil Servant*, 19.

11. Geoffrey Gorer, *The Life and Ideas of The Marquis de Sade* (London: Peter Owen, 1962), 162.

12. Interview between Bernard Braden and Quentin Crisp. https://www.youtube.com/watch?v=HFPqDUQKmt8.

13. Crisp, *The Naked Civil Servant*, 153.

14. Coldstream, *Dirk Bogarde*, 12.

15. Crisp, *The Naked Civil Servant*, 83.

16. Christine Geraghty, *British Cinema in the Fifties—Gender, Genre and the "New Look"* (London: Routledge, 2000), 143–144.

17. Dirk Bogarde, *A Postillion Struck by Lightning* (London: Chatto & Windus, 1977), 160.

18. Robert Murphy, *Sixties British Cinema* (London: British Film Institute, 1992), 39.

19. Coldstream, *Dirk Bogarde*, 271.

20. Dirk Bogarde, *Snakes and Ladders* (London: Chatto & Windus, 1978), 202.

21. Coldstream, *Dirk Bogarde*, 271.

22. *Ibid.*, 272.

23. Gordon Burn, "Ghoul of the Month" *Sunday Times Magazine*, 14 August 1977, 39.

24. *Cutting Room Floor: Veronica Carlson 2* (Diabolique Films, 2017), https://www.youtube.com/watch?v=ydYvORVXppI.

25. Coldstream, *Dirk Bogarde*, 272.

26. Bogarde, *Snakes and Ladders*, 202.

27. Crisp, *The Naked Civil Servant*, 80.

28. *Dirk Bogarde—By Myself* (dir. Paul Joyce, 1992).

29. Coldstream, *Dirk Bogarde*, 281.

30. *Ibid.*, 293.

31. *Ibid.*, 294.

32. David Caute, *Joseph Losey—A Revenge on Life* (London: Faber and Faber, 1994), 7.

33. John Lash, *Twins and the Double* (London: Thames and Hudson, 1993), 17.

34. Bram Stoker, *Dracula* (London: Constable, 1904), 18.

35. *Ibid.*, 28.

36. *Ibid.*, 315.

37. *Ibid.*, 40.

38. Edmund White, "Nabokov's 'great gay comic novel,'" in *The Times Literary Supplement*, 3 August 2016, https://www.the-tls.co.uk/articles/public/80834/.

39. Robert Tanitch, *Dirk Bogarde—The Complete Career Illustrated* (London: Ebury Press, 1988), 119.

40. Coldstream, *Dirk Bogarde*, 332.

41. *Ibid.*, 334.

42. Vladimir Nabukov, *Despair* (London: Panther, 1969), 70.

43. *Ibid.*, 73.

44. *Ibid.*, 155.

45. Dirk Bogarde, *An Orderly Man* (London: Chatto & Windus, 1983), 261–262.

46. Lev Grossman, "The gay Nabokov," in *Salon*, San Francisco, 17 May 2000, https://www.salon.com/2000/05/17/nabokov_5/.

47. Wladimir Troubetzkoy, "Vladimir Nabukov's *Despair*: The Reader as April Fool," http://revel.unice.fr/cycnos/index.html?id=1451.

Chapter Six

1. Susan Sontag, "Notes on Camp," 275–292, in *Against Interpretation* (London: Vintage, 1994), 284.

2. *Ibid.*, 280.

3. *Ibid.*, 288.

4. *Ibid.*, 279.

5. *Ibid.*, 280.

6. *Ibid.*, 277.

7. *Ibid.*, 288.

8. *Ibid.*, 290.

9. David Caute, *Joseph Losey—A Revenge on Life* (London: Faber and Faber, 1994), 209.

10. *Ibid.*, 211.

11. Laurence Durrell, *The Alexandria Quartet* (London: Faber and Faber, 1972), 210.

12. Robert Tanitch, *Dirk Bogarde—The Complete Career Illustrated* (London: Ebury Press), 1988, 154.

13. Durrell, *The Alexandria Quartet*, 343.

14. *Ibid.*, 344.

15. Laurence Durrell, "Vampire in Venice" in *A Clutch of Vampires*, ed. Raymond T. McNally, 195–199 (Greenwich, CT: New York Graphic Society, 1974), 196.

16. Durrell, *The Alexandria Quartet*, 208.

17. *Dirk Bogarde—Above the Title* (Yorkshire Television, dir. Nick Gray, 1986).

18. Tanitch, *Dirk Bogarde*, 174.

19. John Coldstream, *Dirk Bogarde*, 321.

Chapter Seven

1. Dirk Bogarde, *Snakes and Ladders* (London: Chatto & Windus, 1978), 221.

2. Robert Tanitch, *Dirk Bogarde—The Com-*

plete Career Illustrated (London: Ebury Press), 1988, 113.

3. Anthony Burgess, *A Clockwork Orange* (Harmondsworth: Penguin, 1971), 92.

4. A.C. Benson, "Basil Netherby" in *The Temple of Death—The Ghost Stories of A.C. & R.C. Benson*, 105–128 (Ware: Wordsworth Editions, 2007), 112.

5. *Dirk Bogarde—Above the Title* (Yorkshire Television, dir. Nick Gray, 1986).

6. Dirk Bogarde, *A Short Walk from Harrods* (London: Penguin Viking, 1993), 209–210.

7. John Coldstream, *Dirk Bogarde—The Authorized Biography* (London: Weidenfeld & Nicolson, 2004), 499.

8. Dirk Bogarde, *Cleared for Take-Off* (London: Penguin Viking, 1995), 87.

9. *Ibid.*, 88.

10. *Ibid.*, 90.

11. Coldstream, *Dirk Bogarde*, 5.

12. Tanitch, *Dirk Bogarde*, 166.

13. Bogarde, *Snakes and Ladders*, 300.

14. Tanitch, *Dirk Bogarde*, 166.

15. *Ibid.*

Chapter Eight

1. *The Bible*, "Ruth" 1:66–67.

2. W. Somerset Maugham, "The Alien Corn" in *The World Over—The Collected Stories*, vol. 1, 399–432 (London: The Reprint Society/Heinemann, 1954), 418.

3. *Ibid.*, 420.

4. *Ibid.*, 429.

5. *Ibid.*

6. George Bernard Shaw, "The Doctor's Dilemma" in *The Complete Plays of Bernard Shaw*, 503–546 (London: Odhams Press, no date), 526.

7. *Ibid.*, 540.

8. Richard Wagner (trans. William Ashton Ellis), "An End in Paris" in *Pilgrimage to Beethoven and Other Essays*, 46–68 (Lincoln: University of Nebraska Press, 1994), 66.

9. Shaw, "The Doctor's Dilemma" in *The Complete Plays*, 545.

10. *Ibid.*, 517.

11. *Ibid.*, 530.

12. John Coldstream, *Dirk Bogarde—The Authorized Biography* (London: Weidenfeld & Nicolson, 2004), 240.

13. Bogarde, *Snakes and Ladders*, 182.

14. *Ibid.*, 183.

15. Harold Schonberg, *The Great Pianists* (London: Victor Gollancz, 1964), 126.

16. Alan Walker, *Franz Liszt—The Weimar*

Years 1848–1861 (London: Faber and Faber, 1989), 27.

17. Bogarde, *Snakes and Ladders*, 260.

18. *Ibid.*, 255.

19. *Ibid.*, 194.

20. *Ibid.*, 201.

21. Coldstream, *Dirk Bogarde*, 266.

22. *Ibid.*, 490.

23. Robert Tanitch, *Dirk Bogarde—The Complete Career Illustrated* (London: Ebury Press), 1988, 95.

Chapter Nine

1. Dirk Bogarde, *Snakes and Ladders* (London: Chatto & Windus, 1978), 309.

2. *Ibid.*, 311.

3. Thomas Mann (trans. Richard and Clara Winston), *Thomas Mann Diaries 1918–1939* (London: Robert Clark, 1985), 7.

4. *Ibid.*, 42.

5. *Ibid.*, 100.

6. *Ibid.*, 101.

7. *Ibid.*

8. Ronald Hayman, *Thomas Mann* (London: Bloomsbury, 1995), 250.

9. Dirk Bogarde, *An Orderly Man* (London: Chatto & Windus, 1983), 80.

10. Friedrich Nietzsche (trans. Walter Kaufmann), "The Birth of Tragedy" in *The Birth of Tragedy and The Case of Wagner*, 15–151 (New York: Random House/Vintage, 1967), 35.

11. *Ibid.*, 36.

12. *Ibid.*, 37.

13. Thomas Mann, "Death in Venice" in *Stories of Three Decades*, 378–437 (London: Martin Secker & Warburg, 1946), 384.

14. *Ibid.*, 431.

15. Laurence Schifano, *Luchino Visconti—The Flames of Passion* (London: Collins, 1990), 379.

16. Thomas Mann (ed. Richard and Clara Winston), Letter to Carl Maria Weber, 4 July 1920 in *Selected Letters of Thomas Mann* (Harmondsworth: Penguin, 1975), 94–95.

17. Richard Winston, *Thomas Mann—The Making of an Artist, 1875–1911* (London: Constable, 1982), 273–274.

18. Hayman, *Thomas Mann*, 170.

19. Mann (trans. Winston), *Thomas Mann Diaries*, 210.

20. Mann, "Death in Venice" in *Stories of Three Decades*, 418.

21. Hayman, *Thomas Mann*, 64.

22. Schifano, *Luchino Visconti*, 327.

23. *Ibid.*, 378.

24. John Coldstream, *Dirk Bogarde—The*

Authorized Biography (London: Weidenfeld & Nicolson, 2004), 272.

25. Dirk Bogarde, *A Postillion Struck by Lightning* (London: Chatto & Windus, 1977), 191.

26. Schifano, *Luchino Visconti*, 76.

27. Mann, "Death in Venice" in *Stories of Three Decades*, 384.

28. Friedrich Nietzsche (trans. R. J. Hollingdale), *Thus Spoke Zarathustra* (Harmondsworth: Penguin, 1980), 244.

29. *Ibid.*, 331–332.

30. Friedrich Nietzsche (trans. R. J. Hollingdale), *Ecce Homo* (Harmondsworth: Penguin, 1982), 133.

31. Coldstream, *Dirk Bogarde*, 520.

32. *Dirk Bogarde—Above the Title* (Yorkshire Television, dir. Nick Gray, 1986).

33. Walter Kaufmann, *Nietzsche—Philosopher, Psychologist, Antichrist,* Fourth Edition (Princeton: Princeton University Press, 1974), 232.

34. *Afternoon Plus* (Thames Television, 1981), https://ru-clip.net/video/i1kT9RZi-ZU/dirk-bogarde-interview-thames-tv-1981.html.

Chapter Ten

1. Kenneth Williams (ed. Russell Davies), *The Kenneth Williams Diaries* (London: Harper-Collins, 1993), 215.

2. *Ibid.* (Sept. 2, 1961), 175.

3. *Ibid.* (Oct. 27, 1981), 643.

4. Dirk Bogarde, *Cleared for Take-Off* (London: Penguin Viking, 1995), 227.

5. Williams (ed. Davies), *The Kenneth Williams Diaries* (Aug. 1 & Aug. 2, 1985), 721.

6. John Coldstream, *Dirk Bogarde—The Authorized Biography* (London: Weidenfeld & Nicolson, 2004), 272.

7. *Ibid.*, 51.

8. *Ibid.*, 204.

9. *Ibid.*, 279.

10. Alec Guinness, *My Name Escapes Me—The Diary of a Retiring Actor* (London: Hamish Hamilton, 1996), 28.

11. Oscar Wilde, "De Profundis" in *Complete Works of Oscar Wilde*, with an introduction by Vivian Holland, 873–957 (London: Collins, 1977), 876.

12. Robert Murphy, *Sixties British Cinema* (London: British Film Institute, 1992), 124.

13. David Caute, *Joseph Losey—A Revenge on Life* (London: Faber and Faber, 1994), 229.

14. Robert Tanitch, *Dirk Bogarde—The Complete Career Illustrated* (London: Ebury Press, 1988), 141.

15. *Ibid.*, 142.

16. Dirk Bogarde, *Snakes and Ladders* (Chatto & Windus, 1978), 115.

17. Coldstream, *Dirk Bogarde*, 321.

18. Caute, *Joseph Losey*, 242.

19. Johann Joachim Winckelmann (trans. G Henry Lodge), *History of Ancient Art*, vol. 1 (Boston, 1880), 338.

20. Walter Pater, *The Renaissance—Studies in Art and Poetry* (London: Folio Society, 2013), 202.

21. Caute, *Joseph Losey*, 184.

Conclusion

1. John Coldstream, *Dirk Bogarde—The Authorized Biography* (London: Weidenfeld & Nicolson, 2004), 480.

2. Dirk Bogarde, *Cleared for Take-Off* (London: Penguin Viking, 1995), 225.

3. Dirk Bogarde, *A Short Walk from Harrods* (London: Penguin Viking, 1993), 235–236.

Bibliography

Adam, Peter, *Arts of the Third Reich* (London: Thames and Hudson, 1992).

Benson, A. C., *The Temple of Death—The Ghost Stories of A.C. & R.C. Benson* (Ware: Wordsworth Editions, 2007).

Bogarde, Dirk, *Cleared for Take-Off* (London: Penguin Viking, 1995).

Bogarde, Dirk, *For the Time Being* (London: Penguin Viking, 1998).

Bogarde, Dirk, *An Orderly Man* (London: Chatto & Windus/The Hogarth Press, 1983).

Bogarde, Dirk, *A Particular Friendship* (London: Penguin Viking, 1989).

Bogarde, Dirk, *A Postillion Struck by Lightning* (London: Chatto & Windus, 1977).

Bogarde, Dirk, *A Short Walk from Harrods* (London: Penguin Viking, 1993).

Bogarde, Dirk, *Snakes and Ladders* (London: Chatto & Windus, 1978).

Buchan, John, *The Four Adventures of Richard Hannay*, with an introduction by Robin W. Winks (Boston: David R. Godine, 1988).

Burgess, Anthony, *A Clockwork Orange* Harmondsworth: Penguin, 1971).

Burke, Edmund, *A Philosophical Enquiry into the Origin of our Ideas of the Sublime and Beautiful* (Oxford: Oxford University Press, 1990).

Burleigh, Michael, *The Third Reich: A New History* (New York: Farrar, Straus and Giroux, 2001).

Carlyle, Thomas, *Sartor Resartus* (London: Dent, 1940).

Carpenter, Humphrey, *Benjamin Britten—A Biography* (London: Faber & Faber, 1992).

Caute, David, *Joseph Losey—A Revenge on Life* (London: Faber & Faber, 1994).

Coldstream, John, *Dirk Bogarde—The Authorized Biography* (London: Weidenfeld & Nicolson, 2004).

Coleridge, Samuel Taylor (ed. Stephen Potter), *Select Poetry & Prose* (London: Nonesuch Press, 1971).

Conradi, Peter, *Hitler's Piano Player—The Rise and Fall of Ernst Hanfstaengl, Confidant of Hitler, Ally of FDR* (London: Duckworth, 2006).

Crisp, Quentin, *The Naked Civil Servant* (London: Penguin, 2006).

Davenport-Hines, Richard, *Gothic—Four Hundred Years of Excess, Horror, Evil and Ruin* (London: Fourth Estate, 1998).

Durrell, Laurence, *The Alexandria Quartet* (London: Faber & Faber, 1972).

Easthope, Antony, *What a Man's Gotta Do—The Masculine Myth in Popular Culture* (London: Palladin/Grafton Books, 1986).

Eksteins, Modris, *Rites of Spring—The Great War and the Birth of the Modern Age* (London: Papermac, 2000).

Esslin, Martin, *The Age of Television* (London: Routledge, 2017).

France, Anatole (trans. Alfred Allinson), *The Merrie Tales of Jacques Tournebroche* (London: John Lane, 1910).

Freud, Sigmund (trans. James Strachey), *The Interpretation of Dreams* (Harmondsworth: Penguin, 1983).

Geraghty, Christine, *British Cinema in the Fifties—Gender, Genre and the "New Look"* (London: Routledge, 2000).

Gill, A. A., *A A Gill Is Away* (New York: Simon & Schuster, 2007).

Gorer, Geoffrey, *The Life and Ideas of The Marquis de Sade* (London: Peter Owen, 1962).

Guinness, Alec, *My Name Escapes Me—The Diary of a Retiring Actor* (London: Hamish Hamilton, 1996).

Hadleigh, Boze, *The Lavender Screen: The Gay and Lesbian Films—Their Stars, Makers, Characters, and Critics* (rev. ed.) (New York: Citadel Press, 2001).

Hanson, Ellis, *Out Takes: Essays on Queer Theory and Film* (Durham: Duke University Press, 1999).

Hart-Davies, Rupert, *Hugh Walpole—A Biography* (London: Macmillan, 1952).

Hayman, Ronald, *Thomas Mann* (London: Bloomsbury, 1995).

Herr, Michael, *Dispatches* (London: Pan Macmillan, 1978).

Hitler, Adolf (trans. Ralph Manheim), *Mein Kampf* (London: Hutchinson, 1980).

Hyde, H. Montgomery (ed.), *Notable British Trials—The Trials of Oscar Wilde* (London: William Hodge, 1948).

Kaufmann, Walter, *Nietzsche—Philosopher, Psychologist, Antichrist,* Fourth Edition (Princeton: Princeton University Press, 1974).

Kennedy, Michael, *The Dent Master Musicians—Britten* (London: Dent, 1993).

Lash, John, *Twins and the Double* (London: Thames and Hudson, 1993).

Lawrence, T. E., *Seven Pillars of Wisdom* (London: Penguin, 2000).

Machtan, Lothar (trans. John Brownjohn), *The Hidden Hitler* (Oxford: The Perseus Press, 2001).

Mann, Thomas, *Stories of Three Decades* (London: Martin Secker & Warburg, 1946).

Mann, Thomas (ed. Richard and Clara Winston), *Selected Letters of Thomas Mann* (Harmondsworth: Penguin, 1975).

Mann, Thomas (trans. Richard and Clara Winston), *Thomas Mann Diaries 1918–1939* (London: Robert Clark, 1985).

Maugham, W. Somerset, *The World Over—The Collected Stories,* vol. 1 (London: The Reprint Society/Heinemann, 1954).

McNally, Raymond T. (ed.), *A Clutch of Vampires* (Greenwich, CT: New York Graphic Society, 1974).

Murphy, Robert, *Sixties British Cinema* (London: British Film Institute, 1992).

Nicolson, Adam, *The Mighty Dead—Why Homer Matters* (London: William Collins, 2014).

Nietzsche, Friedrich (trans. Walter Kaufmann), *The Birth of Tragedy and the Case of Wagner* (New York: Random House/Vintage, 1967).

Nietzsche, Friedrich (trans. R. J. Hollingdale), *Ecce Homo* (Harmondsworth: Penguin, 1982).

Nietzsche, Friedrich (trans. Josefine Nauckhoff), *The Gay Science* (Cambridge: Cambridge University Press, 2001).

Nietzsche, Friedrich (trans. R. J. Hollingdale), *Thus Spoke Zarathustra* (Harmondsworth: Penguin, 1980).

Pater, Walter, *The Renaissance—Studies in Art and Poetry* (London: Folio Society, 2013).

Raphael, Frederic, *Somerset Maugham and His World* (London: Thames and Hudson, 1976).

Rhodes, Gary R., *Tod Browning's Dracula* (Sheffield: Tomahawk Press, 2014).

Rilke, Rainer Maria (trans. Stanley Appelbaum, "Der Knabe" in *Selected Poems* (New York: Dover, 2011).

Ruskin, John, *Sesame and Lilies* (London: George Allen, 1902).

Sade, the Marquis de (trans. Meredith X), *Philosophy in the Boudoir* (London: Creation Books, 1995).

Schifano, Laurence, *Luchino Visconti—The Flames of Passion* (London: Collins, 1990).

Schonberg, Harold, *The Great Pianists* (London: Victor Gollancz, 1964).

Shaw, George Bernard, *The Complete Plays of Bernard Shaw* (London: Odhams Press, no date).

Sontag, Susan, *Against Interpretation* (London: Vintage, 1994).

Stoker, Bram, *Dracula* (London: Constable, 1904).

Swofford, Anthony, *Jarhead: A Marine's Chronicle of the Gulf War and Other Battles* (New York: Scribner's, 2003).

Tanitch, Robert, *Dirk Bogarde—The Complete Career Illustrated* (London: Ebury Press, 1988).

Taylor, Brandon and Wilfried van der Will, *The Nazification of Art—Art, Design, Music, Architecture & Film in the Third Reich* (Winchester: The Winchester Press, 1990).

Wagner, Richard (trans. William Ashton Ellis), *Pilgrimage to Beethoven and Other Essays* (Lincoln: University of Nebraska Press, 1994).

Walker, Alan, *Franz Liszt—The Weimar Years 1848–1861* (London: Faber & Faber, 1989).

Walpole, Hugh, *Four Fantastic Tales* (London: Macmillan, 1932).

Walpole, Hugh, *Rogue Herries* (London: Macmillan, 1935).

Walpole, Hugh, *Wintersmoon* (London: Macmillan, 1933).

Wheatley, Dennis, *The Satanist* (London: Heron, 1972.

Wilde, Oscar, *Complete Works of Oscar Wilde,* with an introduction by Vivian Holland (London: Collins, 1977).

Williams, Kenneth (ed. Russell Davies), *The Kenneth Williams Diaries* (London: HarperCollins, 1993).

Winckelmann, Johann Joachim (trans. G. Henry Lodge), *History of Ancient Art,* vol. 1 (Boston, 1880).

Winston, Richard, *Thomas Mann—The Making of an Artist, 1875–1911* (London: Constable, 1982).

Woolf, Virginia (ed. Anne Oliver Bell), *A Moment's Liberty—The Shorter Diary of Virginia Woolf* (London: The Hogarth Press 1990).

Journals and websites

Afternoon Plus (Thames Television, 1981) https://ru-clip.net/video/ilkT9RZi-ZU/dirk-bogarde-interview-thames-tv-1981.html.

Arena: "The Private Dirk Bogarde" (BBC, dir. Adam Low, 2001).

Cutting Room Floor: Veronica Carlson 2 (Diabolique Films, 2017), https://www.youtube.com/watch?v=ydYvORVXppI.

"Cassandra." "Crying All the Way to the Bank...," *Daily Mirror*, 26 September 1956.

Desert Island Discs (BBC Radio 4), first broadcast 24 October 1993.

Dirk Bogarde—Above the Title (dir. Nick Gray, 1986).

Dirk Bogarde—By Myself (dir. Paul Joyce, 1992).

Gordon, Burn, "Ghoul of the Month" *Sunday Times Magazine*, 14 August 1977, 39.

Grossman, Lev. "The Gay Nabokov," in *Salon*, San Francisco, 17 May 2000, https://www.salon.com/2000/05/17/nabokov_5/.

Hammer—The Studio that Dripped Blood (BBC, dir. David Thompson, 1987).

Interview between Bernard Braden and Quentin Crisp. https://www.youtube.com/watch?v=HFPqDUQKmt8.

Last Laugh in Vegas, Episode 3 (ITV, dir. Iain Thompson, 2018).

Man Alive: "Consenting Adults: The Men" (prod. Tom Conway, 1967).

White, Edmund. "Nabokov's 'great gay comic novel'" in *The Times Literary Supplement*, 3 August 2016, https://www.the-tls.co.uk/articles/public/80834/.

Wladimir Troubetzkoy: "Vladimir Nabokov's *Despair*: The Reader as April Fool," http://revel.unice.fr/cycnos/index.html?id=1451.

Index